AF411560

THE UNITED STATES AND THE KOREAN PROBLEM

DOCUMENTS 1943–1953

AMS PRESS

NEW YORK

83D CONGRESS
1st Session } SENATE { DOCUMENT
No. 74

THE UNITED STATES AND THE KOREAN PROBLEM

DOCUMENTS 1943–1953

PRESENTED BY MR. WILEY

JULY 30, 1953.—Ordered to be printed

———

UNITED STATES
GOVERNMENT PRINTING OFFICE
WASHINGTON : 1953

37358

Library of Congress Cataloging in Publication Data

United States. Congress. Senate. Committee on Foreign
    Relations.
    The United States and the Korean problem.

    Reprint of the 1953 ed., published by U. S. Govt. Print. Off.,
Washington, which was issued as 83d Congress, 1st session, 1953.
Senate document no. 74.
    1. Korea—History—1945-   —Sources. 2. United States—
Foreign relations—Korea—Sources. 3. Korea—Foreign relations—
United States—Sources. I. Title. II. Series: United States. 83d
Congress, 1st session, 1953. Senate. Document; no. 74.
[DS917.U52 1976]   951.9'04   72-38089
ISBN 0-404-56962-5

AMS PRESS, INC.
NEW YORK, N.Y.

FOREWORD

This collection of official documents bearing on the Korean problem has been compiled by the staff of the Committee on Foreign Relations at the direction of the committee. It makes no pretense of being all-inclusive, but it represents instead an effort to bring together in a single volume the more important international agreements, United Nations resolutions and reports, and statements by United States officials having to do with the independence and unification of Korea and the Korean armistice negotiations.

The documents were selected by the staff of the committee on the basis of their usefulness in any discussion of the Korean settlement. This is the second collection of documents on Korea compiled by the Congress; the first, which was entitled "Background Information on Korea," was prepared in 1950 by the House Committee on Foreign Affairs.

The committee gratefully acknowledges the assistance of the Department of State and the Legislative Reference Service of the Library of Congress.

ALEXANDER WILEY, *Chairman.*

AUGUST 10, 1953.

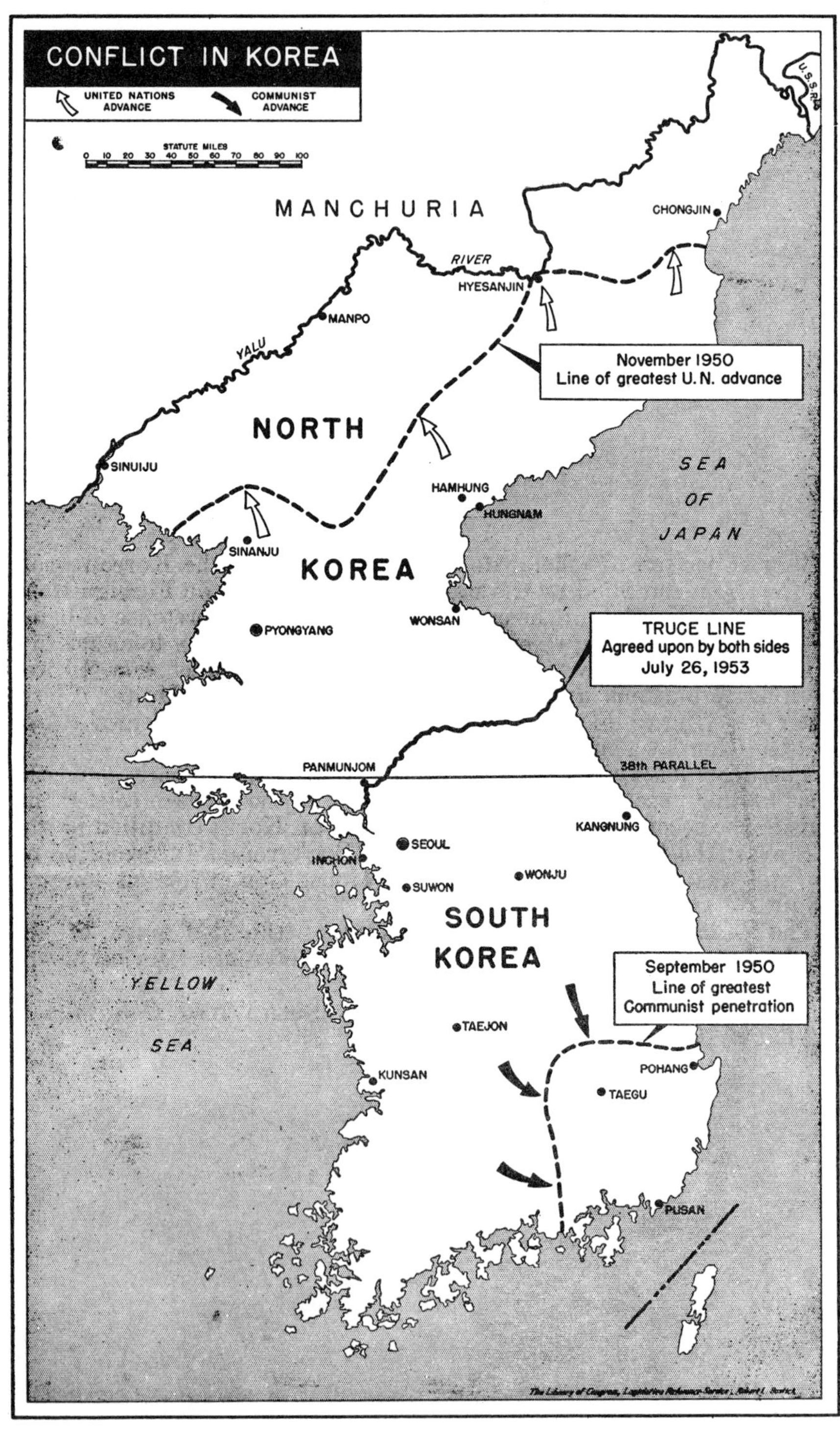

CONFLICT IN KOREA
UNITED NATIONS ADVANCE
COMMUNIST ADVANCE
STATUTE MILES
0 10 20 30 40 50 60 70 80 90 100
MANCHURIA
U.S.S.R.
CHONGJIN
RIVER
HYESANJIN
MANPO
YALU
November 1950
Line of greatest U. N. advance
NORTH
SINUIJU
SEA
OF
JAPAN
HAMHUNG
HUNGNAM
KOREA
SINANJU
PYONGYANG
WONSAN
TRUCE LINE
Agreed upon by both sides
July 26, 1953
PANMUNJOM
38th PARALLEL
KANGNUNG
SEOUL
INCHON
WONJU
SUWON
SOUTH
KOREA
YELLOW
September 1950
Line of greatest
Communist penetration
SEA
TAEJON
POHANG
TAEGU
KUNSAN
PUSAN
The Library of Congress, Legislative Reference Service, Robert L. Rowtck

CONTENTS

APPENDIX

THE UNITED STATES AND THE KOREAN PROBLEM

I. WARTIME AGREEMENTS

1. THE CAIRO DECLARATION—STATEMENT BY PRESIDENT ROOSEVELT, GENERALISSIMO CHIANG KAI-SHEK, AND PRIME MINISTER CHURCHILL, DECEMBER 1, 1943 [1]

The several military missions have agreed upon future military operations against Japan. The Three Great Allies expressed their resolve to bring unrelenting pressure against their brutal enemies by sea, land, and air. This pressure is already rising.

The Three Great Allies are fighting this war to restrain and punish the aggression of Japan. They covet no gain for themselves and have no thought of territorial expansion. It is their purpose that Japan shall be stripped of all the islands in the Pacific which she has seized or occupied since the beginning of the first World War in 1914, and that all the territories Japan has stolen from the Chinese, such as Manchuria, Formosa, and the Pescadores, shall be restored to the Republic of China. Japan will also be expelled from all other territories which she has taken by violence and greed. The aforesaid three great powers, mindful of the enslavement of the people of Korea, are determined that in due course Korea shall become free and independent.

With these objects in view the three Allies, in harmony with those of the United Nations at war with Japan, will continue to persevere in the serious and prolonged operations necessary to procure the unconditional surrender of Japan.

2. THE POTSDAM PROCLAMATION DEFINING TERMS FOR JAPANESE SURRENDER, JULY 26, 1945 [2]

[Excerpt]

(1) We—the President of the United States, the President of the National Government of the Republic of China, and the Prime Minister of Great Britain representing the hundreds of millions of our countrymen, have conferred and agree that Japan shall be given an opportunity to end this war.

*   *   *   *   *   *   *

(8) The terms of the Cairo Declaration shall be carried out * * *

3. U. S. S. R. DECLARATION OF WAR AGAINST JAPAN, AUGUST 8, 1945 [3]

Foreign Commissar of the U. S. S. R. Comrade Molotov received Japanese Ambassador Sato and in the name of the Soviet Govern-

---

[1]. Toward the Peace—Documents, Department of State publication 2298, p. 14; Department of State Bulletin, December 4, 1943.
[2] Department of State Bulletin, July 29, 1945, pp. 137–138.
[3] Embassy of the Union of Soviet Socialist Republics, Information Bulletin, Vol. V, No. 82, August 11, 1945.

ment gave him the following statement for transmission to the Government of Japan:

After the defeat and capitulation of Hitlerite Germany, Japan remained the only great power which still stands for the continuation of the war.

The demand of the three powers, the United States, Great Britain, and China, of July 26 for the unconditional surrender of the Japanese armed forces was rejected by Japan. Thus, the proposal made by the Japanese Government to the Soviet Union for mediation in the Far East has lost all foundation.

Taking into account the refusal of Japan to capitulate, the Allies approached the Soviet Government with a proposal to join the war against Japanese aggression and thus shorten the duration of the war, reduce the number of casualties, and contribute toward the most speedy restoration of peace.

True to its obligation as an Ally, the Soviet Government has accepted the proposal of the Allies and has joined in the declaration of the Allied powers of July 26.

The Soviet Government considers that this policy is the only means able to bring peace nearer, to free the people from further sacrifice and suffering, and to give the Japanese people the opportunity of avoiding the danger of destruction suffered by Germany after her refusal to accept unconditional surrender.

In view of the above, the Soviet Government declares that from tomorrow, that is, from August 9, the Soviet Union will consider herself in a state of war against Japan.

4. ESTABLISHMENT OF BOUNDARY AT THE 38TH PARALLEL

A. STATEMENT BY UNDER SECRETARY OF STATE WEBB [4]

The circumstances surrounding the establishment of the thirty-eighth-degree parallel line in Korea were as follows:

Japan's first offer of surrender was made on August 10, 1945. On the following day, August 11, the Secretary of War submitted to the Secretary of State a draft of General Order No. 1, which General MacArthur, as Supreme Commander for the Allied Powers, was to cause the Japanese Government to issue to all of its armed forces; this order directed Japanese commanders to surrender to various designated Allied commanders as indicated in paragraph 1 thereof. As regards Korea, paragraph 1 provided that Japanese forces north of 38° north latitude were to surrender to the Soviet commander, while those south of that line were to surrender to the American commander.

The War Department's draft of General Order No. 1 was discussed by the State-War-Navy Coordinating Committee at its meetings on August 11 and 12, 1945. At the latter meeting the Committee agreed to defer consideration of General Order No. 1 "until it has been reviewed and revised as deemed necessary" by the Joint Chiefs of Staff.

The review of General Order No. 1 by the Joint Chiefs of Staff was concluded on August 14, following which it was approved by the State-War-Navy Coordinating Committee and submitted to the President for his approval.

---

[4] Statement made before the House Committee on Foreign Affairs, Background Information on Korea, H. Rept. 2495, 81st Cong., p. 2.

Following approval of the President, General Order No. 1 was telegraphed by the Joint Chiefs of Staff to General MacArthur in Manila on August 15, 1945. At the same time, General Order No. 1 was sent to General Deane, commanding general, United States Military Mission to the U. S. S. R., in Moscow, for his information.

The text of General Order No. 1 was thereupon communicated to Generalissimo Stalin, as well as to the British Government. In his reply of August 16, Generalissimo Stalin, while suggesting certain amendments which were subsequently accepted by the United States Government, made no reference to those provisions of the order having to do with the 38° parallel line.

It is worthy of note that Soviet military forces entered north Korea on August 12, 1945, while General Order No. 1 was still under discussion.

General Order No. 1, including the provision concerning the 38° parallel line, was issued by General MacArthur on September 2, 1945.

B. General Order No. 1, September 7, 1945 [5]

[*Excerpt*]

General Headquarters,
United States Army Forces, Pacific,
Office of the Commanding General,
Yokohama, Japan, September 7, 1945.

To the People of Korea:

As Commander in Chief, United States Army Forces, Pacific, I do hereby proclaim as follows:

By the terms of the instrument of surrender, signed by command and in behalf of the Emperor of Japan and the Japanese Government and by command and in behalf of the Japanese Imperial General Headquarters, the victorious military forces of my command will today occupy the territory of Korea south of 38° north latitude.

Having in mind the long enslavement of the people of Korea and the determination that in due course Korea shall become free and inedependent, the Korean people are assured that the purpose of the occupation is to enforce the instrument of surrender and to protect them in their personal and religious rights. In giving effect to these purposes, your active aid and compliance are required.

By virtue of the authority vested in me as Commander in Chief, United States Army Forces, Pacific, I hereby establish military control over Korea south of 38° north latitude and the inhabitants thereof, and announce the following conditions of the occupation:

All powers of Government over the territory of Korea south of 38° north latitude and the people thereof will be for the present exercised under my authority.

*   *   *   *   *   *   *

Given under my hand at Yokohama, this seventh day of September 1945.

Douglas MacArthur,
General of the Army of the United States,
Commander in Chief, United States Army Forces, Pacific.

---

[5] Background Information on Korea, H. Rept. 2495, 81st Cong., pp. 3–4.

II. THE UNITED STATES-U. S. S. R. JOINT COMMISSION

5. THE MOSCOW AGREEMENT, DECEMBER 27, 1945 [6]

[Excerpt]

III. KOREA

1. With a view to the re-establishment of Korea as an independent state, the creation of conditions for developing the country on democratic principles and the earliest possible liquidation of the disastrous results of the protracted Japanese domination in Korea, there shall be set up a provisional Korean democratic government which shall take all the necessary steps for developing the industry, transport. and agriculture of Korea and the national culture of the Korean people.

2. In order to assist the formation of a provisional Korean government and with a view to the preliminary elaboration of the appropriate measures, there shall be established a Joint Commission consisting of representatives of the United States command in southern Korea and the Soviet command in northern Korea. In preparing their proposals the Commission shall consult with the Korean democratic parties and social organizations. The recommendations worked out by the Commission shall be presented for the consideration of the Governments of the Union of Soviet Socialist Republics, China, the United Kingdom and the United States prior to final decision by the two governments represented on the Joint Commission.

3. It shall be the task of the Joint Commission, with the participation of the provisional Korean democratic government and of the Korean democratic organizations to work out measures also for helping and assisting (trusteeship) the political, economic, and social progress of the Korean people, the development of democratic self-government and the establishment of the national independence of Korea.

The proposals of the Joint Commission shall be submitted, following consultation with the provisional Korean Government for the joint consideration of the Governments of the United States, Union of Soviet Socialist Republics, United Kingdom, and China for the working out of an agreement concerning a four-power trusteeship of Korea for a period of up to five years.

6. EXCHANGE OF LETTERS BETWEEN THE UNITED STATES AND THE U. S. S. R. REGARDING FOUR-POWER CONVERSATIONS, AUGUST 28, SEPTEMBER 4, AND SEPTEMBER 17, 1947

(A) ACTING SECRETARY OF STATE LOVETT TO SOVIET FOREIGN MINISTER MOLOTOV, AUGUST 28, 1947 [7]

DEAR MR. MOLOTOV: In your letter of August 23, 1947, to Secretary Marshall the position of the Soviet Delegation to the Joint Commission has been set forth in terms which corroborate a recent report received by this Government from the United States Delegation to the Joint Commission. The report of the United States Delegation was

[6] A Decade of American Foreign Policy, 1941–49, S. Doc. 123, 81st Cong., p. 63.
[7] Department of State Bulletin, September 7, 1947, pp. 473–475. The letter was delivered by Ambassador W. Bedell Smith at the Soviet Foreign Office on August 28, 1947.

in compliance with the desire of Secretary Marshall as set forth in his letter to you of August 12 that a report from the Joint Commission should be submitted by August 21 in order that our governments might immediately consider what further steps may be useful to achieve the long-delayed unification and independence of Korea. The report of the United States Delegation makes it clear that the Joint Commission has been unable to reach agreement regarding the basis on which representatives of democratic Korean parties and social organizations shall be consulted by the Joint Commission. The United States Delegation also reports that it has been unable to obtain the agreement of the Soviet Delegation to any alternative method of completing the task of the Joint Commission.

As pointed out in your letter it was agreed in the interchange of correspondence in May of this year that "the Joint Commission should consult with those democratic parties and social organizations which fully support the Moscow Decision on Korea." [8] You will, however, recall that in your letter of May 7 you expressly agreed to the interpretation of the above phrase as proposed by the United States Commander in Korea that "signing the declaration in Communiqué No. 5 will be accepted as declaration of good faith with respect to upholding fully the Moscow Decision and will make the signatory party or organization eligible for initial consultation." The parties and organizations mentioned by you as belonging to the Anti-Trusteeship Committee did sign Communiqué No. 5 and are, in the opinion of the United States Government, eligible for initial consultation. Your letter of May 7 also provided that any decision excluding individuals, parties, and social organizations for active opposition to the work of the Joint Commission "shall be by agreement of the Joint Commission." Accordingly, the United States Delegation has repeatedly, but without success, attempted to obtain from the Soviet Delegation agreement to criteria for consultation with Korean parties and social organizations applying for such consultation in accordance with the terms embodied in your letter. The Soviet Delegation has insisted on the unilateral right to exclude parties which have expressed distaste for "trusteeship," even though such parties have declared and reiterated their intention fully to support the Joint Commission and have in fact, since signing the declaration not instigated active opposition to the work of the Commission. The Soviet position is not only contrary to the specific terms of the agreement between you and Secretary Marshall, it is also contrary to the democratic principle of freedom of opinion.

In Secretary Marshall's letter to you of August 11, 1947,[9] reference was made to the fact that the United States Delegation has several times offered to limit oral consultations to parties and organizations with membership in excess of one thousand, or any other reasonable figure proposed by the Soviet Delegation. The United States Delegation reports, however, that when the Soviet Delegation proposed limiting consultation to parties of 10,000 or more, the Soviet Delegation submitted a list which omitted 24 such parties which claimed total membership of 15,200,000 and refused to consider any other list or alternative proposal.

---

[8] Department of State Bulletin, May 11, 1947, p. 947; May 18, 1947, p. 995; May 25, 1947, p. 1043.
[9] Department of State Bulletin, August 24, 1947, p. 398.

The United States Government denies categorically that there has been oppression or persecution of Korean parties or individuals in the United States zone as charged in your letter.   The arrests which you mention have been necessary to control subversive activities aimed at the destruction of constituted government and law and order in the American zone.   United States forces are charged with the responsibility for maintaining law and order in south Korea without interference with democratic rights.   That they have done so successfully is amply proven by the freedom with which all shades of political opinion are expressed and respected in the United States zone.

It is noted that you have no objection to the proposal that the Joint Commission furnish an agreed report to our two governments. The United States Delegation has accordingly been instructed to take immediate steps to reach agreement on a joint report of the status of the deliberations of the Joint Commission.   In view of the position set forth in your letter and the report already rendered by the United States Delegation, however, it is apparent that a joint report can accomplish little other than a formal delineation of the issues which have prevented the fulfillment of the Moscow Agreement.

For almost two years the Government of the United States has devoted its utmost efforts to carrying out the terms of the Moscow Agreement on Korea.   The present stalemate in the Joint Commission negotiations and the failure of that Commission to accomplish even the first task of its mission have made it abundantly clear to all that bilateral negotiations on the subject of consultation with Korean political parties and organizations will only serve to delay the implementation of this agreement and defeat its announced purpose of bringing about early independence for Korea.   The United States Government cannot in good conscience be a party to any such delay in the fulfillment of its commitment to Korean independence and purposes that the four powers adhering to the Moscow Agreement meet to consider how that agreement may be speedily carried out.

The United States Government therefore submits for the consideration of your government the enclosed outline of proposals designed to achieve the aims of the Moscow Agreement on Korea.   The United States Government proposes that these suggestions be considered at an early date by the powers adhering to that Agreement.   It is therefore hoped that the Soviet Chargé d'Affaires at Washington or an authorized deputy may be designated to participate in four-power conversations on this problem at Washington beginning on September 8, 1947.

It is believed that the Joint Commission's report on the status of its deliberations might be helpful in consideration of the United States proposals during these four-power conversations.   The United States Delegation has accordingly been instructed to endeavor to reach agreement with the Soviet Delegation on a joint report to be submitted not later than September 5, 1947.

Copies of this letter are being transmitted to the Foreign Ministers of the United Kingdom and China together with invitatitons to participate in the four-power conversations referred to above.

Please accept [etc.]

ROBERT A. LOVETT.

UNITED STATES PROPOSALS REGARDING KOREA

1. In both the U. S. S. R. and U. S. zones of Korea there shall be held early elections to choose wholly representative provisional legislatures for each zone. Voting shall be by secret, multi-party ballot on a basis of universal suffrage and elections shall be held in accordance with the laws adopted by the present Korean legislatures in each zone.

2. These provisional zonal legislatures shall choose representatives in numbers which reflect the proportion between the populations of the two zones, these representatives to constitute a national provisional legislature. This legislature shall meet at Seoul to establish a provisional government for a united Korea.

3. The resulting Provisional Government of a united Korea shall meet in Korea with representatives of the four Powers adhering to the Moscow Agreement on Korea to discuss with them what aid and assistance is needed in order to place Korean independence on a firm economic and political foundation and on what terms this aid and assistance is to be given.

4. During all the above stages the United Nations shall be invited to have observers present so that the world and the Korean people may be assured of the wholly representative and completely independent character of the actions taken.

5. The Korean Provisional Government and the Powers concerned shall agree upon a date by which all occupation forces in Korea will be withdrawn.

6. The provisional legislatures in each zone shall be encouraged to draft provisional constitutions which can later be used as a basis for the adoption by the national provisional legislature of a constitution for all of Korea.

7. Until such time as a united, independent Korea is established, public and private Korean agencies in each zone shall be brought into contact with international agencies established by or under the United Nations and the presence of Korean observers at official international conferences shall be encouraged in appropriate cases.

B. Soviet Foreign Minister Molotov to Secretary of State Marshall, September 4, 1947 [10]

Dear Mr. Marshall: In acknowledging receipt of Mr. Lovett's letter of August 26, 1947, I consider it necessary to draw to your attention that the preliminary elaboration of measures to assist the formation of a provisional Korean democratic government, in accordance with the decision of the Moscow Conference of the three Ministers for Foreign Affairs, is to be carried out by the Joint Commission consisting of representatives of the Soviet Command in northern Korea and of the United States Command in southern Korea. For the consideration of the four Governments, including the British and Chinese Governments, according to the Moscow decision, there should be submitted the recommendations worked out by the Joint Commission prior to adoption of a final decision. Furthermore, the Governments of Great Britain and China will take part, together

---

[10] Korea. 1945–48, Department of State Publication 3305, pp. 45–47.

with the Governments of the U. S. S. R. and the U. S. A., in the consideration of the proposals worked out by the Joint Soviet-American Commission concerning measures for helping and assisting (trusteeship) the political, economic, and social progress of the Korean people, the development of democratic self-government, and the establishment of the national independence of Korea, in order to work out an agreement concerning a four-power trusteeship with relation to Korea.

The task of the Joint Soviet-American Commission, as is known, is to render assistance in the formation of a single provisional democratic government for all Korea.

The Joint Commission has still, in fact, done little in this direction, but this situation is primarily the result of the position adopted by the American delegation on the question of consultation of the Commission with Korean democratic parties and social organizations, as was pointed out in my last letter to you. If the American delegation had shown the necessary desire to render assistance in the creation of a really democratic government in Korea, the work of the Joint Commission would have been more successful, the task laid upon it would have been fulfilled, and there would not be that stagnant situation in the work of the Joint Commission which in Mr. Lovett's letter is called an *impasse*.

As you know, the Soviet delegation, wishing to resolve the situation which had been created in the Joint Commission and seeking to expedite the work of creating a provisional Korean democratic government, agreed with the proposal of the American delegation not to carry on oral consultations with Korean democratic parties and social organizations, and on August 26, 1947 introduced a new proposal for the establishment of a consultative organ—the provisional general Korean peoples' assembly of representatives of democratic parties and social organizations of all Korea. This proposal in our opinion should meet no objection on the part of the American delegation in as much as it might remove the difficulties which the Joint Commission has encountered.

I consider it necessary to add to the above that the successful realization of the measure set forth in the proposal of the Soviet delegation is possible only on the basis of free and unfettered activity of the democratic parties and organizations, representatives of which at the present time in southern Korea are subjected to arrests and other repressions, which is incompatible with the principles of democracy and legality and also with the obligations which the Governments of the U. S. A. and the U. S. S. R. took upon themselves with respect to Korea.

In connection with the assertions contained in Mr. Lovett's letter concerning the position of the Soviet delegation to the Joint Commission, the sense of which is that the Soviet delegation does not display sufficient understanding of the proposals of the American delegation, I see no necessity for stopping on these assertions in view of their obvious unsoundness.

At the same time I cannot fail to express regret concerning unilateral acts undertaken by you such as the despatch of an invitation to the Governments of Great Britain and China to take part in the discussion of this question, fixing the place and date for the conference.

The Soviet Government considers inexpedient your proposal to submit the question of the establishment of a provisional Korean democratic government to the consideration of the Governments of the four countries in as much as the Joint Commission is still far from exhausting all its possibilities for working out agreed recommendations, which is entirely possible. The "United States proposals concerning Korea" set forth in Mr. Lovett's letter are also unacceptable.

These proposals cannot fail to entail the further division of Korea in as much as they envisage the establishment of separate provisional legislative assemblies in the south and in the north of Korea (in the Soviet and American zones) whereas the vital task is to achieve as rapidly as possible the establishment of a single, even though provisional, organ of authority—the General Korean Provisional Democratic Government. The American proposal does not correct the situation now existing in Korea—the division of the country into two zones, to the liquidation of which all efforts should be directed—but on the contrary consolidates this abnormal situation.

Having in mind that the proposal for the consideration of the question of Korea is a joint conference of the representatives of the four powers does not stem from the Moscow decision of the three Ministers for Foreign Affairs concerning Korea, and taking into consideration the views set forth above, the Soviet Government sees no possibility of accepting the proposals advanced in Mr. Lovett's letter.

Copies of this letter are being sent by me to the Governments of Great Britain and China.

Please accept [etc.]   V. M. MOLOTOV.

C. The Acting Secretary of State Lovett to Soviet Foreign Minister Molotov, September 17, 1947 [11]

DEAR MR. MOLOTOV: The decision of the Soviet Government as conveyed in your letter of September 4, not to participate in Four Power discussions of proposals of the United States Government designed to achieve the speedy realization of the aims of the Moscow Agreement on Korea is deeply regretted. For almost two years the United States Government has been faithfully endeavoring to reach agreement with the Soviet Government to carry out the terms of the Moscow Agreement but with no appreciable success. It has even proved impossible for the Soviet and United States Delegations on the Joint Commission in Korea to agree upon a joint report of the status of their deliberations up to the present. There is no sign of the early setting up of a Korean Provisional Government. Korea remains divided and her promised independence unrealized.

The United States Government believes that this situation must not be permitted to continue indefinitely. In view of the fact that bilateral negotiations have not advanced Korean independence and that the Soviet Government does not agree to discussions among the powers adhering to the Moscow Agreement, there is but one course remaining. It is the intention therefore, of my Government to refer the problem of Korean independence to the forthcoming session of the General Assembly of the United Nations. It is suggested that the members of the Joint Commission hold themselves in readiness to give such aid and assistance to the General Assembly as may be required during the Assembly's consideration of this problem.

---

[11] Korea's Independence, Department of State Publication 2933, pp. 59–60.

It is the hope of my Government that consideration of this problem by the General Assembly may result in bringing about the early restoration of freedom and independence to the long suffering people of Korea.

Copies of this letter have been furnished to the Governments of the United Kingdom and China.

Accept [etc.]

ROBERT A. LOVETT,
Acting Secretary of State.

III. EARLY U. N. EFFORTS AT UNIFICATION

7. ADDRESS BY SECRETARY OF STATE MARSHALL BEFORE THE GENERAL ASSEMBLY OF THE UNITED NATIONS, SEPTEMBER 17, 1947 [12]

[Excerpt]

I turn now to the question of the independence of Korea. At Cairo in December 1943, the United States, the United Kingdom, and China joined in declaring that in due course Korea should become free and independent. This multilateral pledge was reaffirmed in the Potsdam Declaration of July 1945 and subscribed to by the Union of Soviet Socialist Republics when it entered the war against Japan. In Moscow in December of 1945, the Foreign Ministers of the U. S. S. R., the United Kingdom, and the United States concluded an agreement designed to bring about the independence of Korea. This agreement was later adhered to by the Government of China. It provided for the establishment of a Joint U. S.–U. S. S. R. Commission to meet in Korea and, through consultations with Korean democratic parties and social organizations, to decide on methods for establishing a provisional Korean government. The Joint Commission was then to consult with that provisional government on methods of giving aid and assistance to Korea, any agreement reached being submitted for approval to the four powers adhering to the Moscow Agreement.

For about two years the United States Government has been trying to reach agreement with the Soviet Government, through the Joint Commission and otherwise, on methods of implementing the Moscow Agreement, and thus bringing about the independence of Korea. The United States representatives have insisted that any settlement of the Korean problem must in no way infringe the fundamental democratic right of freedom of opinion. That is still the position of my Government. Today the independence of Korea is no further advanced than it was two years ago. Korea remains divided at the 38th parallel with Soviet forces in the industrial north and United States forces in the agricultural south. There is little or no exchange of goods or services between the two zones. Korea's economy is thus crippled.

The Korean people, not former enemies but a people liberated from 40 years of Japanese oppression, are still not free. This situation must not be allowed to continue indefinitely. In an effort to make progress the United States Government recently made certain proposals designed to achieve the purposes of the Moscow Agreement and requested the powers adhering to that Agreement to join in discussion of these proposals. China and the United Kingdom agreed to this procedure.

---

[12] Korea's Independence, Department of State Publication 2933, pp. 15–16.

The Soviet Government did not. Furthermore, the United States and Soviet Delegations to the Joint Commission have not even been able to agree on a joint report on the status of their deliberations. It appears evident that further attempts to solve the Korean problem by means of bilateral negotiations will only serve to delay the establishment of an independent, united Korea.

It is therefore the intention of the United States Government to present the problem of Korean independence to this session of the General Assembly. Although we shall be prepared to submit suggestions as to how the early attainment of Korean independence might be effected, we believe that this is a matter which now requires the impartial judgment of the other members. We do not wish to have the inability of two powers to reach agreement delay any further the urgent and rightful claims of the Korean people to independence.

8. RESOLUTION OF THE GENERAL ASSEMBLY ESTABLISHING THE UNITED NATIONS TEMPORARY COMMISSION ON KOREA, NOVEMBER 14, 1947 [13]

I

INASMUCH AS the Korean question which is before the General Assembly is primarily a matter for the Korean people itself and concerns its freedom and independence, and

RECOGNIZING that this question cannot be correctly and fairly resolved without the participation of representatives of the indigenous population;

The General Assembly

1. *Resolves* that elected representatives of the Korean people be invited to take part in the consideration of the question;

2. *Further resolves* that in order to facilitate and expedite such participation and to observe that the Korean representatives are in fact duly elected by the Korean people and not mere appointees by military authorities in Korea, there be forthwith established a United Nations Temporary Commission on Korea, to be present in Korea, with right to travel, observe, and consult throughout Korea.

II

The General Assembly,

RECOGNIZING the urgent and rightful claims to independence of the people of Korea;

BELIEVING that the national independence of Korea should be reestablished and all occupying forces then withdrawn at the earliest practicable date;

RECALLING its previous conclusion that the freedom and independence of the Korean people cannot be correctly or fairly resolved without the participation of representatives of the Korean people, and its decision to establish a United Nations Temporary Commission on Korea (hereinafter called the "Commission") for the purpose of facilitating and expediting such participation by elected representatives of the Korean people:

[13] The United States and the United Nations: Report by the President to the Congress for the Year 1947, Department of State Publication 3024, pp. 157–159.

1. *Decides* that the Commission shall consist of representatives of Australia, Canada, China, El Salvador, France, India, Philippines, Syria, Ukrainian Soviet Socialist Republic;

2. *Recommends* that the elections be held not later than 31 March 1948 on the basis of adult suffrage and by secret ballot to choose representatives with whom the Commission may consult regarding the prompt attainment of the freedom and independence of the Korean people and which representatives, constituting a National Assembly, may establish a National Government of Korea. The number of representatives from each voting area or zone should be proportionate to the population, and the elections should be under the observation of the Commission;

3. *Further recommends* that as soon as possible after the elections, the National Assembly should convene and form a National Government and notify the Commission of its formation;

4. *Further recommends* that immediately upon the establishment of a National Government, that Government should, in consultation with the Commission: (*a*) constitute its own national security forces and dissolve all military or semimilitary formations not included therein, (*b*) take over the functions of government from the military commands and civilian authorities of north and south Korea, and (*c*) arrange with the occupying Powers for the complete withdrawal from Korea of their armed forces as early as practicable and if possible within ninety days;

5. *Resolves* that the Commission shall facilitate and expedite the fulfilment of the foregoing programme for the attainment of the national independence of Korea and withdrawal of occupying forces, taking into account its observations and consultations in Korea. The Commission shall report, with its conclusions, to the General Assembly and may consult with the Interim Committee with respect to the application of this resolution in the light of developments;

6. *Calls upon* the Member States concerned to afford every assistance and facility to the Commission in the fulfilment of its responsibilities;

7. *Calls upon* all Members of the United Nations to refrain from interfering in the affairs of the Korean people during the interim period preparatory to the establishment of Korean independence, except in pursuance of the decisions of the General Assembly; and thereafter, to refrain completely from any and all acts derogatory to the independence and sovereignty of Korea.

9. REPORT OF THE UNITED NATIONS TEMPORARY COMMISSION ON KOREA ON THE ELECTIONS OF MAY 10, 1948, IN SOUTH KOREA, JULY 21, 1948 [14]

[Excerpt]

CHAPTER VI. SUMMARY AND CONCLUSIONS ON THE FIRST PART OF THE REPORT (TECHNICAL ASPECTS OF THE ELECTIONS)

A. PRELIMINARY CONSIDERATIONS

1. Before going into the subject matter of the present chapter, it may be useful to recall that the problem of the reestablishment of

[14] United Nations, General Assembly, official records: Third session, Supplement No. 9 (A/575), pp. 39–47.

Korean independence had its genesis in the Cairo Declaration of 1 December 1943, the Potsdam Conference of July 1945, and the Moscow Agreement of December 1945.[15] The latter agreement established the United States-Soviet Joint Commission on Korea,[16] which, after a series of inconclusive meetings, finally reached a deadlock in September 1947. Subsequently the United States Government submitted the problem to the General Assembly of the United Nations in September 1947.[17]

2. Following considerable debate, the General Assembly, on 14 November 1947, adopted two resolutions[18] which recognized "the urgent and rightful claims to independence of the people of Korea" and laid down the principle of the participation of Korean representatives in the discussion of the problem. For that purpose a temporary commission on Korea was established with the right to travel, observe, and consult throughout the country.

3. The terms of reference of the Commission, as stated in the resolution, may be summarized as follows:

(a) To facilitate and expedite the participation of Korean representatives in the consideration of the problem, the Commission shall observe that these representatives be duly elected;

(b) To facilitate and expedite the fulfilment of the programme laid down for the attainment of the independence of Korea and the withdrawal of the occupying forces, the elected representatives, constituting a National Assembly, may etablish a National Government and enter into consultations with the Commission.

4. Since the resolutions referred clearly to Korea as a whole, and since the United States Government had formally made known its intention to cooperate, the Commission felt it to be its first duty, following its arrival in Seoul in January 1948, to make special efforts to ascertain the degree of cooperation that would be accorded to it by the interested Powers through their occupying forces.

5. The United States military authorities in the South declared themselves ready to extend facilities and assistance. On the other hand, no answer was received to that effect from the Soviet Military Commander in North Korea, but the negative attitude of the Government of the Union of Soviet Socialist Republics was reaffirmed by the Soviet representative of the United Nations.[19]

6. The Commission therefore regretfully drew the conclusion that it would not be possible, for the time being, to implement its terms of reference in that part of Korea occupied by the forces of the Union of Soviet Socialist Republics.

7. In these circumstances, the Commission decided to consult the Interim Committee for the purpose of obtaining its views on the course to be followed in the light of developments.[20]

8. The Interim Committee, on 26 February 1948, expressed the view that "it is incumbent upon the United Nations Temporary Commission on Korea" to implement the programme as outlined in resolution II of the General Assembly, "in such parts of Korea as are accessible to the Commission." The Commission thereupon decided to

<hr>

[15] See ch. III, par. 2.
[16] See ch. III, par. 18–21.
[17] See ch. I, par. 1–6.
[18] See ch. I, par. 34.
[19] See ch. IV, pars. 1–12.
[20] See ch. IV, pars. 15–17.

observe the elections in South Korea announced by the United States Commanding Officer to be held on 10 May 1948,[21] taking into account the recommendations contained in the letter of the Chairman of the Interim Committee to the Chairman of the Commission.

9. This decision did not imply any essential change in the opinion of the members of the Commission that they were primarily concerned with Korea as a whole.

The background of the situation in Korea

10. In the course of acquainting itself with the background of the situation in Korea since its arrival in January 1948, the Commission had noted certain salient features, bearing upon the political developments, which might be enumerated as follows.

11. The Koreans from both North and South Korea belong to the same race, speak the same language, cherish the same customs and traditions, and have the same fervent love of country. Forty years of Japanese occupation and traditions of feudalistic rule have neither dampened the fervour and political passion of the Korean people nor weakened their historical, ethnic, economic, and cultural unity as a people. Both this passion and this unity have periodically manifested themselves in patriotic outbursts.

12. Having discarded certain aspects of their past, they nevertheless continued to conform to old patterns insofar as their cultural and family life was concerned. Language, national dress, and way of life outlived the Japanese occupation. The modern tendency to accord equality of rights to women has not lessened the influence and authority of the paterfamilias.

13. In addition to this concept, in rural areas, the village headman continues to speak and decide for his community on important matters relating to agricultural, social, and political life.

14. In this context, the Japanese occupation did not find it too difficult to establish an administrative and police network which had so entrenched itself that, even after the liberation of the country, the administrative organization of Korea continued to be influenced by deeply rooted systems of vertical authoritarian rule.

15. Moreover, denied access to accurate sources of information and deprived of the freedom usually associated with the Press, the Korean people, under Japanese rule, had spent a number of years in a state of unawareness, particularly with reference to international affairs.

16. On the eve of liberation, therefore, the Korean people, in spite of certain traces of indigenous democratic practices, were not prepared for an immediate and general application of modern systems of democracy.

17. Following the disappearance of Japanese rule, the development of the political situation in the part of Korea occupied by the Soviet military forces and in the part occupied by the United States military forces took divergent courses. Thus, this artificial division of the country into two parts of the thirty-eighth parallel,[22] which the Korean people considered as disquieting from the very beginning, was sharpened by the drifting of North and South Korean politics in opposite directions. This unfortunate situation could not but have the most disturbing effects on the political and economic life of the country.

---

[21] See ch. IV, pars. 23–34.
[22] See ch. III, pars. 2 and 3.

The situation in the Northern zone, on the basis of such fragmentary information as the Commission was able to gather, is described in chapter III, paragraphs 4–7. As for South Korea, the American occupation authorities were faced in the initial stages either with the prospect of a complete breakdown of government or with a continued use of Japanese-trained personnel. This embarrassment was heightened by the fact that Korea was a liberated and not a conquered country. The Military Government, while being compelled to leave a broad measure of authority to such elements as were necessary for the maintenance of law and order, gradually introduced, whenever possible, reforms directly inspired by the American conception of democracy.[23]

18. In addition to a long history of feudalistic rule, the suppression of political activities during forty years of Japanese occupation had deprived the Koreans of opportunities to acquire adequate political experience. This helps to explain the existing weakness in organization of political parties in South Korea, their multiplicity and—possibly—the tendency of such parties and organizations to gravitate more towards personalities than towards issues, resulting in constant shifting of political alignments.

19. Certain rightist parties, having the support of some elements in the Korean administration, had been able to build up an extensive network of provincial and local party organizations.[24] The moderate groups, being of recent origin, were not as successful as the rightists in extending their party organizations in the provinces, in spite of the fact that some of their outstanding members had, until recently, occupied high positions in the Korean Interim Government.[25] The extreme left, whose political machinery was brought to the foreground by the establishment of a "People's Republic" at the time of liberation, had already lost their advantages since the establishment of a military government. Subsequently, they were forced to operate underground and to confine their activities to sporadic attempts at sabotage and violence.[26]

B. PROBLEMS OF THE ELECTION

20. In this political atmosphere, the Commission sought to bring about a greater measure of freedom before the election and to expedite as much as possible the democratization process in South Korea. Through its hearings of Korean personalities and interviews with competent American authorities, such issues as civil liberties, reform of criminal procedure, certain phases of the activities of the police and youth organizations, political prisoners, means of public information, and electoral procedures, came to the attention of the Commission.

21. In due time, extensive recommendations towards obtaining a freedom of atmosphere were transmitted by the Commission to the Commanding General, United States Army Forces in Korea. These recommendations were made in conformity with recognition of the responsibility of the United States authorities for the maintenance of law and order in the country. The United States Command in Korea

---

[23] See ch. III, pars. 46, 47, and 48.
[24] See ch. III, par. 36.
[25] See ch. III, par. 42.
[26] See ch. III, pars. 8, 15, 25, 31, 45.

subsequently took a number of steps in the direction the Commission had advocated as desirable.

22. The following changes regarded as an important step in ensuring civil liberties were effected by the American authorities:

(*a*) A Korean Bill of Rights, issued by the Commanding General, United States Army Forces in Korea, enumerated the inherent liberties of the Korean people. The proclamation contained the ordinary constitutional rights and freedoms such as generally prevail in democratic countries;[27]

(*b*) On 20 March, the Military Governor approved an ordinance on criminal procedures,[28] which had been under consideration for some time by the United States Command. Among other things, the new ordinance provided that there would be no arrests without warrant, or in certain specified cases, where arrests without warrant were permitted, no detention would be for longer than forty-eight hours without subsequent warrant. It also contained provisions for bail, counsel, and punitive measures for abuse of power, all new features for Korea.

23. Realizing that neither laws, ordinances nor proclamations in themselves would provide sufficient guarantees for a free atmosphere for elections, the Commission directed its attention to the national police and the youth organizations which had been described, in a number of complaints, as often resorting to abusive practices (arbitrary arrests, threats or pressure, etc.).

24. Though concrete evidence of such abuses was not actually presented by the complainants, the Commission nevertheless recognized that the national police might play an important role in the application and execution of laws and ordinances relating to elections. For this reason, it took the decision to observe the attitude of the police very closely during the preelection and the election periods.[29]

25. With respect to "youth organizations"[30] it appeared that with the exception of the National Youth Organization—a group supported by the United States Military Government—they were dependent on private initiative only, and most of them were affiliated to political parties. Almost all of them were markedly prone to organize bellicose demonstrations against their political opponents, thus giving frequent indications of a dangerous lack of tolerance towards the ideas they did not share. The Commission noted, moreover, that the membership of these youth organizations included a large number of adults.

26. A number of recommendations were made in this connection and the respective youth organizations were informed that their behaviour would constitute an important element in the decision of the Commission as to the free atmosphere for elections.

27. From the outset, the Commission had been concerned with the problem of political prisoners.[31] In its recommendations to the Commanding General, United States Army Forces in Korea, the Commission, recognizing the ambiguity of the term "political prisoners," indicated its attitude by specifying those categories of prisoners on whose behalf it did not feel itself justified in interceding. On the other hand, it advocated the release of all those who had been im-

---

[27] Document A/AC.19/62 ; see ch. V, par. 20.
[28] Ordinance 176, effective April 1, 1948, Document A/AC.19/W.40.
[29] See ch. III, par. 74.
[30] The proper translation of "Chong Yong Dan" is "Young Men's Organization."
[31] The question was first raised by the Syrian representative at the opening meeting on January 12, 1948.

prisoned for crimes of a political nature and "had not been guilty of any act of violence or fraud." Furthermore, the Commission recommended that prisoners of the latter category, provided their release did not endanger public order, should benefit by a special pardon.

28. As result of those recommendations, the Military Governor, on 31 March 1948, signed 3,140 pardons restoring to those released full civil rights and allowing them to register as voters and stand as candidates if they so desired.[32] In this regard, the Commission, on 15 April 1948, expressed its gratification to the Commanding General, United States Army Forces in Korea.[33]

29. Although some efforts had been made since the liberation to improve means of public information, the Commission felt it necessary to stress the importance of recognizing and respecting the freedom of the Press. Furthermore, in view of the elections, it made a number of recommendations concerning the dissemination of information, distribution of newsprint and radio time.

30. The Commission undertook a detailed examination as well as a comparative study of the electoral laws of North and South Korea.[34] It was, however, unable to consult the North Korean and Soviet authorities on the matter. Such hearings and interviews as conducted by the Commission were thus confined to competent American authorities and a group of representatives of the Legislative Assembly of South Korea.[35] Subsequent recommendations with respect to the revision of the electoral law and regulations were transmitted to the United States authorities; their purpose was to bring the electoral provisions into greater conformity with the General Assembly's resolutions concerning adult suffrage and secret ballot and, in general, to promote as complete and as free an expression of popular will as possible.[36] With minor exceptions, these recommendations were embodied in the revised electoral law.

31. The Commission, in observing the election programme in South Korea, sought to determine whether these recommendations had been complied with at all levels of authority.

(C) OBSERVATION OF THE ELECTIONS OF 10 MAY 1948

32. By extensive field observations, the Commission witnessed the election programme in the most important areas during the period of preelection preparations and on the date of election itself.

Registration of the electorate (first observation tour)

33. The observation groups found a fair standard of efficiency and organization at all levels of authority. The members of the various election committees were reasonably well informed of the procedures they had to implement and their work in this respect was carried out in orderly fashion.

34. This was the first formal occasion since the liberation when the Korean people had the opportunity of demonstrating their desire for independence through the medium of elections. The whole administrative machinery was mobilized to acquaint qualified voters with the

---

[32] Document A/AC.19/61/Add.1.
[33] Document A/AC.19/61/Add.2.
[34] See ch. V, pars. 41 and 54.
[35] See ch. V, pars. 42 and 45.
[36] See ch. V, pars. 41 and 52.

procedure of registration and with the significance of the elections. At the end of the registration period, 7,837,504 voters had actually registered.[37]

35. The observation groups were not able to collect any concrete evidence of threats or violence against nonregistrants. However, the following complaints about malpractices in the conduct of the registration were received:

> (*a*) In some cases registration was taking place in local administrative offices which, among other functions, issued rice ration cards;
>
> (*b*) Threatened confiscation of rice ration cards resulted, in some instances, in compulsory registration;
>
> (*c*) Against the background of Japanese rule, the advice given by the police and youth organizations to register was regarded as a form of coercion.

36. Regarding the complaints noted in paragraph 35, subparagraphs (*a*) and (*b*), the Commission did not find any evidence of actual confiscation of rice ration cards as a means to compel registration. As to the so-called compulsion through the police or youth groups, the election committees repudiated any suggestion of unlawful pressure being exerted on the people. It would appear, however, that a number of those who were opposed to the elections registered because they did not wish their friends and neighbours to doubt their patriotism at a time when the election was being widely publicized as a decisive step towards national independence. Such minor infractions as were noted by the observation groups were remedied by the election committees.

37. Following the first observation period, the Military Governor was invited to appear before the Main Committee for an extensive exchange of views. Members of the Commission gave a detailed account of their impressions of registrations and of deficiencies observed and received assurances from the Military Governor that he would do everything within his power to remedy the situation.[38] The effect of his intervention in the direction desired by the Commission was noted by the field groups in their subsequent observations.

38. The extreme left seemed to have confined itself mostly to conducting a vigorous campaign of anti-election activities, many of which were of a violent nature. In addition to threats to members of the election committees, registration officials, and voters, there were scattered instances of poll registers being stolen or burnt, registration offices being set on fire and persons associated with registration being wounded or murdered. These activities, exaggerated in some instances by the law-enforcement officers in their reports, were continued

---

[37] From the figures compiled by the Office of Administration (Census Division), South Korean Interim Government the estimated population in South Korea on April 1, 1948, was 19,947,000. The total possible registrants, based on the percentage of 49.3 as derived from the 1947 National Registration (7½ million sample) were 9,834,000. On this basis, the number of registrants would appear as representing some 79.7 percent of the potential electorate. See also Document A/AC.19/66/Add.3 (vol. II, annex VII).

[38] Documents A/AC.19/SC.4/SR.4, A/AC.19/SC.4/SR.5, A/AC.19/SC.5/SR.9, par. 13, A/AC.19/SC.8/SR.1 see vol. III).

throughout the election period. From 7 February to 9 May 1948, inclusive, acts of violence resulted in 245 persons being killed and 559 wounded.[39] Similarly, on Election Day itself, 44 persons were killed and 62 wounded.[40] Means of transportation and communication were disrupted in a number of places.

These threats and acts of violence, however, were not as a whole supported by the people. With the exception of North Cheju Gun,[41] where the situation was rather confused, registration was duly completed in accordance with the electoral provisions.

Registration of candidates (second observation tour)

39. There were 942 candidates [42] originally registered for 200 available seats, ranging from eleven candidates in Cheju-Do for three available seats, to 145 in Kyonggi-Do for twenty-nine available seats.[43] In an electoral district, it was not unusual for four or five candidates, in some instances as many as ten or more, to contest one available seat. There were also instances where two or more candidates from the same party contested the election in the same district.

40. The nomination of the great number of "independent" candidates may be attributed to several factors:

(*a*) Candidates affiliated with a political party, but not standing as the official nominee of the party in a given district, tended to try their luck by campaigning as independents notwithstanding orders from their party headquarters in Seoul;

(*b*) It is possible that certain rightist parties, fearing that their nominees would be prejudiced by the local prevailing political situation, put forward some of their candidates as independents;

(*c*) Members of certain parties opposing the elections might have attempted to seek election by standing as independent candidates;

(*a*) It seemed that a certain number of independents entered the contest relying on their appeal to certain sections of the Korean electorate dissatisfied with the existing parties.

41. The Commission's observation groups made every effort to acquaint themselves with the political views of the candidates. In addition to voicing their opposition to communism and the artificial division of their country, most of these declared themselves in favour of the elections as the method of effecting the unity and independence of Korea. During those interviews it also appeared that many candidates favoured the establishment of a National Government following the elections.

In actual campaigning before the electorate, all candidates pleaded for the support of the elections as a step toward achieving the inde-

---

[39] Documents A/AC.19/W.39/Add.4, Add.6, and Add.8.
[40] Documents A/AC.19/W.39/Add.7 and Add.8.
[41] Documents A/AC.19/SC.5/SR.5 and 6 (see vol. III), A/AC.19/SC.4/6/Add.3 (not reproduced) and A/AC.19/66/Add.3 (vol. II, annex VII).
[42] Of 942 candidates originally registered for 200 seats, 57 did not stand for election. Of this figure, 50 withdrew their candidacy, 2 were assassinated, 1 died of natural causes, 4 were disqualified.
[43] For detailed classifications of registered candidates and subsequent elections, see par. 51.

pendence of Korea. This aspect of the campaign was of such over-riding importance that discussions on domestic issues and party platforms were noticeably absent. Beyond this question of supporting the elections, the electorate was rarely faced by the candidates with other views as to how unity and independence were to be attained. However, most of the people were fully aware of the meaning of the campaign led by the opposition against the elections.

42. Organized campaigning was local in nature, rather than nationally coordinated. It was frequently restricted to local rivalry between competing candidates whose personalities seemed to play a major part. Because of this, certain elected candidates spent only insignificant sums, whereas defeated candidates had devoted sizable funds to their campaigns.

43. During the second observation tour, the candidates, on the whole, declared that they were able to campaign freely and without interference. However, many complaints did later reach the Commission. Specific ones were duly transmitted to the National Election Committee, whose subsequent decisions were regarded as conforming generally to the electoral procedures.

The elections (third observation tour)

44. The Commission divided itself into nine observation groups, which visited the City of Seoul and all the provinces in South Korea for the purpose of observing the conduct of the elections.

45. The preparations made for the actual mechanics of voting were generally satisfactory. Although the arrangements in some cases appeared to be makeshift and might be described as rudimentary, the secrecy of the balloting was, on the whole, ensured. Such minor defections as were noted by the observation groups were immediately rectified by the election committees.

46. Of the 7,837,504 who had registered, 7,036,750, or 95.2 percent of the total registrants,[44] actually took part in the voting. This represents 75 percent [45] of the total potential electorate. The Commission observed that a large percentage of the registered voters, often as many as 90 percent, had cast their ballots during the first four hours, so that in many cases voting was practically completed hours before closing time.

47. These features seemed to indicate a real enthusiasm on the part of the people, as well as of the election officials. There can be little doubt that the Korean electorate responded willingly to the appeal that had been made to them by those interested in the success of the elections, and that the election officials, in spite of the threats made— and often carried out—by the opposition, performed their duties with a zeal and a degree of efficiency that the Commission could hardly expect to find in a country recently opened to modern forms of democracy. This might be explained to a large extent by patriotic motives,

---

[44] The figures mentioned are based on statistics compiled by the Census Division, South Korean Interim Government (document A/AC.19/66/Add.3) (vol. II, annex VII). Computation of percentage is exclusive of 445,622 registrants in noncontested areas. See also footnote to par. 34.

[45] It should be kept in mind that registration was neither automatic nor compulsory. Thus, 25 percent represents the total abstention.

although an undeniable curiosity for an entirely new experience in
a general election on the part of the electorate and of the election
officials themselves might have been a contributing factor. The
observation groups also found a general display of good will and
eagerness to perform electoral duties.

48. As to the administrative and electoral authorities, complaints
were again received that they had interfered with the normal course
of the elections. These complaints were, however, even more vague
in character than those received during the period of registration.
Concrete facts were rarely reported. Such words as "threats" and
"violence" were again freely used to describe irresponsible acts which
constitute, even in the most advanced democracies, the quasi-ritual
accompaniment of individual or even party propaganda. It should
be noted that, while these complaints were still numerous on the
eve of the elections, their number decreased substantially after the
results had been made known. As a whole, the evidence produced
was not such as to impress the Commission that the outcome of the
elections had been appreciably affected, the more so when the extreme
left parties—which the police and the youth organizations were ac-
cused of trying to suppress—were abstaining. Those cases which appeared to be serious enough to deserve careful consideration were,
however, referred to the United States military authorities, who gave
to the Commission a detailed account of the results of the inquiries
conducted at their request.

49. As regards the national police as a whole, it might be pointed
out that, had they ever thought of interfering with the course of the
elections, in spite of the Military Governor's specific instructions not
to do so, they would have had neither the time nor the means to
exert their influence on the days preceding the elections and on
Election Day itself. The active campaign of violence conducted by the
extreme leftists created among the police a feeling of apprehension
and watchfulness. They had thus practically no respite during that
period. Being primarily occupied with the maintenance of order,
they gave no grounds for criticism to the Commission. Few among the
complaints received were connected with their activities on Election
Day.

50. As to the youth organizations, which belonged mostly to the
extreme right, they appeared to have refrained from active interference in the course of the elections. Their activities were directed
towards assisting the authorities in protection of polling places and
the protection of voters or even of candidates. A good number of
their members had volunteered in the "Community Protection
Groups" created in view of the elections to assist the police in maintaining order. These groups were not allowed to carry arms and were
placed under the supervision of the police. It would thus appear that,
having been warned by the authorities of the concern of the Commission regarding their activities, the youth organizations adroitly
refrained from any unlawful interference, leaving to the extreme
left the monopoly of violence.

51. The party affiliations of registered candidates and elected representatives were officially listed as follows: [46]

Candidates' affiliations	Number of candidates	Number of elected representatives
Independents	366	85
National Association for the Rapid Realization of Korean Independence (NARRKI)	247	55
Hankook Democratic Party	100	28
Tae Dong Youth Group	90	12
National Youth Corps	22	6
Dae Han Labour League	22	2
Christian Organization	13	1
Korean Independence Party	8	1
Buddhist Organization	5	
Patriotic Women's Association	3	
Farmer's Party	1	1
Chungyou Youth Group	1	
Former Members of Korean Interim Legislative Assembly	6	
Military Government Officials	6	
Confucian Organization	5	
Liberals	4	
People's Independence Party	2	
Young Men's Christian Association	1	
Catholic	1	
Korean Youth Association	1	
Gold Miners' Association	1	
Chundo Religion	1	
Korean Agriculture	1	
Chosen Democratic Party		1
Tan Min Party		1
General Headquarters for Korean National Unification		1
Education Association	31	1
Korea Republic Party		1
No. 15 Club, Pusan		1
Tai Sun Association		1
Others		

52. In attempting to interpret the significance of party affiliations of elected representatives, the following factors should be given careful consideration:

(*a*) Party discipline in Korea seemed relatively loose. The candidates had at their disposal a certain amount of leeway to act independently of the parties to which they were affiliated.

(*b*) Personalities played an important role in Korean politics. Constant shiftings in party affiliations were not uncommon. It is difficult, therefore, to determine to what extent the people, in electing a candidate to the Assembly, were influenced by his personality and to what extent by his party.

In view of the above, just how and how far the elected representatives may conform to party lines cannot now be foreseen.

53. Of 85 independents elected, allowance should be made for the fact that an indefinite number belonged to either the rightists or opposition parties. The actual alignments of independents can be ascertained only by analysing their forthcoming votes in the Assembly on specific issues.

54. As long as the party affiliations of the independents remain uncertain, the two major political parties in South Korea—the National Association for the Rapid Realization of Korean Independence and the Hankook Democratic Party—would not appear, either alone or together, to have polled a clear majority of the seats.

<hr>

[46] Documents A/AC.19/66/Add.5 (vol. II, annex VII), A/AC.19/75 (vol. II, annex VII) and A/AC.19/W.54.

55. With regard to the boycott of the elections by various parties and organizations,[47] three different methods of protest were available under the conditions in which the elections were held: [48]

    (*a*) Abstaining from registering;

    (*b*) Registering but abstaining from voting;

    (*c*) Registering and casting a blank or a void ballot.

56. No doubt a certain number of South Koreans, for political reasons, followed one or other of the above-mentioned courses. However having regard to the inexperience of voters, the relatively high degree of illiteracy, and normal disabilities of old age and sickness, not all who did so acted for political reasons.

57. The fact that 75 per cent [49] of the potential voters actually went to the polls would be regarded in most countries as an impressive popular response. Even after making full allowance for the possible effects of social pressure on some of the voters and for the habits of subordination to authority in producing a large vote, this response still signified on the part of the people a widespread endorsement of the elections as a means of achieving Korean independence, and an acceptance of those parties and individuals that campaigned for the elections. Of the 25 per cent who abstained from voting, how many did so for political reasons and how many for non-political reasons could not be ascertained. However, such an abstention, whatever the percentage for political reasons may be, might serve as a basis for those who opposed the elections to claim that their views were shared by large numbers of their fellow countrymen. At the same time, it might be pointed out that this abstention constituted a refutation of the charges made by certain circles that the free will of the electorate could not be exercised at all.

D. CONCLUSIONS ON THE ELECTIONS OF 10 MAY 1948

58. The Commission, having taken into account the facts noted above, is of the opinion that:

(*a*) There existed in South Korea during the period of preparation for the elections and on Election Day itself, a reasonable degree of free atmosphere wherein democratic rights of freedom of speech, Press and assembly were recognized and respected;

(*b*) The United States Army Forces in Korea and the South Korean Interim Government complied with the recommendations of the Commission on electoral procedures and the conduct of the elections conformed generally to the electoral laws and regulations;

(*c*) The elections were regarded as a step in the reestablishment of the independence of Korea and, as such, were the only substantial issue placed before the electorate, resulting in the large percentage both of registration and balloting; the candidates who stood for election were in favour of this method of effecting the unity and independence of Korea and therefore did not place any fundamentally conflicting issues before the electorate; and opposition to the issues

---

[47] See ch. III, pars. 56, 57, 59, and 60–64.

[48] From the data compiled by the Census Division of the South Korean Interim Government about 20.3 percent of the potential electorate failed to register, 4.8 percent of those who registered failed to vote, and 3.8 percent of those who voted cast blank or void ballots.

[49] See footnotes to par. 46.

involved in the elections took the form of a boycott of the elections themselves;

(*d*) Having taken into account the reports of its observation groups, and the conclusions noted above, and bearing in mind the traditional and historical background of the people of Korea, the results of the ballot of 10 May 1948 are a valid expression of the free will of the electorate in those parts of Korea which were accessible to the Commission and in which the inhabitants constitute approximately two-thirds of the people of all Korea.

10. UNITED STATES POSITION ON WITHDRAWAL OF OCCUPATION FORCES FROM KOREA, SEPTEMBER 20, 1948 [50]

It has been the consistent view of this government that the best interests of the Korean people would be served by the withdrawal of all occupying forces from Korea at the earliest practicable date. This same view was embodied in the United Nations General Assembly resolution of November 14, 1947, in which provision was made for such withdrawal as soon as practicable after the establishment of the Korean Government which it was the intention of that resolution to bring into being. Had the Soviet Union cooperated in carrying out the provisions of the resolution of November 14, 1947, the question of troop withdrawal from Korea would doubtless have been already resolved.

The United States Government regards the question of the withdrawal of occupying forces as but one facet of the entire question of the unity and independence of Korea. The General Assembly of the United Nations has taken cognizance of this larger question as evidenced by the resolution referred to above, and it may be expected to give further consideration to the matter at its forthcoming meeting.

11. RESOLUTION OF THE GENERAL ASSEMBLY, DECEMBER 12, 1948, ON THE ESTABLISHMENT OF THE REPUBLIC OF KOREA AND THE UNITED NATIONS COMMISSION ON KOREA (UNCOK) [51]

The General Assembly,

Having regard to its resolution 112 (II) of 14 November 1947 concerning the problem of the independence of Korea,

Having considered the report of the United Nations Temporary Commission on Korea (hereinafter referred to as the "Temporary Commission"), and the report of the Interim Committee of the General Assembly regarding its consultation with the Temporary Commission,

Mindful of the fact that, due to difficulties referred to in the report of the Temporary Commission, the objectives set forth in the resolution of 14 November 1947 have not been fully accomplished, and in particular that unification of Korea has not yet been achieved.

1. *Approves* the conclusions of the reports of the Temporary Commission;

2. *Declares* that there has been established a lawful government (the Government of the Republic of Korea) having effective control and jurisdiction over that part of Korea where the Temporary Commission

---

[50] Korea 1945–48, Department of State Publication 3305, p. 116.
[51] United States Policy in the Korean Conflict, July 1950–February 1951, Department of State Publication 4263, pp. 42–43.

was able to observe and consult and in which the great majority of the people of all Korea reside; that this Government is based on elections which were a valid expression of the free will of the electorate of that part of Korea and which were observed by the Temporary Commission; and that this is the only such Government in Korea;

3. *Recommends* that the occupying Powers should withdraw their occupation forces from Korea as early as practicable;

4. *Resolves* that, as a means to the full accomplishment of the objectives set forth in the resolution of 14 November 1947, a Commission on Korea consisting of Australia, China, El Salvador, France, India, the Philippines, and Syria shall be established to continue the work of the Temporary Commission and carry out the provisions of the present resolution, having in mind the status of the Government of Korea as herein defined, and in particular to:

(a) Lend its good offices to bring about the unification of Korea and the integration of all Korean security forces in accordance with the principles laid down by the General Assembly in the resolution of 14 November 1947;

(b) Seek to facilitate the removal of barriers to economic, social, and other friendly intercourse caused by the division of Korea;

(c) Be available for observation and consultation in the further development of representative government based on the freely expressed will of the people;

(d) Observe the actual withdrawal of the occupation forces and verify the fact of withdrawal when such has occurred; and for this purpose, if it so desires, request the assistance of military experts of the two occupying Powers;

5. *Decides* that the Commission:

(a) Shall, within thirty days of the adoption of the present resolution, proceed to Korea, where it shall maintain its seat;

(b) Shall be regarded as having superseded the Temporary Commission established by the resolution of 14 November 1947;

(c) Is authorized to travel, consult, and observe throughout Korea;

(d) Shall determine its own procedures;

(e) May consult with the Interim Committee with respect to the discharge of its duties in the light of developments, and within the terms of the present resolution;

(f) Shall render a report to the next regular session of the General Assembly and to any prior special session which might be called to consider the subject matter of the present resolution, and shall render such interim reports as it may deem appropriate to the Secretary-General for distribution to Members;

6. *Requests* that the Secretary-General shall provide the Commission with adequate staff and facilities, including technical advisers as required; and authorizes the Secretary-General to pay the expenses and *per diem* of a representative and an alternate from each of the State members of the Commission;

7. *Calls upon* the Member States concerned, the Government of the Republic of Korea, and all Koreans to afford every assistance and facility to the Commission in the fulfillment of its responsibilities;

8. *Calls upon* Member States to refrain from any acts derogatory to the results achieved and to be achieved by the United Nations in bringing about the complete independence and unity of Korea;

9. *Recommends* that Member States and other nations, in establishing their relations with the Government of the Republic of Korea, take into consideration the facts set out in paragraph 2 of the present resolution.

Hundred and eighty-seventh plenary meeting,
12 December 1948.

12. UNITED STATES RECOGNITION OF THE REPUBLIC OF KOREA, JANUARY 1, 1949 [52]

On December 12, 1948, the United Nations General Assembly adopted a resolution approving the conclusions of the report of the United Nations Temporary Commission on Korea and declaring in part "that there has been established a lawful government (the Government of the Republic of Korea), having effective control and jurisdiction over that part of Korea where the Temporary Commission was able to observe and consult and in which the great majority of the people of all Korea reside; that this Government is based on elections which were a valid expression of the free will of the electorate of that part of Korea and which were observed by the Temporary Commission; and that this is the only such Government in Korea." The resolution of December 12 concluded with the recommendation that member states and other nations take the foregoing facts into consideration in establishing their relations with the Government of Korea.

In the light of this action by the General Assembly, and taking into account the facts set forth in the statement issued by this Government on August 12, 1948, concerning the new Korean Government, the United States Government has decided to extend full recognition to the Government of the Republic of Korea. Incidental to this step it is anticipated that, by agreement with that Government, the Mission of the United States Special Representative in Korea will in the near future be raised to Embassy rank.

In conformity with the General Assembly resolution of December 12, the United States Government will endeavor to afford every assistance and facility to the new United Nations Commission on Korea established thereunder in its efforts to help the Korean people and their lawful Goverment to achieve the goal of a free and united Korea.

13. STATEMENT BY THE DEPARTMENT OF STATE ON THE WITHDRAWAL OF UNITED STATES TROOPS FROM KOREA, JUNE 8, 1949 [53]

On January 1 of this year the United States Government extended full recognition to the Government of the Republic of Korea. In so doing, the United States welcomed into the community of free nations a new Republic, born of the efforts of the United Nations, and of the United States as a principally interested Power, to give effect to the urgent and rightful claims of the Korean people to freedom and national independence.

The United States Government, inspired by its historic ties of friendship with the Korean people and by its sincere interest in the

[52] Department of State Bulletin, January 9, 1949, pp. 59–60.
[53] Department of State Press Release No. 429, June 8, 1949.

spread of free institutions and representative government among the peoples of the world, entertains a particularly deep and sympathetic concern for the welfare of the Republic of Korea. As evidence of this concern, the United States is currently carrying out in Korea a program of economic and technical assistance designed to provide the economic stability without which political stability would be impossible. A request for authorization to continue and to strengthen this program during the coming fiscal year has already been submitted to the Congress. The United States has, moreover, maintained in Korea a military training mission whose function it has been to advise and assist the Government of the Republic of Korea in the development of its own security forces, in consonance with the United Nations General Assembly's Resolution of November 14, 1947, and has transferred to that Government for those forces substantial amounts of military equipment and supplies under the authority of the Surplus Property Act. The transfer of such equipment and supplies is continuing, while the military training mission has recently been placed on a more formal basis with the establishment of a United States Military Advisory Group to the Republic of Korea (see Department of State Press Release No. 428 of this date). Other forms of assistance, such as that in the fields of education and vocational training, also have been and are being given to the Republic of Korea by the United States Government.

In pursuance of the recommendation contained in the General Assembly's Resolution of December 12, 1948, to the effect that the occupying Powers should "withdraw their occupation forces from Korea as early as practicable," the United States Government will soon have completed the withdrawal of its occupation forces from that country. As is clear from the broad program of assistance outlined above, this withdrawal in no way indicates a lessening of United States interest in the Republic of Korea, but constitutes rather another step toward the normalization of relations with that Republic and a compliance on the part of the United States with the cited provision of the December 12 Resolution of the General Assembly.

While the United States has given unstintingly of its material assistance and political support in order that the Republic of Korea might grow and prosper, this Government recognizes that the Korean problem remains one of international concern and that it is only through continued support by the entire community of nations to which that Republic owes its existence that the security and stability of this new nation can be assured during the critical months and years that lie ahead. So long as the authority of the Republic of Korea continues to be challenged within its own territory by the alien tyranny which has been arbitrarily imposed upon the people of north Korea, the need for such support will be a vital one.

The United States Government has already pledged its support to the United Nations Commission on Korea in its efforts to assist the Korean people toward the goal of a free and united Korea. It believes, however, that this goal can be achieved only through the continued strengthening of the freely elected and democratic Government of the Republic of Korea as an embodiment of the hopes and aspirations of all Koreans to the freedom and independence for which they have worked and waited so long.

14. RESOLUTION OF THE GENERAL ASSEMBLY CONTINUING UNCOK, OCTOBER 21, 1949 [54]

THE GENERAL ASSEMBLY

HAVING REGARD to its resolutions 112 (II) of 14 November 1947 and 195 (III) of 12 December 1948 concerning the problem of the independence of Korea,

HAVING CONSIDERED the report of the United Nations Commission on Korea, and having taken note of the conclusions reached therein,

MINDFUL of the fact that, due to difficulties referred to in the report of the Commission, the objectives set forth in the resolutions referred to have not been fully accomplished, and in particular that the unification of Korea and the removal of barriers to economic, social, and other friendly intercourse caused by the division of Korea have not yet been achieved.

HAVING NOTED that the Commission has observed and verified the withdrawal of United States occupation forces, but that it has not been accorded the opportunity to observe or verify the reported withdrawal of Soviet occupation forces,

RECALLING its declaration of 12 December 1948 that there has been established a lawful government (the Government of the Republic of Korea) having effective control and jurisdiction over that part of Korea where the United Nations Temporary Commission on Korea was able to observe and consult and in which the great majority of the people of Korea reside; that this Government is based on elections which were a valid expression of the free will of the electorate of that part of Korea and which were observed by the Temporary Commission; and that this is the only such Government in Korea;

CONCERNED lest the situation described by the Commission in its report menace the safety and well-being of the Republic of Korea and of the people of Korea and lead to open military conflict in Korea.

1. *Resolves* that the United Nations Commission on Korea shall continue being with the following membership: Australia, China, El Salvador, France, India, Philippines, and Turkey and, having in mind the objectives set forth in the General Assembly resolutions of 14 November 1947 and 12 December 1948 and also the status of the Government of the Republic of Korea as defined in the latter resolution, shall:

(a) Observe and report any developments which might lead to or otherwise involve military conflict in Korea;

(b) Seek to facilitate the removal of barriers to economic, social and other friendly intercourse caused by the division of Korea; and make available its good offices and be prepared to assist, whenever in its judgment a favorable opportunity arises, in bringing about the unification of Korea in accordance with the principles laid down by the General Assembly in the resolution of 14 November 1947;

(c) Have authority, in order to accomplish the aims defined under subparagraphs (a) and (b) of the present paragraph, in its discretion to appoint observers, and to utilize the services and good offices of one or more persons whether or not representatives on the Commission;

---

[54] General Assembly Roundup, Fourth Regular Session, Press Release GA/600, 10 December 1949.

(d) Be available for observation and consultation throughout Korea in the continuing development of representative government based on the freely-expressed will of the people, including elections of national scope;

(e) Verify the withdrawl of Soviet occupation forces insofar as it is in a position to do so;

2. DECIDES that the Commission:

(a) Shall meet in Korea within thirty days from the date of the present resolution;

(b) Shall continue to maintain its seat in Korea;

(c) Is authorized to travel, consult and observe throughout Korea;

(d) Shall continue to determine its own procedures;

(e) May consult with the Interim Committee of the General Assembly (if it be continued) with respect to the discharge of its duties in the light of developments and within the terms of the present resolution;

(f) Shall render a report to the next regular session of the General Assembly and to any prior special session which might be called to consider the subject matter of the present resolution, and shall render such interim reports as it may deem appropriate to the Secretary-General for transmission to Members;

(g) Shall remain in existence pending a new decision by the General Assembly;

3. CALLS UPON Member States, the Government of the Republic of Korea, and all Koreans to afford every assistance and facility to the Commission in the fulfilment of its responsibilities, and to refrain from any acts derogatory to the purposes of the present resolution;

4. REQUESTS the Secretary-General to provide the Commission with adequate staff and facilities, including technical advisers and observers as required; and authorizes the Secretary-General to pay the expenses and *per diem* of a representative and an alternate from each of the States members of the Commission and of such persons as may be appointed in accordance with paragraph 1 (c) of the present resolution.

IV. U. S. ASSISTANCE TO KOREA

15. MESSAGE OF PRESIDENT TRUMAN TO CONGRESS, JUNE 7, 1949, ON ECONOMIC ASSISTANCE TO KOREA [55]

To the Congress of the United States:

I recommend that the Congress authorize the continuation of economic assistance to the Republic of Korea for the fiscal year ending June 30, 1950.

The United States is now providing relief and a small amount of assistance in rehabilitation to the Republic of Korea under Pubic Law 793—80th Congress. The continuation of that assistance is of great importance to the successful achievement of the foreign policy aims of the United States. The authority of the present Act extends only until June 30, 1949. For this reason legislation is urgently needed and I am hopeful that the Congress may give it early consideration.

---

[55] A Decade of American Foreign Policy, 1941–1949, S. Doc. 123, 81st Cong., pp. 679–682.

The people of the United States have long had sympathetic feelings for the Korean people. American missionaries, supported by American churches of many denominations, brought spiritual guidance, education and medical aid to the Korean people during their forty years of Japanese bondage. All Americans who have come to know the Korean people appreciate their fierce passion for freedom and their keen desire to become an independent nation.

Early in the war with Japan, it was resolved that Korea should be liberated. In the Cairo Declaration of December, 1943, the United States joined with the United Kingdom and China to express their determination that in due course Korea should become free and independent. This pledge was reaffirmed in the Potsdam Declaration of July 26, 1945, with which the Soviet Union associated itself upon its entrance into the war against Japan in the following month. With our victory over Japan, it was hoped that the Korean nation would be reborn. Unfortunately, however, only the people of Korea south of the 38° parallel have thus far attained their freedom and independence.

The present division of Korea along the 38° parallel was never intended by the United States. The sole purpose of the line along the 38° parallel was to facilitate acceptance by the Soviet and United States forces of the surrender of Japanese troops north and south of that line. Immediately after the completion of the Japanese surrender the United States through direct negotiations with the Soviet Union sought to restore the unity of Korea.

For two years these efforts were rendered unavailing by the attitude of the Soviet Union. When it became apparent that further delay would be injurious to the interests of the Korean people, the United States submitted the matter to the General Assembly of the United Nations, in the hope that the United Nations could assist the people of Korea to assume their rightful place as an independent, democratic nation.

By vote of an overwhelming majority, the General Assembly adopted a resolution on November 14, 1947, calling for an election, under the observation of a United Nations Temporary Commission on Korea, to choose a representative National Assembly for the purpose of drafting a democratic constitution and establishing a national government. The Soviet Union refused to permit the United Nations Commission to enter its zone. Consequently, the right of the Korean people to participate in a free election to establish a free government was confined to south Korea. As a result of this election, the Government of the Republic of Korea was inaugurated August 15, 1948.

The General Assembly of the United Nations at its next session considered the report of its Commission and in December, 1948, adopted a resolution holding the Government of the Republic of Korea to be the validly elected, lawful government of the area in which elections were held under the Commission's observation—and the only such government in Korea. The General Assembly established a re-constituted Commission to consult with the occupying powers on the withdrawal of their forces and to continue to work for the unification of Korea under representative government.

The United States terminated its military government in Korea upon the inauguration of the Government of the Republic of Korea and recognized the new government on New Year's Day, 1949.

The December, 1948, resolution of the General Assembly called on the occupying powers to withdraw their forces as soon as practicable. The United States has thus far retained a small number of troops in Korea at the request of the Government of the Republic to give the Republic an opportunity to establish forces adequate to protect itself against internal disturbances and external attacks short of an aggressive war supported by a major power. A military advisory group requested by the Korean Government for training purposes will be retained in Korea after the withdrawal of United States troops.

The debilitated state in which the Korean economy was left by the Japanese has been accentuated by the separation of the hydroelectric power, coal and metal and fertilizer industries of the north from the agricultural and textile industries of the south and by the effects of continuing communist agitation. The United States has furnished the people of south Korea with basic relief during the period of military government. Despite such assistance, however, the Republic is still far short of being able to support itself, even at the present modest standard of living of its people. It is in urgent need of further assistance in the difficult period ahead until it can stand on its own feet economically.

The aid now being provided to Korea is essentially for basic relief. Without the continuation of such relief, its economy would collapse— inevitably and rapidly. Bare relief alone, however, would not make it possible for the Republic to become self-supporting. The Republic would remain dependent upon the continuation of relief from the United States at a costly level into the indefinite future—and subject to the same inevitable collapse at any time the relief should be withdrawn. For these reasons the aid granted should be not for more relief but for recovery. The kind of program which is needed is the kind which the Congress has authorized for the countries of Western Europe and under which those countries have achieved such rapid progress toward recovery during the past year. Full advantage should be taken of the broad and successful experience in Western Europe by continuing responsibility for the administration of the Korean aid program in the Economic Cooperation Administration, which has been administering aid to Korea since January 1 of this year.

Prior to January 1 of this year, aid to Korea was administered by the Army as a part of its program for government and relief in occupied areas. The Budget which I submitted to the Congress in January contemplated that economic assistance to Korea would be continued outside of the Army's program for government and relief in occupied areas. The needs of the Republic of Korea for economic assistance have been carefully studied in the light of the latest available information. I am convinced that the sum of $150,000,000 is the minimum aid essential during the coming year for progress toward economic recovery.

Such a recovery program will cost only a relatively small amount more than a bare relief program. Yet a recovery program—and only a recovery program—will enable the Republic of Korea to commence building up the coal production, electric power capacity and fertilizer production which are fundamental to the establishment of a self-supporting economy and to the termination of the need for aid from the United States. Aid in the restoration of the Korean economy should be less costly to the United States in the end than a continued program of relief.

The recovery program which is recommended is not only the soundest course economically but also the most effective from the standpoint of helping to achieve the objectives of peaceful and democratic conditions in the Far East.

Korea has become a testing ground in which the validity and practical value of the ideals and principles of democracy which the Republic is putting into practice are being matched against the practices of communism which have been imposed upon the people of north Korea. The survival and progress of the Republic toward a self-supporting, stable economy will have an immense and far-reaching influence on the people of Asia. Such progress by the young Republic will encourage the people of southern and southeastern Asia and the islands of the Pacific to resist and reject the Communist propaganda with which they are besieged. Moreover, the Korean Republic, by demonstrating the success and tenacity of democracy in resisting communism, will stand as a beacon to the people of northern Asia in resisting the control of the Communist forces which have overrun them.

The Republic of Korea, and the freedom-seeking people of north Korea held under Soviet domination, seek for themselves a united, self-governing and sovereign country, independent of foreign control and support and with membership in the United Nations. In their desire for unity and independence, they are supported by the United Nations.

The United States has a deep interest in the continuing progress of the Korean people toward these objectives. The most effective, practical aid which the United States can give toward reaching them will be to assist the Republic to move toward self-support at a decent standard of living. In the absence of such assistance, there can be no real hope of achieving a unified, free and democratic Korea.

If we are faithful to our ideals and mindful of our interest in establishing peaceful and prosperous conditions in the world, we will not fail to provide the aid which is so essential to Korea at this critical time.

16. FAR EASTERN ECONOMIC ASSISTANCE ACT OF 1950, PUBLIC LAW 447, EIGHTY-FIRST CONGRESS [S. 2319], 64 STAT. 5, APPROVED FEBRUARY 14, 1950, AS AMENDED BY SECTION 107 OF TITLE I OF PUBLIC LAW 535, EIGHTY-FIRST CONGRESS [H. R. 7797], 64 STAT. 202, APPROVED JUNE 5, 1950 [56]

AN ACT To provide economic assistance to certain areas of the Far East

Be it enacted by the Senate and House of Representatives of the United States of America in Congress assembled, That this Act be cited as the "Far Eastern Economic Assistance Act of 1950".

* * *

SEC. 3. (a) The Administrator for Economic Cooperation is hereby authorized to furnish assistance to the Republic of Korea in conformity with—

---

[56] Mutual Security Legislation and Related Documents, Committee on Foreign Affairs, House of Representatives, Committee Print, November 1952, pp. 68–70.

(1) the provisions of the Economic Cooperation Act of 1948, as amended, wherever such provisions are applicable and not inconsistent with the intent and purposes of this section 3; and

(2) the agreement on aid between the United States of America and the Republic of Korea signed December 10, 1948, or any supplementary or succeeding agreement which shall not substantially alter the basic obligations of either party.

(b) Notwithstanding the provisions of any other law, the Administrator shall immediately terminate aid under this section in the event of the formation in the Republic of Korea of a coalition government which includes one or more members of the Communist Party or of the party now in control of the government of northern Korea.

(c) Notwithstanding the provisions of any other law, the Administrator is authorized to make available to the Republic of Korea merchant vessels of tonnage not in excess of two thousand five hundred gross tons each, in a number not to exceed ten at any one time, with a stipulation that such vessels shall be operated only in east Asian waters and must be returned forthwith upon demand of the Administrator and in any event not later than June 30, 1952.[57] Any agency of the United States Government owning or operating any such vessel is authorized to make such vessel available to the Administrator for the purposes of this section upon his application, notwithstanding the provisions of any other law and without reimbursement by the Administrator, and title to any such vessel so supplied shall remain in the United States Government.

NOTE.—Section 303 of the Mutual Security Act of 1951, as amended, provides:
"(e) The functions of the Administrator for Economic Cooperation under the provisions of section 3 of the Far Eastern Economic Assistance Act of 1950, as amended (22 U. S. C. 1551), shall hereafter be performed by such departments or agencies of the Government as the President shall direct."

(d) In order to carry out the provisions of this section 3, there is hereby authorized to be appropriated to the President, in addition to sums already appropriated, not to exceed $60,000,000 for the fiscal year ending June 30, 1950, and $100,000,000 for the fiscal year ending June 30, 1951.[58]

(e) Notwithstanding the provisions of any other law, until such time as an appropriation shall be made pursuant to subsection (d) of this section, the Reconstruction Finance Corporation is authorized and directed to make advances not to exceed in the aggregate $30,000,-000 to carry out the provisions of this section, in such manner, at such times, and in such amounts as the Administrator shall request, and no interest shall be charged on advances made by the Treasury to the Reconstruction Finance Corporation for this purpose. The Reconstruction Finance Corporation shall be repaid without interest for advances made by it hereunder; from funds made available for the purposes of this section 3.

---

[57] Sec. 107 (a) of Public Law 535, 81st Cong., changed the date in this sentence from June 30, 1951, as originally provided, to June 30, 1952.
[58] Sec. 107 (b) of Public Law 535 authorized the additional amount for fiscal year 1951. The changes made in this subsection by sec. 107 (b) of Public Law 535 are shown as follows:
"(d) In order to carry out the provisions of this sec. 3, there is hereby authorized to be appropriated to the President, in addition to sums already appropriated, not to exceed $60,000,000 for the fiscal year ending [June 30, 1950.] *June 30, 1950, and $100,000,000 for the fiscal year ending June 30, 1951.*"

SEC. 4. The authorization for appropriations in this Act is limited to the period ending June 30, 1951,[59] in order that any subsequent authorizations may be separately passed on, and is not to be construed as an express or implied commitment to provide further authorizations or appropriations.[60]

17. UNITED STATES NONMILITARY ASSISTANCE TO REPUBLIC OF KOREA, JULY 1, 1945–MARCH 31, 1953 [61]

Grants:

Army Civilian Supplies	$297, 890, 000
Civilian Relief in Korea	277, 534, 000
Technical and Economic Assistance (ECA/MSA)	123, 191, 000
Foreign Relief Program (Public Law 84)	72, 000
Chinese-Korean Students Relief	47, 000
United Nations Korean Rehabilitation Agency (UNKRA)	35, 000, 000
United Nations Relief and Rehabilitation Agency (UNRRA)	546, 000
Subtotal	734, 280, 000
Credits: Surplus property	24, 928, 000
Total	759, 208, 000

V. THE OUTBREAK OF AGGRESSION

18. TELEGRAM FROM THE UNITED NATIONS COMMISSION ON KOREA TO SECRETARY-GENERAL TRYGVE LIE [62]

[SEOUL, June 25, 1950.]

Government of Republic of Korea states that about 04: 00 hrs. 25 June attacks were launched in strength by North Korean forces all along the 38th parallel.   Major points of attack have included Ongjin Peninsula, Kaesong area and Chunchon and east coast where seaborne landings have been reported north and south at Kanknung. Another seaborne landing reported imminent under air cover in Pohang area on southeast coast.   The latest attacks have occurred along the parallel directly north of Seoul along shortest avenue of approach. Pyongyang radio allegation at 13: 35 hrs. of South Korean invasion across parallel during night declared entirely false by President and Foreign Minister in course of conference with Commission members and principal secretary.   Allegations also stated Peoples Army instructed repulse invading forces by decisive counterattack and placed responsibility for consequences on South Korea.   Briefing on situation by President included statement thirty-six tanks and armoured cars used in northern attacks at four points.   Following emergency Cabinet meeting Foreign Minister issuing broadcast to people of South Korea encouraging resistance against dastardly attack.   President expressed complete willingness for Commission broadcast urging cease-fire and for communication to United Nations to inform of gravity of situation.   Although North Korean declaration of war rumoured at 11: 00 hrs. over Pyongyang radio, no confirmation avail-

[59] Sec. 107 (c) of Public Law 535, 81st Cong., changed the date in this sentence from June 30, 1950, as originally provided, to June 30, 1951.

[60] Authorizations for fiscal year 1952 appropriations are contained in sec. 303, Mutual Security Act of 1951, as amended.

[61] *Foreign Aid*, Office of Business Economics, U. S. Department of Commerce.   Military assistance figures are classified security information.

[62] United States Policy in the Korean Crisis, Department of State Publication 3922, p. 12; UN doc. S/1496.

able from any source. President not treating broadcast as official notice. United States Ambassador, appearing before Commission, stated his expectation Republican Army would give good account of itself.

At 17:15 hrs. four yak-type aircraft strafed civilian and military airfields outside Seoul destroying planes, firing gas tanks and attacking jeeps. Yongdungpo railroad station on outskirts also strafed.

Commission wishes to draw attention of Secretary-General to serious situation developing which is assuming character of full-scale war and may endanger the maintenance of international peace and security. It suggests that he consider possibility of bringing matter to notice of Security Council. Commission will communicate more fully considered recommendation later.

19. RESOLUTION OF THE SECURITY COUNCIL, JUNE 25, 1950 [63]

The Security Council

Recalling the finding of the General Assembly in its resolution of 21 October 1949 that the Government of the Republic of Korea is a lawfully established government "having effective control and jurisdiction over that part of Korea where the United Nations Temporary Commission on Korea was able to observe and consult and in which the great majority of the people of Korea reside; and that this Government is based on elections which were a valid expression of the free will of the electorate of that part of Korea and which were observed by the Temporary Commission; and that this is the only such Government in Korea";

Mindful of the concern expressed by the General Assembly in its resolutions of 12 December 1948 and 21 October 1949 of the consequences which might follow unless Member States refrained from acts derogatory to the results sought to be achieved by the United Nations in bringing about the complete independence and unity of Korea; and the concern expressed that the situation described by the United Nations Commission on Korea in its report menaces the safety and well-being of the Republic of Korea and of the people of Korea and might lead to open military conflict there;

Noting with grave concern the armed attack upon the Republic of Korea by forces from North Korea,

Determines that this action constitutes a breach of the peace,

I. *Calls for* the immediate cessation of hostilities; and

Calls upon the authorities of North Korea to withdraw forthwith their armed forces to the thirty-eighth parallel;

II. *Requests* the United Nations Commission on Korea

(a) To communicate its fully considered recommendations on the situation with the least possible delay;

(b) To observe the withdrawal of the North Korean forces to the thirty-eighth parallel; and

(c) To keep the Security Council informed on the execution of this resolution;

III. *Calls upon* all Members to render every assistance to the United Nations in the execution of this resolution and to refrain from giving assistance to the North Korean authorities.

---

[63] United States Policy in the Korean Crisis, Department of State Publication 3922, p. 16. UN doc. S/1501.

20. STATEMENT BY PRESIDENT TRUMAN, JUNE 26, 1950 [64]

I conferred Sunday evening with the Secretaries of State and Defense, their senior advisers, and the Joint Chiefs of Staff about the situation in the Far East created by unprovoked aggression against the Republic of Korea.

The Government of the United States is pleased with the speed and determination with which the United Nations Security Council acted to order a withdrawal of the invading forces to positions north of the 38th parallel. In accordance with the resolution of the Security Council, the United States will vigorously support the effort of the Council to terminate this serious breach of the peace.

Our concern over the lawless action taken by the forces from North Korea, and our sympathy and support for the people of Korea in this situation, are being demonstrated by the cooperative action of American personnel in Korea, as well as by steps taken to expedite and augment assistance of the type being furnished under the Mutual Defense Assistance Program.

Those responsible for this act of aggression must realize how seriously the Government of the United States views such threats to the peace of the world. Willful disregard of the obligation to keep the peace cannot be tolerated by nations that support the United Nations Charter.

21. STATEMENT BY PRESIDENT TRUMAN, JUNE 27, 1950, ORDERING U. S. AIR AND NAVAL FORCES TO ASSIST THE REPUBLIC OF KOREA [65]

In Korea the Government forces, which were armed to prevent border raids and to preserve internal security, were attacked by invading forces from North Korea. The Security Council of the United Nations called upon the invading troops to cease hostilities and to withdraw to the thirty-eighth parallel. This they have not done, but on the contrary have pressed the attack. The Security Council called upon all members of the United Nations to render every assistance to the United Nations in the execution of this resolution. In these circumstances I have ordered United States air and sea forces to give the Korean Government troops cover and support.

The attack upon Korea makes it plain beyond all doubt that communism has passed beyond the use of subversion to conquer independent nations and will now use armed invasion and war. It has defied the orders of the Security Council of the United Nations issued to preserve international peace and security. In these circumstances the occupation of Formosa by Communist forces would be a direct threat to the security of the Pacific area and to United States forces performing their lawful and necessary functions in that area.

Accordingly I have ordered the Seventh Fleet to prevent any attack on Formosa. As a corollary of this action I am calling upon the Chinese Government on Formosa to cease all air and sea operations against the mainland. The Seventh Fleet will see that this is done. The determination of the future status of Formosa must await the restoration of security in the Pacific, a peace settlement with Japan, or consideration by the United Nations.

---

[64] United States Policy in the Korean Crisis, Department of State Publication 3922, pp. 16–17.

[65] Background Information on Korea, H. Rept. No. 2495, 81st Cong., pp. 45–46.

I have also directed that United States forces in the Philippines be strengthened and that military assistance to the Philippine Government be accelerated.

I have similarly directed acceleration in the furnishing of military assistance to the forces of France and the associated States in Indochina and the dispatch of a military mission to provide close working relations with those forces.

I know that all members of the United Nations will consider carefully the consequences of this latest aggression in Korea in defiance of the Charter of the United Nations. A return to the rule of force in international affairs would have far-reaching effects. The United States will continue to uphold the rule of law.

I have instructed Ambassador Austin, as the representative of the United States to the Security Council, to report these steps to the Council.

22. RESOLUTION OF THE SECURITY COUNCIL, JUNE 27, 1950 [66]

The Security Council,
Having determined that the armed attack upon the Republic of Korea by forces from North Korea constitutes a breach of the peace,
Having called for an immediate cessation of hostilities, and
Having called upon the authories of North Korea to withdraw forthwith their armed forces to the 38th parallel, and
Having noted from the report of the United Nations Commission for Korea that the authorities in North Korea have neither ceased hostilities nor withdrawn their armed forces to the 38th parallel and that urgent military measures are required to restore international peace and security, and
Having noted the appeal of the Republic of Korea to the United Nations for immediate and effective steps to secure peace and security,
Recommends that the Members of the United Nations furnish such assistance to the Republic of Korea as may be necessary to repel the armed attack and to restore international peace and security in the area.

23. STATEMENT OF PRESIDENT TRUMAN, JUNE 30, 1950 [67]

At a meeting with congressional leaders at the White House this morning the President, together with the Secretary of Defense, the Secretary of State, and the Joint Chiefs of Staff, reviewed with them the latest developments of the situation in Korea.

The congressional leaders were given a full review of the intensified military activities.

In keeping with the United Nations Security Council's request for support to the Republic of Korea in repelling the North Korean invaders and restoring peace in Korea, the President announced that he had authorized the United States Air Force to conduct missions on specific military targets in Northern Korea wherever militarily necessary, and had ordered a naval blockade of the entire Korean coast.

General MacArthur has been authorized to use certain supporting ground units.

---

[66] United States Policy in the Korean Crisis, Department of State Publication 3922, p. 24. UN doc. S/1511.
[67] Background Information on Korea, H. Rept. 2495, 81st Cong., pp. 50–51.

24. RESOLUTION OF THE SECURITY COUNCIL, JULY 7, 1950, ESTABLISHING THE UNIFIED COMMAND UNDER THE UNITED STATES [68]

The Security Council,

Having determined that the armed attack upon the Republic of Korea by forces from North Korea constitutes a breach of the peace,

Having recommended that Members of the United Nations furnish such assistance to the Republic of Korea as may be necessary to repel the armed attack and to restore international peace and security in the area,

1. *Welcomes* the prompt and vigorous support which governments and peoples of the United Nations have given to its Resolutions of 25 and 27 June 1950 to assist the Republic of Korea in defending itself against armed attack and thus to restore international peace and security in the area;

2. *Notes* that Members of the United Nations have transmitted to the United Nations offers of assistance for the Republic of Korea;

3. *Recommends* that all Members providing military forces and other assistance pursuant to the aforesaid Security Council resolutions make such forces and other assistance available to a unified command under the United States;

4. *Requests* the United States to designate the commander of such forces;

5. *Authorizes* the unified command at its discretion to use the United Nations flag in the course of operations against North Korean forces concurrently with the flags of the various nations participating;

6. *Requests* the United States to provide the Security Council with reports as appropriate on the course of action taken under the unified command.

25. RESOLUTION OF THE SECURITY COUNCIL, JULY 31, 1950 [69] ON CIVILIAN RELIEF IN KOREA

The Security Council,

Recognizing the hardships and privations to which the people of Korea are being subjected as a result of the continued prosecution by the North Korean forces of their unlawful attack; and

Appreciating the spontaneous offers of assistance to the Korean people which have been made by governments, specialized agencies, and nongovernmental organizations;

Requests the Unified Command to exercise responsibility for determining the requirements for the relief and support of the civilian population of Korea, and for establishing in the field the procedures for providing such relief and support;

Requests the Secretary-General to transmit all offers of assistance for relief and support to the Unified Command;

Requests the Unified Command to provide the Security Council with reports, as appropriate, on its relief activities;

Requests the Secretary-General, the Economic and Social Council in accordance with Article 65 of the Charter, other appropriate United Nations principal and subsidiary organs, the specialized agencies in accordance with the terms of their respective agreements with

[68] United States Policy in the Korean Crisis, Department of State Publication, 4263, pp. 66–67.   UN doc. S/1588.

[69] United States Policy in the Korean Conflict, July 1950–February 1951, Department of State Publication 4263, pp. 11–12.   UN Doc. S/1657.

the United Nations, and appropriate nongovernmental organizations to provide such assistance as the Unified Command may request for the relief and support of the civilian population of Korea, and as appropriate in connection with the responsibilities being carried out by the Unified Command on behalf of the Security Council.

26. REPORT OF THE UNITED NATIONS COMMISSION ON KOREA, SEPTEMBER 4, 1950 [70]

[Excerpt]

PART 4. ANALYSIS AND CONCLUSIONS

A. RESPONSIBILITY FOR THE AGGRESSION

202. The invasion of the territory of the Republic of Korea by the armed forces of the North Korean authorities, which began on 25 June 1950, was an act of aggression initiated without warning and without provocation, in execution of a carefully prepared plan.

203. This plan of aggression, it is now clear, was an essential part of the policy of the North Korean authorities, the object of which was to secure control over the whole of Korea. If control could not be gained by peaceful means, it would be achieved by overthrowing the Republic of Korea, either by undermining it from within or, should that prove ineffective, by resorting to direct aggression. As the methods used for undermining the Republic from within proved unsuccessful, the North Korean authorities launched an invasion of the territory of the Republic of Korea.

ORIGIN AND NATURE OF THE CONFLICT

204. The origin of the conflict is to be found in the artificial division of Korea and in the failure, in 1945, of the occupying Powers to reach agreement on the method to be used for giving independence to Korea. This failure was not due to anything inherent in the attitude of the people of Korea themselves, but was a reflection of those wider and more fundamental differences of outlook and policy which have become so marked a feature of the international scene.

205. This artificial division was consolidated by the exclusion from North Korea of the United Nations Temporary Commission, which had been charged by the General Assembly to observe the holding of elections on a democratic basis in the whole of Korea. In the circumstances, it was decided to hold such elections in South Korea alone.

206. Had internationally supervised elections been allowed to take place in the whole of Korea, and had a unified and independent Korea thereby come into existence, the present conflict could never have arisen.

C. PROSPECTS OF UNIFICATION

207. The Korean people, one in race, language, and culture, fervently desire to live in a unified and independent Korea. Unification can be the only aim regarding Korea. It did, however, appear to the Commission, before the aggression took place, that unification through

---

[70] General Assembly Official Records: Fifth Session, Supplement No. 16 (A/1350), pp. 32–33.

negotiation was unlikely to be achieved if such negotiation involved the holding of internationally supervised elections on a democratic basis in the whole of Korea. Experience suggested that the North Korean authorities would never agree to such elections

208. It was hoped that, at some stage, it might be possible to break down the economic and social barriers between the two political entities as a step toward unification. That too proved illusory, as the North Korean authorities persisted in their policy of aiming at the overthrow of the Republic of Korea.

209. After the consolidation of the division of Korea, propaganda and hostile activities on the part of the North Korean authorities accentuated tension which, in turn, stiffened the attitude of the Government and people of the Republic of Korea, and even further prejudiced such possibility of unification by negotiation as might have remained. Notwithstanding the continued efforts of the Commission, it appeared on the eve of the aggression that the Korean Peninsula would remain divided indefinitely, or at least until international tension had slackened.

D. DEVELOPMENT OF REPRESENTATIVE GOVERNMENT IN THE REPUBLIC OF KOREA

210. The necessity to safeguard the stability and security of the Republic of Korea from the threat from the North gradually became a controlling factor in all the major activities of the administration of the Republic, and absorbed energies and resources which were needed to develop the new form of representative government and to carry out the economic and social reconstruction programme.

211. The first two years of the new National Assembly reflected clearly the difficulties which it would be normal to expect in a body dealing with a new and unfamiliar political structure. It had become clear, long before the act of aggression occurred, that the Legislature was making good progress in its efforts to exert parliamentary control over all departments of government, and would not rest content until its relations with the Executive had been satisfactorily adjusted. The growing civic responsibility shown by the Legislature augured well for the future of representative government in Korea.

212. At the elections of 30 May 1950, the people showed very considerable enthusiasm, and the electoral machinery functioned well. Among the cases of interference with candidates which occurred, some were explainable in the light of the stringent precautions which the Government found it necessary to take in order to safeguard the stability and security of the State against the threat from the North. Although there appeared to be little justification for interference in some other cases, the results of the elections, in which many candidates critical of the Administration were returned, showed that the voters were in fact able to exercise their democratic freedom of choice among candidates, and had cast their votes accordingly. The results also showed popular support of the Republic, and a determination to improve the Administration by constitutional means.

213. The division of Korea added to the economic difficulties that had arisen at the end of the Japanese domination, and made it most difficult for the Republic of Korea to become self-supporting. Funds which might have been expended for the execution of the social and economic programme of the Republic were consumed by heavy de-

fence expenditures. Nevertheless, when the aggression occurred, substantial progress was being made with that programme.

E. KOREAN NEEDS AND ASPIRATIONS

214. Serious problems of reconstruction and rehabilitation, particularly the grave refugee problem, already confront the country. To these problems will be added problems of yet greater magnitude when the military conflict comes to an end. It will be quite beyond the capacity of the country to provide from its own resources means for rehabilitation. A healthy and viable democracy in Korea cannot come into being unless very considerable aid and assistance are provided from outside Korea.

215. Finally, as the division of the country and the resulting antagonisms were artificial, the Commission believes that, when the conditions under which they arose disappear, it will be possible for the Korean people of both North and South to come again together, to live in peace and to build the strong foundations of a free, democratic Korea.

DONE in a single copy in the English language at House No. 328 at Camp Hialeah, Pusan, Korea, this fourth day of September in the year nineteen hundred and fifty.

(*Signed*)
Anup SINGH (*Chairman*) (*India*)
A. B. JAMIESON (*Rapporteur*) (*Australia*)
LIU Yu-Wan (*China*)
Angel Gochez MARIN (*El Salvador*)
Henri BRIONVAL (*France*)
Bernabe AFRICA (*The Philippines*)
Kamil IDIL (*Turkey*)
Bertil A. RENBORG (*Principal Secretary*)

VI. EARLY U. N. ATTEMPTS AT SETTLEMENT OF KOREAN WAR

27. RESOLUTION OF THE GENERAL ASSEMBLY, OCTOBER 7, 1950,[71] ESTABLISHING THE UNITED NATIONS COMMISSION FOR THE UNIFICATION AND REHABILITATION OF KOREA (UNCURK)

The General Assembly,

Having regard to its resolutions of November 14, 1947, of December 12, 1948, and of October 21, 1949,

Having received and considered the report of the United Nations Commission on Korea,

Mindful of the fact that the objectives set forth in the resolutions referred to above have not been fully accomplished and, in particular, that the unification of Korea has not yet been achieved, and that an attempt has been made by an armed attack from North Korea to extinguish by force the Government of the Republic of Korea,

Recalling the General Assembly declaration of December 12, 1948, that there has been established a lawful government (the Government of the Republic of Korea) having effective control and jurisdiction

---

[71] United States Policy in the Korean Conflict, July 1950–February 1951, Department of State Publication 4263, pp. 17–18. UN doc. A/1435.

over that part of Korea where the United Nations Temporary Commission on Korea was able to observe and consult and in which the great majority of the people of Korea reside; that this Government is based on elections which were a valid expression of the free will of the electorate of that part of Korea and which were observed by the Temporary Commission; and that this is the only such Government in Korea,

Having in mind that United Nations armed forces are at present operating in Korea in accordance with the recommendations of the Security Council of June 27, 1950, subsequent to its resolution of June 25, 1950, that Members of the United Nations furnish such assistance to the Republic of Korea as may be necessary to repel the armed attack and to restore international peace and security in the area,

Recalling that the essential objective of the resolutions of the General Assembly referred to above was the establishment of a unified, independent, and democratic Government of Korea,

1. *Recommends* that

(a) All appropriate steps be taken to ensure conditions of stability throughout Korea;

(b) All constituent acts be taken, including the holding of elections, under the auspices of the United Nations, for the establishment of a unified, independent, and democratic Government in the sovereign State of Korea;

(c) All sections and representative bodies of the population of Korea, South and North, be invited to cooperate with the organs of the United Nations in the restoration of peace, in the holding of elections, and in the establishment of a unified Government;

(d) United Nations forces should not remain in any part of Korea otherwise than so far as necessary for achieving the objectives specified in subparagraphs (a) and (b) above;

(e) All necessary measures be taken to accomplish the economic rehabilitation of Korea;

2. *Resolves* that

(a) The Commission consisting of Australia, Chile, Netherlands, Pakistan, Philippines, Thailand, and Turkey, to be known as the United Nations Commission for the Unification and Rehabilitation of Korea, be established to (i) assume the functions hitherto exercised by the present United Nations Commission in Korea; (ii) represent the United Nations in bringing about the establishment of a unified, independent and democratic government of all Korea; (iii) exercise such responsibilities in connection with relief and rehabilitation in Korea as may be determined by the General Assembly after receiving the recommendations of the Economic and Social Council. The United Nations Commission for the Unification and Rehabilitation of Korea should proceed to Korea and begin to carry out its functions as soon as possible.

(b) Pending the arrival in Korea of the United Nations Commission for the Unification and Rehabilitation of Korea, the Governments of the States represented on the Commission should form an interim committee composed of representatives meeting at the seat of the United Nations to consult with and advise the United Nations Unified Command in the light of the above recommendations; the interim committee should begin to function immediately upon the approval of the present resolution by the General Assembly;

(c) The Commission shall render a report to the next regular session of the General Assembly and to any prior special session which might be called to consider the subject matter of the present resolution, and shall render such interim reports as it may deem appropriate to the Secretary-General for transmission to Members;

The General Assembly furthermore,

Mindful of the fact that at the end of the present hostilities the task of rehabilitating the Korean economy will be of great magnitude,

3. *Requests* the Economic and Social Council, in consultation with the specialized agencies, to develop plans for relief and rehabilitation on the termination of hostilities and to report to the General Assembly within three weeks of the adoption of the present resolution by the General Assembly;

4. *Also recommends* the Economic and Social Council to expedite the study of long-term measures to promote the economic development and social progress of Korea, and meanwhile to draw the attention of the authorities which decide requests for technical assistance to the urgent and special necessity of affording such assistance to Korea;

5. *Expresses* its appreciation of the services rendered by the members of the United Nations Commission on Korea in the performance of their important and difficult task;

6. *Requests* the Secretary-General to provide the Commission with adequate staff facilities, including technical advisers as required; and authorizes the Secretary-General to pay the expenses and *per diem* of a representative and alternate from each of the States members of the Commission.

28. SPECIAL REPORT OF THE UNITED NATIONS COMMAND ON COMMUNIST CHINESE INTERVENTION, NOVEMBER 5, 1950 [72]

[NEW YORK,] *November 6, 1950*

The Representative of the United States to the United Nations presents his compliments to the Secretary-General of the United Nations and has the honor to refer to Paragraph 6 of the Resolution of the Security Council of July 7, 1950, requesting the United States to provide the Security Council with reports, as appropriate, on the course of action taken under the United Nations Command.

In compliance with this Resolution, there is enclosed herewith, for circulation to the members of the Security Council, a Special Report of the Commanding General, United Nations Command.

Following is text of special report from Commanding General, United Nations Command.

November 5, 1950

I herewith submit a special report of the United Nations Command operations in Korea which I believe should be brought to the attention of the United Nations.

Introduction

The United Nations Forces in Korea are continuing their drive to the north and their efforts to destroy further the effectiveness of the enemy as a fighting force are proving successful. However, presently

---

in certain areas of Korea, the United Nations Forces are meeting a new foe. It is apparent to our fighting forces, and our intelligence agencies have confirmed the fact, that the United Nations are presently in hostile contact with Chinese Communist military units deployed for action against the forces of the United Command.

The fact of intervention

Hereafter, in summary form, are confirmed intelligence reports substantiating the fact that forces other than Korean are resisting our efforts to carry out the resolutions of the United Nations:

A. 22 August: Approximately 50 bursts heavy anti-aircraft fire from Manchurian side of Yalu River against RB–29 flying at 7000 feet over Korea in the vicinity of the Sui-Ho reservoir; damage, none; time 1600 K; weather, 10 miles visibility, high broken clouds.

B. 24 August: Approximately 40 bursts heavy antiaircraft fire from Manchurian side of Yalu River against RB–29 flying at 10,000 feet over Korea in the vicinity of Sinuiju; damage, none, time 1500 K; weather, 20 miles visibility.

C. 15 October: Antiaircraft fire from the Manchurian side of Yalu River against a flight of 4 F–51's flying near Sinuiju airfield on the Korean side of river; damage, 1 aircraft total loss; time 14451; weather, overcast at 8,000 feet; 8 to 10 miles visibility.

D. 16 October: The 370th Regiment of the 124th Division of the Chinese Communist 42nd Army, consisting of approximately 2,500 troops, crossed Yalu River (Korean border) at Wan Po Jin, and proceeded to the area of Chosen and Fusen Dams in North Korea where they came in contact with United Nations forces approximately 40 miles north of Hamhung.

E. 17 October: Approximately 15 bursts heavy antiaircraft fire from Manchurian side of Yalu River against RB–29 flying at 10,000 feet over Korea in the vicinity of Sinuiju; damage, none; time 1200 I; weather, 8 miles visibility, low clouds 2,300 feet.

F. 20 October: A Chinese Communist Task Force known as the "56th" unit, consisting of approximately 5,000 troops crossed the Yalu River (Korean border) at Antung and deployed to positions in Korea south of the Sui-Ho Dam. A captured Chinese Communist soldier of this Task Force states that his group was organized out of the regular Chinese Communist 40th Army stationed at Antung, Manchuria.

G. 1 November: A flight of F–51's was attacked early in the afternoon by 6 to 9 Jet aircraft which flew across the Yalu River into Manchuria. No damage was done to United States aircraft. A red star was observed on the top of the right wing on one of the Jet aircraft.

H. 1 November: Antiaircraft fire from the Manchurian side of the Yalu River directed against a flight of 13–F–80 aircraft was observed in the vicinity of Sinuiju at 1345 hours. This resulted in the total loss of 1 United Nations aircraft.

I. 30 October: Interrogation of 19 Chinese prisoners of war identified two additional regiments of 124 CCF Division, the 371 and the 372 in the vicinity of Changjin.

J. 2 November: Interrogation of prisoners of war indicates the 54 CCF unit in Korea. This unit is reported to have same organization as 55 and 56 units, but to be drawn from the 112, 113, and 114 Divisions of the 38 CCF Army.

K. 3 November: Further interrogation of Chinese prisoners of war indicates 56 CCF unit organized from elements of 118, 119, and 120 CCF Divisions of the 40 CCF Army.

L. 4 November: As of this date, a total of 35 CCF prisoners had been taken in Korea.

The continued employment of Chinese Communist forces in Korea and the hostile attitude assumed by such forces, either inside or outside Korea, are matters which it is incumbent upon me to bring at once to the attention of the United Nations.

29. JOINT RESOLUTION IN THE SECURITY COUNCIL, NOVEMBER 10, 1950 [73] [74]

The Security Council,

Recalling its resolution of June 25, 1950, determining that the North Korean forces had committed a breach of the peace and calling upon all Members of the United Nations to refrain from giving assistance to the North Korean authorities,

Recalling the resolution adopted by the General Assembly on October 7, 1950, which sets forth the policies of the United Nations in respect to Korea,

Having noted from the special report of the United Nations Command in Korea dated November 5, 1950, that Chinese Communist military units are deployed for action against the forces of the United Nations in Korea,

Affirming that United Nations forces should not remain in any part of Korea otherwise than so far as necessary for achieving the objectives of stability throughout Korea and the establishment of a unified independent and democratic government in the sovereign State of Korea, as set forth in the resolution of the General Assembly dated October 7, 1950,

Insistent that no action be taken which might lead to the spread of the Korean conflict to other areas and thereby further endanger international peace and security,

Calls upon all States and authorities, and in particular those responsible for the action noted above, to refrain from assisting or encouraging the North Korean authorities, to prevent their nationals or individuals or units of their armed forces from giving assistance to North Korean forces and to cause the immediate withdrawal of any such nationals, individuals, or units which may presently be in Korea;

Affirms that it is the policy of the United Nations to hold the Chinese frontier with Korea inviolate and fully to protect legitimate Chinese and Korean interests in the frontier zone;

Calls attention to the grave danger which continued intervention by Chinese forces in Korea would entail for the maintenance of such a policy;

Requests the Interim Committee on Korea and the United Nations Commission for the Unification and Rehabilitation of Korea to consider urgently and to assist in the settlement of any problems relating to conditions on the Korean frontier in which States or authorities on the other side of the frontier have an interest, and suggests that the

---

[73] United States Policy in the Korean Conflict, July 1950–February 1951, Department of State Publication 4263, p. 22.   UN doc. S/1894.

[74] Sponsored by Cuba, Ecuador, France, Norway, the United Kingdom, and the United States; vetoed by the Soviet Union, Nov. 30, 1950.

United Nations Commission for the Unification and Rehabilitation of Korea proceed to the area as soon as possible, and, pending its arrival, that it utilize the assistance of such States members of the Commission as now have representatives in the area for this purpose.

30. RESOLUTION OF THE GENERAL ASSEMBLY, DECEMBER 1, 1950 [75] ESTABLISHING THE UNITED NATIONS KOREAN RECONSTRUCTION AGENCY (UNKRA)

[Excerpt]

The General Assembly.

Having regard to its resolution of October 7, 1950 on the problem of the independence of Korea,

Having received and considered a report of the Economic and Social Council submitted in accordance with that resolution,

Mindful that the aggression by North Korean forces and their warfare against the United Nations seeking to restore peace in the area has resulted in great devastation and destruction which the Korean people cannot themselves repair,

Recognizing that as a result of such aggression the people of Korea are desperately in need of relief supplies and materials and help in reconstructing their economy.

Deeply moved by the sufferings of the Korean people and determined to assist in their alleviation,

Convinced that the creation of a United Nations programme of relief and rehabilitation for Korea is necessary both to the maintenance of lasting peace in the area and to the establishment of the economic foundations for the building of a unified and independent nation,

Considering that, under the said resolution of October 7, 1950, the United Nations Commission for the Unification and Rehabilitation of Korea is the principal representative of the United Nations in Korea, and hence must share in the responsibility for the work undertaken by the United Nations in furtherance of the objects and purposes mentioned in the said resolution,

Considering that it is nevertheless desirable to set up a special authority with broad powers to plan and supervise rehabilitation and relief and to assume such functions and responsibilities related to planning and supervision, to technical and administrative matters, and to questions affecting organization and implementation as are to be exercised under the plans for relief and rehabilitation approved by the General Assembly, such authority to carry out its responsibilities in close cooperation with the Commission,

1. *Establishes* the United Nations Korean Reconstruction Agency (UNKRA) under the direction of a United Nations Agent General, who shall be assisted by one or more deputies. The Agent General shall be responsible to the General Assembly for the conduct (in accordance with the policies established by the General Assembly, and having regard to such general policy recommendations as the United Nations Commission for the Unification and Rehabilitation of Korea may make) of the programme of relief and rehabilitation in Korea, as that programme may be determined from time to time by the General Assembly;

---

[75] United States Policy in the Korean Conflict, July 1950–February 1951, Department of State Publication 4263, pp. 24–25.   UN doc. A/1595.

2. *Authorizes* the United Nations Commission for the Unification and Rehabilitation of Korea:

(a) To recommend to the Agent General such policies concerning the United Nations Korean Reconstruction Agency's programme and activities as the Commission may consider necessary for the effective discharge of the Commission's responsibilities in relation to the establishment of a unified, independent and democratic government in Korea;

(b) To determine, after consultation with the Agent General, the geographical areas within which the Agency shall operate at any time;

(c) To designate authorities in Korea with which the Agent General may establish relationships; and to advise the Agent General on the nature of such relationships;

(d) To take such steps as may be needed to support the Agent General in fulfilling his task in accordance with the policies established by the General Assembly for relief and rehabilitation;

(e) To consider the reports of the Agent General to the General Assembly and to transmit any comments thereon to the Economic and Social Council and the General Assembly;

(f) To call for information on those aspects of the work of the Agent General which the Commission may consider necessary for the proper performance of its work.

31. RESOLUTION OF THE GENERAL ASSEMBLY, DECEMBER 14, 1950 [76]

The General Assembly,

Viewing with grave concern the situation in the Far East,

Anxious that immediate steps should be taken to prevent the conflict in Korea spreading to other areas and to put an end to the fighting in Korea itself, and that further steps should then be taken for a peaceful settlement of existing issues in accordance with the Purposes and Principles of the United Nations,

Requests the President of the General Assembly to constitute a group of three persons, including himself, to determine the basis on which a satisfactory cease-fire in Korea can be arranged and to make recommendations to the General Assembly as soon as possible.

REPORT OF THE GROUP ON CEASE-FIRE IN KOREA TO THE FIRST COMMITTEE OF THE GENERAL ASSEMBLY, JANUARY 2, 1951 [77]

On 14 December 1950 the General Assembly adopted the following resolution which had been sponsored by thirteen Asian Powers: . . .

2. In pursuance of the resolution, the President forthwith constituted a group consisting of Mr. L. B. Pearson of Canada, Sir Benegal N. Rau of India and himself, and announced this fact to the General Assembly. The Group met almost immediately afterwards and decided to associate the Secretary-General of the United Nations with its work.

3. A copy of the resolution was sent on 15 December to Ambassador Wu, the representative of the Central People's Government of the People's Republic of China who was then in New York.

---

[76] United States Policy in the Korean Conflict, July 1950–February 1951, Department of State Publication 4263, p. 27.   UN doc. A/1742.

[77] United States Policy in the Korean Conflict, July 1950–February 1951, Department of State Publication 4263, pp. 28–32.   UN doc. A/C.1/643.

4. On 15 December, as a first step in carrying out its task the Group consulted the representatives of the Unified Command as to what they considered to be a satisfactory basis for a cease-fire. The suggestions which emerged from this consultation and which in the circumstances the Group felt constituted a reasonable basis for discussion, are summarized below:

(1) All governments and authorities concerned, including the Central People's Government of the People's Republic of China and the North Korean authorities, shall order and enforce a cessation of all acts of armed force in Korea. This cease-fire shall apply to all of Korea.

(2) There shall be established a demilitarised area across Korea of approximately twenty miles in depth with the southern limit following generally the line of the 38th parallel.

(3) All ground forces shall remain in position or be withdrawn to the rear; forces, including guerillas, within or in advance of the demilitarised area must be moved to the rear of the demilitarized area; opposing air forces shall respect the demilitarized zone and the areas beyond the zone; opposing Naval forces shall respect the waters contiguous to the land areas occupied by the opposing armed forces to the limit of 3 miles from shore.

(4) Supervision of the cease-fire shall be by a United Nations Commission whose members and designated observers shall insure full compliance with the terms of the cease-fire. They shall have free and unlimited access to the whole of Korea. All governments and authorities shall cooperate with the Cease-Fire Commission and its designated observers in the performance of their duties.

(5) All governments and authorities shall cease promptly the introduction into Korea of any reinforcing or replacement units or personnel, including volunteers, and the introduction of additional war equipment and material. Such equipment and material will not include supplies required for the maintenance of health and welfare and such other supplies as may be authorized by the Cease-Fire Commission.

(6) Prisoners of war shall be exchanged on a one-for-one basis, pending final settlement of the Korean question.

(7) Appropriate provision shall be made in the cease-fire arrangements in regard to steps to insure (a) the security of the forces; (b) the movement of refugees; and (c) the handling of other specific problems arising out of the cease-fire, including civil government and police power in the demilitarized zone.

(8) The General Assembly should be asked to confirm the cease-fire arrangements, which should continue in effect until superseded by further steps approved by the United Nations.

5. The Group then attempted to consult the Central People's Government of the People's Republic of China and, for this purpose, sent a message by hand to Ambassador Wu and repeated it by cable to the Minister for Foreign Affairs in Peking. The text of this message is reproduced below:

DEAR AMBASSADOR WU, As you have already been informed by Resolution 1717, a copy of which was sent to you yesterday, a Committee was set up by the General Assembly of the United Nations on the previous day, December 14, consisting of myself and my two colleagues, Sir Benegal Rau of India, and Mr.

L. B. Pearson of Canada, charged with the duty of determining whether it is possible to arrange appropriate and satisfactory conditions for a cease-fire in Korea. The purpose of this cease-fire in Korea will be to prevent the conflict from spreading to other areas, to put an end to the fighting in Korea, and to provide an opportunity for considering what further steps should be taken for a peaceful settlement of existing issues in accordance with the purposes and principles of the United Nations.

The above Committee has now met representatives of the Unified Command in Korea, and has discussed with them, in an exploratory manner, possible conditions upon which a cease-fire might be established. Since the Government of the Communist People's Republic of China has expressed strong views on the future of Korea, and about the present state of warfare in that country, and since Chinese are participating in that warfare, the Committee wishes also to discuss with your Government or its representatives, and with the military authorities in command of the forces operating in North Korea possible conditions upon which a cease-fire might be established. For this purpose, we desire to see you at your earliest convenience, and we should be grateful to know when a meeting can be arranged.

We realised that your Government which sent you here with other objects in mind, may prefer other arrangements by which a cease-fire can be discussed with them. We wish your Government to know that, in the interests of stopping the fighting in Korea and of facilitating a just settlement of the issues there in accordance with the principles of the United Nations Charter, we are prepared to discuss cease-fire arrangements with your Government or its representatives either here or elsewhere, as would be mutually convenient. We urge only that arrangements for these discussions should be made with the least possible delay. With this in mind, we are sending the text of this communication directly to your Government by telegram.

Yours sincerely,

NASROLLAH ENTEZAM

December 16, 1950.

6. On 18 December, Mr. Pearson, on behalf of the Group, submitted a brief preliminary account of its activities to the First Committee, hoping that a fuller report would be made in the near future.

7. On 16 December, the President, acting on behalf of the Group, had availed himself of the good offices of the Swedish Delegation to transmit through the Swedish Embassy in Pekin a request to the Central People's Government that Ambassador Wu be instructed to stay on in New York and discuss with the Group the possibility of arranging a cease-fire. The reply to the request, communicated to the President on 21 December, through the same channel was as follows:

The Central People's Government acknowledges receipt of a message dated 18th December 1950 from Mr. Entezam, President of the General Assembly transmitted via the Swedish Government and ask the Swedish Government to transmit the following reply to Mr. Entezam, President of the General Assembly.

The representative of the People's Republic of China neither participated in nor agreed to the adoption of the Resolution concerning the so-called 3-man Committee for Cease Fire in Korea by United Nations General Assembly. The Central People's Government has repeatedly declared that the Central People's Government would regard as illegal and null and void all major resolutions especially those concerning Asia which might be adopted by the United Nations without the participation and approval of the duly appointed delegates of the People's Republic of China. Therefore the Central People's Government cannot instruct its representative General Wu to continue to remain in Lake Success for negotiations with the above-named 3-men illegal Committee. After the Security Council unreasonably voted against the "Complaint against the United States armed aggression against Taiwan" raised by the People's Republic of China General Wu was instructed by the Central People's Government to continue to stay at Lake Success for participation in the discussion of "the complaint of the U. S. aggression against China" submitted by the U. S. S. R. representative; although he has waited a long time and until the United Nations General

Assembly was declared adjourned, he was still not given the opportunity to speak. Under such circumstances, the Central People's Government deems that there is no more necessity for General Wu and his staff to remain at Lake Success and therefore instructed him to start their homeward journey on December 19.

2. As to the question of how the United Nations may get in touch with the Korean Democratic People's Republic the Central People's Government is of the opinion that United Nations should address direct inquiry to the Government of the Korean Democratic People's Republic.

8. On 19 December, acting on a recommendation from the sponsors of the twelve-Power resolution introduced in the First Committee on 12 December, the Group sent another message to the Foreign Minister of the Central People's Government. This was intended to remove any possible misunderstanding which may have arisen out of the separation of the twelve-Power resolution from the thirteen-Power resolution adopted by the General Assembly on 14 December. The text of the message is given below:

CHOU EN LAI,
 Minister for Foreign Affairs,
  CENTRAL PEOPLE'S GOVERNMENT OF PEOPLE'S REPUBLIC OF CHINA (PEKING, CHINA).

In the consideration which you are giving to our earlier message, we are anxious that there should be no misunderstanding as to the relationship between the United Nations Resolution establishing a cease-fire group, and resolution proposed by twelve Asian Governments, recommending appointment of a committee to meet as soon as possible and make recommendations for peaceful settlement of existing issues in Far East. It is our clear understanding and also that of the twelve Asian sponsors, that once a cease-fire arrangement had been achieved, the negotiations visualized in the second resolution should be proceeded with at once. Indeed, the preamble to cease-fire resolution states specifically that steps should be taken for a peaceful settlement when fighting in Korea is ended. It is also our view, as well as that of the twelve Asian Governments sponsoring the second resolution, that Government of the People's Republic of China should be included in the Negotiating Committee referred to in that resolution. We feel that this Committee should become an effective channel for seeking peaceful solution of existing issues in Far East between the United States, the United Kingdom, the Soviet Union, and China. For that purpose, in our opinion, it should be set up with minimum of doing, but to make that possible a "cease fire" arrangement must be put into effect. This point of view has been communicated to your Delegation which left New York today, and we express the hope that you will give full weight to it.

 Committee of the General Assembly
 NASROLLAH ENTEZAM, *President of the General Assembly*
 SIR BENEGAL RAU
 LESTER B. PEARSON

9. On 23 December, the President of the General Assembly, in his capacity as such, received from the Foreign Minister of the Central People's Government the text of a statement issued by the latter in Peking on 22 December explaining the attitude of the Central People's Government on the Resolution constituting the Cease-Fire Group and on the peaceful settlement of the Korean question. This document is reproduced as an Annex. It appears to be in the nature of an answer to the Group's message of 16 December.

10. In these circumstances and in spite of its best efforts, the Group regrets that it has been unable to pursue discussion of a satisfactory cease-fire arrangement. It therefore feels that no recommendation in regard to a cease fire can usefully be made by it at this time.

33. SUPPLEMENTARY REPORT OF THE GROUP ON CEASE-FIRE IN KOREA TO THE FIRST COMMITTEE OF THE GENERAL ASSEMBLY ("THE FIVE PRINCIPLES") JANUARY 11, 1951 [78]

The objective shall be the achievement, by stages, of the programme outlined below for a cease-fire in Korea, for the establishment of a free and united Korea, and for a peaceful settlement of Far Eastern problems.

1. In order to prevent needless destruction of life and property and while other steps are being taken to restore peace, a cease-fire should be immediately arranged. Such an arrangement should contain adequate safeguards for ensuring that it will not be used as a screen for mounting a new offensive.

2. If and when a cease-fire occurs in Korea, either as a result of a formal arrangement or, indeed, as a result of a lull in hostilities pending some such arrangement, advantage should be taken of it to pursue consideration of further steps to be taken for the restoration of peace.

3. To permit the carrying out of the General Assembly resolution that Korea should be a unified, independent, democratic, sovereign State with a constitution and a government based on free popular elections, all non-Korean armed forces will be withdrawn, by appropriate stages, from Korea, and appropriate arrangements, in accordance with United Nations principles, will be made for the Korean people to express their own free will in respect of their future government.

4. Pending the completion of the steps referred to in the preceding paragraph, appropriate interim arrangements, in accordance with United Nations principles, will be made for the administration of Korea and the maintenance of peace and security there.

5. As soon as an agreement has been reached on a cease-fire, the General Assembly shall set up an appropriate body which shall include representatives of the Governments of the United Kingdom, the United States of America, the Union of Soviet Socialist Republics, and the People's Republic of China with a view to obligations and the provisions of the United Nations Charter, of Far Eastern problems, including among others, those of Formosa (Taiwan) and of representation of China in the United Nations.

34. RESOLUTION OF THE FIRST COMMITTEE OF THE GENERAL ASSEMBLY, JANUARY 13, 1951 [79]

The first committee

Invites the Chairman of the First Committee through the Secretary-General to transmit the principles approved by it on 13 January 1951 to the Central People's Government of the People's Republic of China and invite them to inform him as soon as possible whether they accept these principles as a basis for the peaceful settlement of the

---

[78] United States Policy in the Korean Conflict, July 1950–February 1951, Department of State Publication 4263, pp. 32–33. UN doc. A/C.1/645.
[79] United States Policy in the Korean Conflict, July 1950–February 1951, Department of State Publication 4263, p. 33. UN doc. A/C.1/651.

Korean problem and other Far Eastern problems. Upon the receipt of the reply from the Central People's Government of the People's Republic of China the Chairman of the First Committee will convene the Committee to consider that reply.

35. STATEMENT BY SECRETARY OF STATE ACHESON ON THE U. S. POSITION ON "THE FIVE PRINCIPLES", JANUARY 17, 1951 [89]

There has been a good deal of discussion in this country regarding the latest cease-fire proposal in the United Nations and why this Government voted for it. I should like to comment briefly on this matter.

First. The proposal was put forward by the Cease-Fire Committee—the President of the General Assembly, Mr. Pearson of Canada, Sir Benegal Rau of India. It had the support of the overwhelming majority of the U. N. members. This support was founded on two principal attitudes. One was the belief of many members that the Chinese Communists might still be prevailed upon to cease their defiance of the United Nations. While we did not share this belief we recognized that it was sincerely held by many members.

The second attitude was that, even though there might be little prospect of success in the approach to Peiping, the United Nations should leave no stone unturned in its efforts to find a peaceful solution. Holders of each view believed and stated to us that opposition or abstention by the United States would destroy any possibility of success which the proposal might have.

Peaceful settlement is one of the cardinal purposes of the United Nations. The resort to force in Korea came from the North Koreans first and the Chinese Communists second. The United Nations has constantly demanded that this should end and that the United Nations objectives should be attained by peaceful means—we have stood and still stand for this position. Also it has been our goal to so act as to maintain the unity of the free nations against aggression which has marked the United Nations actions in Korea. Accordingly, we voted for the resolution to demonstrate our adherence to these basic principles even though we did not share the beliefs of other members, mentioned above, that it would achieve its purpose.

Second. As to what the five principles mean:

If they are accepted, first, there would be a cease-fire in Korea. Then, after the fighting has stopped, there would be negotiations among all interested parties to find a peaceful settlement of the Korean question and other outstanding problems in the Far East.

The five principles contain three elements:(1) a termination of hostilities in Korea; after the cease-fire has become effective, two further steps are contemplated: (2) arrangements to ensure the achievement of United Nations objectives of an independent and democratic Korea by peaceful means and the withdrawal by appropriate stages of all non-Korean troops; and (3) a discussion of Far Eastern problems.

---

[89] United States Policy in the Korean Conflict, June 1950–February 1951. Department of State Publication 4263, pp. 33–34.

These principles are entirely consistent with the United Nations Charter, United Nations objectives in Korea, and United States policy. The General Assembly resolution of October 7 made it clear that United Nations forces should not remain in Korea longer than necessary to achieve United Nations objectives there.

We don't want our troops in Korea longer than in absolutely necessary. If satisfactory arrangements for an independent and democratic Korea are put into effect, there is no longer any reason for maintaining United Nations forces in Korea.

The fifth principle provides for discussions on Far Eastern problems and stipulates four of the parties which will participate. It goes without saying that other parties with interests in Far Eastern problems will also participate. It mentions two of the problems which should be considered at a conference on Far Eastern problems— Formosa and Chinese representations in the United Nations. We have discussed these questions freely in the past, stated our views frankly and also stated that the problems should be settled by the peaceful means of discussion and debate. There is no reason why we should oppose discussion of these questions in the future under proper circumstances. If such a conference is held, there will undoubtedly be other items on the agenda, including some which the United States may wish to add. Obviously, we have not committed ourselves on any questions which might be discussed.

36. COMMUNIST CHINESE REJECTION OF "THE FIVE PRINCIPLES," JANUARY 17, 1951 [81]

[Translation]

PEKING, *January 17, 1951*

I have the honour to acknowledge receipt of the cablegram dated 13 January 1951, transmitted by Mr. Owen at the request of the First Committee of the General Assembly, on the principles concerning the Korean and other Far Eastern problems. In the name of the Central People's Government of the People's Republic of China I wish to reply as follows:

1. The Central People's Government of the People's Republic of China has always maintained and still maintains that a rapid termination of the hostilities in Korea should be sought by negotiations among the various countries concerned with a view to the peaceful settlement of the Korean question on the basis of the withdrawal of all foreign troops from Korea and the settlement of Korean domestic affairs by the Koreans themselves; that United States Armed Forces must be withdrawn from Taiwan (Formosa); and that the repre-

[81] United States Policy in the Korean Conflict, July 1950–February 1951, Department of State Publication 4263, pp. 35–36. UN doc. A/C.1/653.

sentatives of the People's Republic of China must assume their rightful place in the United Nations. These principles were also mentioned in my statement of 22 December 1950, transmitted by cable to Mr. Entezam, president of the General Assembly, on the same day, and are now well known to the whole world.

2. On 13 January 1951, the First Committee of the United Nations General Assembly adopted without the participation of the representaive of the People's Republic of China various principles concerning the Korean and other Far Eastern problems, the basic points of which are still the arrangement of a cease-fire in Korea first and the conducting of negotiations among the various countries concerned afterwards. The purpose of arranging a cease-fire first is merely to give the United States troops a breathing space. Therefore, regardless of what the agenda and subject-matter of the negotiations may be, if a cease-fire comes into effect without first conducting negotiations to fix the conditions therefor, negotiations after the cease-fire may entail endless discussions without solving any problems. Besides this fundamental point, the other principles are also not clearly defined. It is not clearly stated whether the so-called existing international obligations refer to the Cairo and Potsdam Declarations, and this may easily be utilized to defend the position of aggression maintained by the United States in Korea, Taiwan and other parts of the Far East. We understand that many countries in the First Committee agreed to the principles adopted on 13 January 1951 because of their desire for peace. It must be pointed out, however, that the principle of a cease-fire first and negotiations afterwards would only help the United States to maintain and extend its aggression, and could never lead to genuine peace.

Therefore the Central People's Government of the People's Republic of China cannot agree to this principle.

3. With a view to a genuine and peaceful solution of the Korean problem and other important Asian problems, I hereby submit, in the name of the Central People's Government of the People's Republic of China, the following proposals to the United Nations:

A. Negotiations should be held among the countries concerned on the basis of agreement to the withdrawal of all foreign troops from Korea and the settlement of Korean domestic affairs by the Korean people themselves, in order to put an end to the hostilities in Korea at an early date.

B. The subject-matter of the negotiations must include the withdrawal of United States Armed Forces from Taiwan and the Taiwan Straits and Far Eastern related problems;

C. The countries to participate in the negotiations should be the following seven countries: the People's Republic of China, the Soviet Union, the United Kingdom, the United States of America, France, India and Egypt, and the rightful place of the Central People's Government of the People's Republic of China in the United Nations should be established as from the beginning of the Seven-Nation Conference;

D. The Seven-Nation Conference should be held in China, at a place to be selected.

4. If the above-mentioned proposals are agreed to by the countries concerned and by the United Nations, we believe that it will be conductive to the prompt termination of the hostilities in Korea and to the peaceful settlement of Asian problems to hold negotiations as soon as possible.

Chou En-Lai

37. RESOLUTION OF THE GENERAL ASSEMBLY BRANDING COMMUNIST CHINESE AS AGGRESSORS, FEBRUARY 1, 1951 [82]

The General Assembly,

Noting that the Security Council, because of lack of unanimity of the permanent members, has failed to exercise its primary responsibility for the maintenance of international peace and security in regard to Chinese Communist intervention in Korea;

Noting that the Central People's Government of the People's Republic of China has not accepted United Nations proposals to bring about a cessation of hostilities in Korea with a view to peaceful settlement, and that its armed forces continue their invasion of Korea and their large-scale attacks upon United Nations forces there;

Finds that the Central People's Government of the People's Republic of China, by giving direct aid and assistance to those who were already committing aggression in Korea and by engaging in hostilities against United Nations forces there, has itself engaged in aggression in Korea;

Calls upon the Central People's Government of the People's Republic of China to cause its forces and nationals in Korea to cease hostilities against the United Nations forces and to withdraw from Korea;

Affirms the determination of the United Nations to continue its action in Korea to meet the aggression;

Calls upon all States and authorities to continue to lend every assistance to the United Nations action in Korea;

Calls upon all States and authorities to refrain from giving any assistance to the aggressors in Korea;

Requests a committee composed of the Members of the Collective Measures Committee as a matter of urgency to consider additional measures to be employed to meet this aggression and to report thereon to the General Assembly; it being understood that the Committee is authorized to defer its report if the Good Offices Committee, referred to in the following paragraph, reports satisfactory progress in its efforts.

Affirms that it continues to be the policy of the United Nations to bring about a cessation of hostilities in Korea and the achievement of United Nations objectives in Korea by peaceful means, and requests the President of the General Assembly to designate forthwith two persons who would meet with him at any suitable opportunity to use their good offices to this end.

---

[82] United States Policy in the Korean Conflict, July 1950–February 1951, Department of State Publication 4263, p. 37. UN doc. A/1771.

38. RESOLUTION OF THE GENERAL ASSEMBLY ON THE APPLICATION OF AN EMBARGO AGAINST COMMUNIST CHINA AND NORTH KOREA, MAY 18, 1951 [88]

The General Assembly.

Noting the report of the Additional Measures Committee dated 14 May 1951.

Recalling its resolution 498 (V) of 1 February 1951,

Noting that:

(*a*) The Additional Measures Committee established by that resolution has considered additional measures to be employed to meet the aggression in Korea,

(*b*) The Additional Measures Committee has reported that a number of States have already taken measures designed to deny contributions to the military strength of the forces opposing the United Nations in Korea,

(*c*) The Additional Measures Committee has also reported that certain economic measures designed further to deny such contributions would support and supplement the military action of the United Nations in Korea and would assist in putting an end to the aggression,

1. *Recommends* that every State:

(*a*) Apply an embargo on the shipment to areas under the control of the Central People's Government of the People's Republic of China and of the North Korean authorities of arms, ammunition, and implements of war, atomic energy materials, petroleum, transportation materials of strategic value, and items useful in the production of arms, ammunition and implements of war;

(*b*) Determine which commodities exoprted from its territory fall within the embargo, and apply controls to give effect to the embargo;

(*c*) Prevent by all means within its jurisdiction the circumvention of controls on shipments applied by other States pursuant to the present resolution;

(*d*) Co-operate with other States in carrying out the purposes of this embargo;

(*e*) Report to the Additional Measures Committee, within thirty days and thereafter at the request of the Committee, on the measures taken in accordance with the present resolution;

2. *Requests* the Additional Measures Committee:

(*a*) To report to the General Assembly, with recommendations as appropriate, on the general effectiveness of the embargo and the desirability of continuing, extending, or relaxing it;

(*b*) To continue its consideration of additional measures to be employed to meet the aggression in Korea, and to report thereon further to the General Assembly, it being understood that the Committee is authorized to defer its report if the Good Offices Committee reports satisfactory progress in its efforts;

3. *Reaffirms* that it continues to be the policy of the United Nations to bring about a cessation of hostilities in Korea, and the achievement of United Nations objectives in Korea by peaceful means, and requests the Good Offices Committee to continue its good offices.

330th plenary meeting,
18 May 1951.

---

[88] United Nations Document A/1805, 21 May 1951.

VII. THE ARMISTICE NEGOTIATIONS

39. SPEECH BY JACOB MALIK, U. S. S. R. REPRESENTATIVE TO THE UNITED NATIONS, JUNE 23, 1951, PROPOSING ARMISTICE NEGOTIATIONS [84]

[Excerpt]

*   *   *   *   *   *   *

The Soviet peoples further believe that the most acute problem of the present day—the problem of the armed conflict in Korea could also be settled.

This would require the readiness of the parties to enter on the path of a peaceful settlement of the Korean question. The Soviet peoples believe that as a first step discussions should be started between the belligerents for a cease fire and an armistice providing for the mutual withdrawal of forces from the thirty-eighth parallel.

Can such a step be taken?

I think it can, provided there is a sincere desire to put an end to the bloody fighting in Korea.

I think that, surely, is not too great a price to pay in order to achieve peace in Korea.

40. EXCHANGE ON ARMISTICE DISCUSSIONS BETWEEN GENERAL RIDGWAY, COMMANDER IN CHIEF, UNITED NATIONS COMMAND, AND THE COMMUNISTS, JUNE 30, JULY 1, 1951 [85]

A. RIDGWAY'S STATEMENT TO THE COMMUNISTS, JUNE 30, 1951

As Commander in Chief of the United Nations Command I have been instructed to communicate to you the following:

"I am informed that you may wish a meeting to discuss an armistice providing for the cessation of hostilities and all acts of armed force in Korea, with adequate guarantees for the maintenance of such armistice.

"Upon the receipt of word from you that such a meeting is desired I shall be prepared to name my representative. I would also at that time suggest a date on which he could meet with your representative. I propose that such a meeting could take place aboard a Danish hospital ship in Wonsan harbor."

B. COMMUNIST REPLY ACCEPTING UNC PROPOSAL FOR MEETING, JULY 1, 1951

*   *   *   *   *   *   *

Gen. Ridgway, Commander-in-Chief of the United Nations forces: Your statement of June 30 this year concerning peace talks has been received.

We are authorized to inform you that we agree to meet your representative for conducting talks concerning cessation of military action and establishment of peace.

We propose that the place of meeting be in the area of Kaesong on the 38th Parallel. If you agree our representatives are prepared to meet your representatives between July 10 and 15, 1951.

---

[84] Department of State selected primary source materials on Korea, 1951–52, pp. 5–6.
[85] Department of State, selected primary source materials on Korea, 1951–52, p. 6.

41. STATEMENT BY SECRETARY OF STATE ACHESON, ON THE WITH-DRAWAL OF FOREIGN TROOPS FROM KOREA AFTER AN ARMISTICE, JULY 19, 1951 [86]

The Communist delegation at Kaesong has raised the question of the withdrawal of all foreign forces from Korea in connection with an armistice. The United Nations Command delegation has stated that it cannot go into this question, which is political in character and can only be settled by the United Nations and the governments concerned.

This is no theoretical argument as to whether the question is political or military. The United Nations forces are in Korea because of decisions made by governments to send them to Korea in response to a request by the United Nations. They are there to repel aggression and to restore international peace and security in the area.

If there is an effective armistice, a United Nations force must remain in Korea until a genuine peace has been firmly established and the Korean people have assurance that they can work out their future free from the fear of aggression. The size of the United Nations force remaining in Korea will depend upon circumstances and, particularly, upon the faithfulness with which an armistice is carried out.

Korea's neighbors know that the presence of United Nations forces in Korea constitutes no danger or threat to themselves. The repeated expressions of policy by the UN and, indeed, the very nature of that organization, furnish them entirely adequate guarantees on this point.

Once before, foreign forces were withdrawn from Korea as a part of a UN plan to reach a final settlement of the Korean problem. The Communists defied this effort and committed aggression against the Republic of Korea. The Korean people can be assured that a repetition of this act will not be tolerated.

42. STATEMENT OF SECRETARY OF DEFENSE MARSHALL ON TRUCE NEGOTIATIONS, JULY 24, 1951 [87]

I wish to make a brief comment concerning the truce negotiations in Korea.

What General Ridgway is trying to accomplish there is the negotiation of a suitable *military armistice*. This negotiation on the battle-field is an entirely different problem from the negotiation of a political settlement. It is essential that the two matters be kept entirely separate and distinct. If an acceptable armistice can be obtained, discussion of the political questions can follow on the highest governmental level.

If the talks resume and get to the substance of an armistice arrangement, there must be agreement upon a military line which will be defensible in the event of any renewal of hostilities; there must be agreement not to reinforce the troops now in Korea; there must be provision for adequate supervision and actual inspection by representatives of both sides to insure against any preparations for a surprise attack and as continuing evidence of good faith; there must be a satisfactory agreement regarding prisoners of war. These are basic

---

[86] Department of State Press Release No. 648, July 19, 1951.
[87] Department of Defense—Minutes of press conference, July 24, 1951.

conditions to an armistice and agreement with respect to them must precede a later effort to reach a final settlement of the Korean question.

Specifically, I am thinking of the Communists' insistence that withdrawal of all foreign troops from Korea be made a firm part of the armistice agenda.

In his statement of July 19, the Secretary of State made it quite clear why the question of the withdrawal of foreign troops from Korea is not a suitable one for consideration in the armistice talks.

The withdrawal of foreign troops from Korea will naturally follow a satisfactory peace settlement. When the proper time comes, removal of these forces should pose no problem if the Communists are sincere in wanting to work out with us a real settlement of the Korean conflict.

The long-range objective of the United Nations in Korea is the creation of conditions that will ultimately make possible a Korea that is unified, master of its own destiny, and free of interference from any outside force.

Meanwhile, the continuing presence and readiness of the United Nations Forces in Korea constitute the only assurance we have of meeting the threat of renewed aggression if the peace talks should break down.

Finally I would add that that necessity for caution is still evident. The discussions thus far have been only on the adoption of an agenda. The real points to be settled have not yet been discussed. There is no agreement as yet as to any of these points.

43. STATEMENT BY GENERAL OF THE ARMY OMAR N. BRADLEY BEFORE THE SENATE ARMED SERVICES COMMITTEE ON MONDAY, JANUARY 14, 1952 [88]

Mr. Chairman and members of the committee, last September 24, when I appeared before your committee to review the worldwide military situation, and specifically the situation in Korea, the truce talks were in recess. The armistice negotiations had broken down after the 5-point armistice agenda had been adopted. An attempt to set a line of military demarcation between the opposing forces had been unsuccessful.

From the 23d of August, when the Communists had called off the negotiations, until the 24th of September, the air had been filled with recriminations, charges and countercharges of violations of the neutral zone.

On September 24—the day I met with your committee—liaison officers of both sides met at Panmunjom to discuss the possibilities of a new site for the negotiations, and to make detailed arrangements to assure the security of the area. General Ridgway insisted that the negotiations be moved from Kaesong, where the Communists were literally in control of the area, to a neutral and more secure area. As long as the negotiations were conducted in Communist-held territory, they continued to act as victors rather than negotiators. At times there was some fear for the actual safety of the United Nations team.

A month later, on the 25th of October, the armistice negotiations were finally resumed at the new site. The discussions on agenda item

---

[88] Department of Defense press release.

No. 2—fixing a military demarcation line between both sides in order to establish a demilitarized zone for the truce—were resumed.

Because peace in Korea might well be a pattern for peace in other troubled spots in the future, it is important to the United Nations that the settlement be based on sound principles. Throughout the negotiations which General Ridgway has so ably conducted, the primary principle has always been and continues to be an earnest and sincere desire for peace. By every means at our command, and at every genuine opportunity for honorable terms, we seek peaceful solutions to international differences. But there is one price we will not pay—appeasement.

The second principle is that any settlement should help to provide deterrents to renewed aggression and, if possible, assurances that hostilities will not break out again. Many of the details and delays of the negotiations hinge upon this principle.

The third principle is a military one: Any settlement we make in Korea must provide adequate safeguards so that the security of the United Nations forces remaining in the area will not be jeopardized. Our agreements must not allow the Communists opportunity for future military "blackmail," or unnecessarily expose the forces in that area.

Within these principles, we have tried for six months to work out the terms of an honorable truce in Korea, in order to put an end to the bloodshed and fighting. As the difficult negotiations have continued, many Americans have considered the possibility that the Communists were gaining a military advantage by delaying the negotiations while they recuperated, and prepared a better defense. In my opinion, the United Nations command has not lost by participting in the truce talks. Militarily, we have continued to press the ground attack wherever it was advisable. And we have continued to inflict the force of air power, on both their ground forces and their supply lines.

Three major issues have already been resolved: the problem of the 38th Parallel; the establishment of a truly neutral meeting place; and a line of demarcation for a military armistice.

In the beginning it was extremely difficult to settle the agenda for the talks because the Communists insisted upon including matters in the agenda which were not related to a military armistice but were more properly the subject of future political negotiation.

The Communists wanted to settle upon the 38th Parallel as a truce line. This would have been intolerable to the United Nations forces because the 38th Parallel is an indefensible line from a military viewpoint. The present battle line—the line of demarcation which was negotiated on November 27—is a militarily sound basis for a military armistice.

I feel sure that many people did not realize why it was so important to move the truce negotiations from Kaesong to Panmunjon. When the negotiations began, Kaesong was in no-man's land. Both sides had patrols in there several times a week. As soon as the negotiations were underway, the Communists took over the area. There was no feeling of security for our team of negotiators, and there was little respect for the United Nations' position. The Communists, because they held the site of the armistice talks, acted as conquerors. General Ridgway insisted on moving to a more neutral area. I believe that this move has contributed greatly to the progress we have made so far.

The security of our own forces is the paramount consideration in item No. 3 of the agenda—concrete arrangements for the cease-fire and armistice, including the organization for carrying out the terms. To date we have reached general agreement on the following points:

(a) There will be a cease-fire within 24 hours of signing the armistice.

(b) An invitation will be extended to non-combatant nations to send representatives to carry out the functions of supervision and inspection. (Sweden, Switzerland, and Norway have indicated that they would accept such an invitation.)

(c) Both sides will withdraw their forces from the demilitarized zone within 72 hours.

(d) The rotation of military personnel in North and South Korea will be allowed, but no increases in strength will be allowed.

There is only one major point of disagreement: the rehabilitation of airfields. The United Nations holds that the unlimited rehabilitation of airfields is a threat against the security of the United Nations forces.

The most difficult agenda item is the exchange of prisoners of war. The United Nations wants to make an agreement which will assure the release of all prisoners of war, but which will permit individuals a freedom of choice about their repatriation, and the supervision by a neutral agency to insure that no duress is placed on any of the prisoners of war.

One of the points about which we feel strongly is that prisoners of war and civilian internees and refugees on both sides have an opportunity to decide for themselves about their repatriation and where they will go at the conclusion of an armistice.

At times it may have appeared that we were unnecessarily persistent in our own point of view. But we have realized that the political discussions, and the settlement of the larger differences concerning Korea, may be some time in the future. The military armistice must be a truce that the United Nations, and especially the Koreans, can live with.

I am hopeful of a conclusive military armistice, one which will provide security and will be a living deterrent to further aggression. General Ridgway and our negotiators for the United Nations have done a remarkable job in most trying and difficult circumstances. They deserve our gratitude and our continued support.

44. RESOLUTION OF THE GENERAL ASSEMBLY ON THE CONVENING OF A SPECIAL SESSION UPON NOTIFICATION OF AN ARMISTICE AGREEMENT, FEBRUARY 5, 1952 [89]

The General Assembly,

Desiring to facilitate to the greatest possible extent the negotiations in Pan-munjom and the conclusion of an armistice in Korea, and

Wishing to avoid premature consideration of items 17 and 27 of the agenda of the present session,

---

[89] United Nations Document A/L. 107, 6 February 1952.

I

Decides that

(a) Upon notification by the Unified Command to the Security Council of the conclusion of an armistice in Korea, the Secretary-General shall convene a special session of the General Assembly at the Headquarters of the United Nations to consider the above-mentioned items, or

(b) When other developments in Korea make desirable consideration of the above-mentioned items, the Secretary-General, acting in accordance with Article 20 of the Charter and with the rules of procedure of the General Assembly, shall convene a special session or an emergency special session of the General Assembly at the Headquarters of the United Nations;

Requests the Negotiating Committee for Extra-Budgetary Funds established by General Assembly resolution of 7 December 1951 to undertake negotiations regarding voluntary contributions to the programme of the United Nations Korean Reconstruction Agency for the relief and rehabilitation of Korea.

45. STATEMENT BY PRESIDENT TRUMAN ON THE ARMISTICE NEGOTIATIONS, MAY 7, 1952 [90]

The United States fully approves and supports without qualification the proposal for reaching an armistice which General Ridgway has offered to the Communist aggressors in Korea.

Last July the United Nations forces had repulsed Communist aggression in Korea, had proved to the Communists that aggression cannot pay, and had brought new hope for peace to free men around the world. The Soviet Union then indicated that Korean hostilities could be terminated by a military armistice. The United Nations Command in good faith and in a sincere desire to find a basis for a peaceful settlement began armistice talks with the Communist in Korea.

After many trying months of negotiation, in which each issue has been dealt with individually, tentative agreement has been reached on all but three issues. It is now apparent that the three remaining issues cannot be resolved separately. The United Nations Command proposal offers a just and a real opportunity to resolve these three issues together and simultaneously. The three-point proposal is:

1. That three shall not be a forced repatriation of prisoners of war—as the Communists have insisted. To agree to forced repatriation would be unthinkable. It would be repugnant to the fundamental moral and humanitarian principles which underlie our action in Korea. To return these prisoners of war in our hands by force would result in misery and bloodshed to the eternal dishonor of the United States and of the United Nations.

We will not buy an armistice by turning over human beings for slaughter or slavery.

The United Nations Command has observed the most extreme care in separating those prisoners who have said they would forcibly oppose return to Communist control. We have offered to submit to an impartial rescreening—after an armistice—of those persons we would hold in our custody.

---

[90] White House press release, May 7, 1952.

Nothing could be fairer. For the Communists to insist upon the forcible return to them of persons who wish to remain out of their control, is an amazing disclosure before the whole world of the operation of their system.

2. That the United Nations Command will not insist on prohibiting reconstruction or rehabilitation of airfields.

3. That the neutral nations supervisory commission should comprise representatives of four countries: Poland and Czechoslovakia chosen by the Communists, Sweden and Switzerland chosen by the United Nations Command.

The three parts of General Ridgway's proposal are all parts of a whole. They must be considered as an entity—not piecemeal. Our agreement is contingent upon acceptance of the whole proposal. This is our position. The Communists thus far have indicated only a willingness to withdraw their proposal that the U. S. S. R. be a member of the neutral inspection commission. This spurious issue was raised by them late in negotiations and its withdrawal is no real concession on their part.

The patience and understanding shown by General Ridgway and the United Nations Command negotiators merit the highest praise. In spite of almost overwhelming provocation, they have made real progress in reaching agreement on many substantial terms for an armistice. General Ridgway's proposal offers a sound and sensible way to settle the remaining issues all at once. It will have compelling appeal to those sincerely desiring peace.

46. SPECIAL REPORT BY THE UNIFIED COMMAND ON THE STATUS OF THE ARMISTICE NEGOTIATIONS, OCTOBER 18, 1952 [91]

LETTER DATED 18 OCTOBER 1952 FROM THE CHAIRMAN OF THE UNITED STATES DELEGATION TO THE GENERAL ASSEMBLY OF THE UNITED NATIONS, ADDRESSED TO THE SECRETARY-GENERAL

NEW YORK, *18 October 1952.*

I have the honour to transmit herewith for the information of the General Assembly of the United Nations a special report by the Unified Command under the United States onthe present status of the military action and the armistice negotiations in Korea.

I would be grateful if you would circulate this report to the Members of the General Assembly.

(Signed) WARREN R. AUSTIN,
Chairman.

OCTOBER 18, 1952.

SPECIAL REPORT OF THE UNIFIED COMMAND ON THE UNITED NATIONS ACTION IN KOREA

I. FOREWORD

The Unified Command transmits herewith a special report on the present status of the military action and the armistice negotiations in Korea, for the information of the General Assembly in connection with its discussion of the problem of Korea.

---

[91] UN Document A/2228, 18 October 1952.

The Security Council resolution of July 7, 1950 established a Unified Command under the United States and entrusted to it the responsibility for the conduct of the military operations in Korea necessitated by the aggression of the North Korean Forces on June 25, 1950. The military action of the United Nations is now in its twenty-eighth month. For fifteen months the United Nations Command has conducted armistice negotiations with representatives of the armed forces of the Chinese Communist and North Korean regimes with a view of bringing the fighting in Korea to an end on a basis consistent with United Nations objectives and principles. In this period a tentative draft armistice agreement has been worked out by both sides, covering all agreed points. * * *

The differences between the United Nations Command and the Communists which have prevented the conclusion of an armistice were narrowed by the end of April 1952, to one question: whether all prinsoners of war should be returned, by force if necessary. Final conclusion of an armistice under the terms of the present draft agreement now depends upon Communist acceptance of a solution to the prisoner of war question consistent with humanitarian principles.

The question of prisoner of war repatriation has been under discussion for more than 8 months. The issue arose because the United Nations Command learned, at an early stage of the hostilities, that many prisoners of war were violently opposed to being returned to the Communists. The United Nations Command is willing to return all prisoners excepting those who would violently resist repatriation. The Communists, however, have insisted on the return of all prisoners by force if necessary.

An issue or principle has thus been posed on which the Unified Command cannot yield without disregard for the fundamental principles of human rights and individual freedom embodied in the Charter.

The United Nations Command has negotiated in good faith and has made every effort to achieve an armistice. It has indicated a willingness to consider any reasonable proposal for solution of the prisoner-of-war question consistent with the principle that prisoners-of-war shall not be returned by force. The United Nations Command has offered numerous proposals for settling the question, but all these proposals have been categorically rejected by the Communists. Not a single constructive proposal has been put forward by the Communists. For months the Communists have not in fact been negotiating but have merely exploited the negotiation sessions for propaganda purposes.

As recently as September 28, the United Nations Command made three new proposals. On October 8, the Communists flatly rejected these suggestions and again insisted on the forced repatriation of prisoners. The United Nations Command Delegation, therefore, called a recess. The duration of the recess is entirely up to the Communists. The negotiations are not terminated. Meetings will resume as soon as the Communists are ready to negotiate in good faith. The United Nations Delegation is prepared to meet with the Communists whenever they come forward with a constructive proposal, or accept any one of the numerous outstanding United Nations Command proposals. The United Nations Command will leave no stone unturned, no promising avenue unexplored, in the effort to conclude an armistice on honorable terms consistent with United Nations objectives in Korea.

II. MILITARY ACTION

The sudden attack of the North Korean forces on June 25, 1950, broke through the Republic of Korea defensive positions along the 38th parallel, inflicted serious casualties on the Republic of Korea forces, and forced a large-scale withdrawal to the South (See UNCOK Reports, S/1496, 1503, 1504, 1505/Rev. 1, 1507; /1350).

Pursuant to the Security Council resolution of June 25 and 27, and July 7, 1950, armed forces of the United States and 15 other United Nations Members have been engaged in military action to assist the Republic of Korea in repelling the aggression of the North Korean, and subsequently the Chinese Communist, armed forces. Fifty-three members of the United Nations have expressed support for the United Nations action in Korea. In addition to the sixteen nations which have provided troops to the Unified Command, five nations have provided medical units and 46 economic assistance to the Unified Command or the United Nations Korean Reconstruction Agency, or both. (The contributing countries to the Unified Command are listed in Annex B.)

During the first weeks of fighting, the initial Communist offensive forced the United Nations forces into a small beachhead perimeter in the Pusan area, where the United Nations lines stiffened. In September 1950, the United Nations forces took the offensive, executing an amphibious landing at Inchon and attacking out of the Pusan perimeter. The United Nations forces soon regained most of the territory of the Republic of Korea and in the process largely destroyed the North Korean army as an effective fighting force. In October, following Communist rejection of the United Nations Command call to stop the fighting and following adoption of the General Assembly resolution of October 7, 1950, the United Nations forces moved into the north of Korea to insure conditions of stability throughout Korea. In early November, the United Nations Commander announced that the Chinese Communist forces had intervened in the Korean conflict. (See S/1884.) In later November, the United Nations troops were forced by a Chinese Communist attack to withdraw southward. The Chinese Communist offensive was stopped south of Seoul in January 1951. In March, the United Nations Command took the initiative and by June had succeeded in advancing to a line across central Korea.

The United Nations Command informed the United Nations in its 23d periodic report covering the period from June 1 to 15, 1951, that the Communist armies were continuing a slow withdrawal under constant pressure and that the enemy's position had deteriorated materially during the preceding few weeks. However, the United Nations Command saw no indication that the enemy would relax his hold on any major portion of North Korea.

Since the opening of armistice negotiations, neither the United Nations forces nor the Communist forces have undertaken sustained offensive action. However, there has been constant, and often heavy, military contact between the United Nations and Communist armed forces. The United Nations forces have sustained serious personnel casualties during the sixteen months' period of the armistice negotiations. During the negotiations the military objective of the United Nations Command has been to safeguard the security of its forces against a potential Communist offensive. The United Nations Command has maintained pressure on the front lines and in the rear areas to secure its defensive positions and to reduce the possibilities of a Communist logistic buildup which, combined with Communist manpower superiority, could seriously threaten the security of the United Nations forces. At the present time the United Nations forces face a Communist army of over 1 million men, mainly Chinese Communist forces, deployed in depth. These forces are well equipped with artillery, tanks, and other heavy military equipment. They have at their disposal an air force of more than 2,000 planes, mostly jet-engined, flown by competent pilots and based in Manchuria, from which they attack United Nations aircraft operating within Korea.

The United Nations Command with the forces now at its disposal is confident of its ability to contain a Communist offensive should the Communists choose this course of action, although additional forces are highly important for the continued effectiveness of the United Nations forces.

Over the past 28 months the United Nations Command has conducted the military operations in Korea for the purpose of repelling aggression and restoring peace and security in Korea. The United Nations Command has not, as alleged in Communist propaganda accusations, attacked any territory outside Korea nor used bacteriological or chemical warfare weapons. The military operations of the United Nations Command have been conducted with the maximum respect for humanitarian considerations and for the lives of civilians.

III. ARMISTICE NEGOTIATIONS

A. Background

From the outset of the Korean hostilities the United Nations Command has at all times demonstrated its willingness to end the fighting in Korea on an honorable basis. It has taken steps to this end on its own initiative and in response to proposals of others. The United Nations Command has insisted, of course, that the cessation of hostilities must be on a basis consistent with the United Nations objective of repelling aggression and restoring peace and security in Korea. As early as July 1950 the United States Government directed its Ambassador to the Soviet Union, Mr. Kirk, to ask the Soviet Government to "use its influence with the North Korean authorities to withdraw their invading forces immediately." In addition, the United Nations Command has on several occasions directed appeals to the Communists to halt the fighting. Fullest cooperation was given to United Nations and other diplomatic efforts to halt the fighting and negotiate a settlement, such as the proposals made by the Cease-Fire Group and the Good Offices Committee established by the General Assembly.

On June 23, 1951, Jacob Malik, Soviet representative on the Security Council, suggested in a radio address: "The Soviet peoples . . . believe that the most acute problem of the present day, the problem of the armed conflict in Korea, could also be settled. . . . The Soviet peoples believe that as a first step discussions should be started between the belligerents for a cease-fire and an armistice. . . ." The United States Government, always prepared to follow up any proposals that might lead to an end to the fighting, immediately sought clarification of certain aspects of Mr. Malik's statement. The United States Ambassador in Moscow called on Soviet Deputy Foreign Minister Gromygo, who explained that in his view an armistice would—

    1. include a cease-fire;

    2. be limited to strictly military questions without involving any political or territorial matters.

The United Nations Command thereupon undertook to establish direct contact with the Communist Command and arrangements were made for the initiation of armistice negotiations.

The United Nations Command entered into the armistice negotiations hopeful of quickly concluding an agreement which would stop the fighting. The United Nations Command was determined, however, that the armistice agreement must assure the achievement of the basic purposes of the United Nations military action in Korea—to repel the aggression against the Republic of Korea and restore peace and security in the area. From the basic purpose of the United Nations' action in Korea flowed the principal United Nations requirements for an armistice agreement:

    1. a line of demarcation consistent with the United Nations objective of repelling aggression, based upon military realities, and affording defensible positions for the opposing forces;

    2. other provisions offering maximum reasonable assurance against a renewal of the aggression;

    3. appropriate arrangements for an exchange of prisoners of war;

    4. avoidance of political issues as not properly related to armistice negotiations.

The United Nations Command negotiators have steadfastly refused to compromise the basic requirements within this framework, and the United Nations Command has at the same time maintained the broadest flexibility in seeking agreement.

B. Negotiations on the agenda and conference site

The initial meetings between the United Nations and Communist armistice negotiators considered the preparation of an agenda. The United Nations Command, while originally proposing a relatively detailed agenda, was primarily concerned with assuring that the agenda adopted should not prejudice subsequent negotiations on the substance of the agenda items. Differences arose over two items in the draft agenda proposed by the Communists. The United Nations Command negotiators opposed a Communist proposal to obtain agreement on agenda language recognizing the 38th Parallel as the line of demarcation for the cease-fire on the grounds that the agenda language proposed prejudiced the substantive question. A separate agenda item on the withdrawal of foreign troops from Korea was rejected as beyond the scope of the military talks. However, the United Nations Command agreed to inclusion on the agenda of an item providing that problems not strictly military in character would be considered for inclusion in recommendations to the Governments concerned. The agenda as agreed upon on July 26, 1951, was as follows:

    1. Adoption of agenda.

    2. Fixing a military demarcation line between both sides so as to establish a demilitarized zone as a basic condition for a cessation of hostilities in Korea.

    3. Concrete arrangements for the realization of a cease-fire and an armistice in Korea, including the composition, authority and functions of a supervising organization.

    4. Arrangements relating to prisoners of war.

    5. Recommendations to the governments of the countries concerned on both sides.

During the agenda discussions, the problem of the neutrality of the conference site arose for the first time. The United Nations Command originally proposed that a Danish hospital ship be anchored near Wonsan for use as the conference site, but in order not to delay the talks it accepted the Communist counterproposal of Kaesong which was in a "no man's land" at the time. At the initial meetings, the United Nations Command negotiators found that the Communists had occupied Kaesong and United Nations access to the conference site was limited. The Communists had also not provided equal treatment to both delegations as originally promised. As a result, General Ridgway suspended the talks on July 12. Meetings were resumed on July 15 after detailed provisions regarding the neutrality of the conference zone were agreed upon.

The neutrality of the conference site once more became an issue in August. The United Nations Command suspended the talks on August 5 because the Kaesong neutral zone was violated by a company of armed Communists. The talks were resumed five days later after the Communists promised to honor the neutrality of the area in the future.

On August 23, during the deadlock in discussions on Agenda item 2, the Communists suspended the discussions because of an alleged bombing and strafing of the conference site by United Nations forces. Investigation by United Nations liaison officers proved the charges to be unfounded. Despite this fact the Communists refused to accept the United Nations Command reply. Negotiations remained suspended for two months until October 24.

During the two-month suspension, the Communists charged additional conference zone violations. Each charge was investigated by the competent United Nations authorities. With the exception of two minor instances, the charges were not substantiated. In the case of the two confirmed violations, the United Nations Command expressed its regrets and took disciplinary action. The Communist charges inevitably raised the question of the suitability of Kaesong as a conference site. After prolonged discussion between liaison officers, the United Nations Command and the Communists shifted the conference site to Panmunjom and agreed upon detailed provisions designed to minimize the possibility of violations of the neutrality of the Panmunjom conference zone and the base camps and the neutral corridors linking these camps to the conference zone.

C. The military demarcation line

The initial substantive agreement reached between the United Nations Command and Communist negotiators was the fixing of a military demarcation line between both sides so as to establish a demilitarized zone. At the outset of negotiations on the demarcation line, the Communists proposed the 38th parallel while the United Nations Command suggested a line directly related to the actual line of contact between the forces of both sides and a demilitarized zone 20 miles wide. The objective of the United Nations Command proposals was to provide maximum defensive safeguards against a possible renewal of aggression. The United Nations Command contended that since an armistice involved military, rather than political, decisions the demarcation line should be based on military requirements. Specifically, a line related to the line of contact and taking advantage of terrain features was considered essential to provide relatively defensible positions. The line of contact was furthermore considered by the United Nations Command as consistent with the United Nations objective of repelling the aggression.

After extended negotiations and following the resumption of meetings in the new conference site of Panmunjom, the Communists accepted in principle the United Nations position that the demarcation line should be based on the line of contact. On November 27, final agreement was reached whereby the existing lines of contact between the two sides should be the demarcation line if an armistice agreement were signed within thirty days; otherwise it should be the line of contact as of the signing of the armistice. The agreement also specified that upon the coming into effect of the armistice both sides were to withdraw two kilometers from this line, creating a four-kilometer demilitarized zone between the military forces so as to minimize the possibility of incidents which could lead to a resumption of hostilities.

D. Recommendations to the governments concerned

While following agreement on agenda item 2, discussion went forward on the 3rd and 4th items, final agreement was next achieved, in fact, on the final agenda item: recommendations to the governments concerned. On February 3, 1952, the Communist delegation had agreed to concurrent discussions of Item 5. Agreement was reached on February 19. Initially, the Communists proposed a political conference covering the whole range of Far Eastern problems. The United Nations delegation pointed out that it was a military negotiating team without authority to deal with political matters. It was, however, prepared to make procedural recommendations concerning a political conference to deal with Korean political problems upon the conclusion of a military armistice. It could not consider recommending a discussion of matters outside of Korea.

The United Nations delegation accepted a revised Communist proposal recommending that within 3 months after the armistice becomes effective "a political conference of a higher level of both sides be held by representatives appointed respectively to settle through negotiation the questions of the withdrawal of all foreign forces from Korea, the peaceful settlement of the Korean question, et cetera." In agreeing to this recommendation, Admiral Joy made a statement for the record concerning the understanding of this proposal by the United Nations Command.

"First, we desire to point out that this recommendation will be made by the Commander in Chief, United Nations Command, to the United Nations as well as to the Republic of Korea. Second, in accepting the term "foreign forces" we are doing so on the basis of your statement that this term means "non-Korean Forces," and third, we wish it clearly understood that we do not construe the word "et cetera" to relate to matters outside of Korea."

E. Arrangements for implementing the armistice

On the same day that agreement was reached on item 2, the delegation began discussion of item 3: supervisory arrangements for carrying out the terms of a cease-fire and armistice. The United Nations Command viewed the discussions on the nature of the supervisory arrangements as crucial to the achievement of a maximum reasonable assurance against the renewal of aggression. To the United Nations Command the principles essential to an acceptable agreement on supervisory arrangements were five fold: (1) cessation of hostilities within twenty-four hours following the armistice signing; (2) withdrawal of all armed forces from the demilitarized zone; (3) no increase in the armed strength of either side; (4) withdrawal of all armed forces from the territory controlled by the other side; and (5) establishment of an organ to supervise the carrying out of the terms of the armistice, the supervisory organ and its observation teams to have access to the territory controlled by both sides. In addition, the United Nations Command sought to assure continued, routine rotation of its troops following the cease-fire. It was within this framework that the United Nations Command negotiators discussed item 3 with the Communists.

In the early discussions and exchange of initial proposals between the United Nations Command and Communist delegations, no serious or prolonged differences arose over the basic principles of the supervisory arrangements. However, extended negotiations were required to reach agreement on the specific details of the supervisory arrangements. There were four main points at issue between the delegations. The United Nations Command delegation in the interests of safeguarding the armistice wanted the broadest possible access to all parts of Korea to assure against the increase of military strength. It was willing to grant corresponding privileges to the Communists. The Communists wanted to limit such inspection claiming that it would be unwarranted interference in their internal affairs of North Korea. It was finally agreed to have inspection teams stationed at five ports of entry on each side plus ten mobile teams to investigate reported violations. Secondly, the Communists initially opposed a provision for the rotation of troops and it was only after lengthy negotiation that a limitation on monthly rotation of 35,000 troops was accepted by both sides. Third, the United Nations Command proposed a ban applicable to both sides on the construction of new military airfields and a ceiling on the number of civilian airfields rehabilitated. This proposal was consistent with a military armistice designed to freeze the military situation pending a final peace settlement. Finally, there were disagreements over the nature of the supervisory organs. Initially, the United Nations Command proposed inspection by joint teams but it accepted the Communist proposal for inspection by observers from neutral countries acceptable to both commands. Final agreement on the neutral nations was forestalled, however, when the Communists proposed as a neutral the Soviet Union. This was unacceptable to the United Nations Command. Final Agreement has not been reached on the last two points: airfield construction and the composition of the neutral supervisory organ.

The area of agreement reached by March 1952 may thus be summarized as follows:

1. There will be a cease-fire within twelve hours of the signing of an armistice.

2. Both sides will withdraw their forces from the demilitarized zone within seventy-two hours after the signing of an armistice.

3. All military forces will be withdrawn from rear areas and the coastal islands and waters of Korea within five days after the signing of an armistice.

4. Both sides shall cease the introduction into Korea of reinforcing military personnel. However, the rotation of 35,000 military personnel a month shall be permitted. Rotated personnel shall enter Korea only through designated ports of entry, under the supervision and inspection of the teams of the Neutral Nations Supervisory Commission.

5. Both sides shall cease the introduction into Korea of reinforcing combat aircraft, armored vehicles, weapons and ammunition. However, the replacement of destroyed, damaged, worn out or used up equipment on the basis of piece-for-piece of the same effectiveness and the same type is permitted. Such replacement shall take place only through designated ports of entry, under the supervision and inspection of teams of the Neutral Nations Supervisory Commission.

6. A Military Armistice Commission, with headquarters at Panmunjom composed of military officers of the United Nations Command and the Communist forces and aided by joint observer teams will—

(*a*) supervise the implementation of the armistice agreement;

(*b*) deal with alleged armistice violations and settle through negotiations any such violations;

(*c*) report all violations of the armistice agreement to the Commanders of the opposing sides;

7. A Neutral Nations Supervisory Commission, with headquarters in proximity to those of the Military Armistice Commission, composed of four senior officers, two of whom shall be appointed by neutral nations nominated by the United Nations Command and two of whom shall be appointed by neutral nations nominated jointly by the Supreme Commander of the Korean People's Army and the Commander of the Chinese People's Volunteers will supervise, observe, inspect, and investigate adherence to the terms of the armistice agreement relative to the introduction into Korea of reinforcing military personnel and equipment. At the request of the Military Armistice Commission or senior member of either side, it can conduct special observation and inspection at places outside the demilitarized zone where violations have been reported. Twenty inspection teams, ten of which will be located at the designated ports of entry, five in North Korea and five in South Korea, with ten mobile teams in reserve, will assist the Commission.

F. Prisoners of war

1. Background.—The prisoner-of-war issue, from the very beginning of the Korean hostilities, has been a major problem for the United Nations Command. There has been a notable difference between the United Nations Command and Communist treatment of prisoners. The United Nations Command has from the beginning of the Korean war scrupulously lived up to the principles of the Geneva Convention relative to the humane treatment of prisoners of war. It sent lists of captured personnel to the International Committee of the Red Cross (ICRC) which in turn transmitted them to the Communists. It admitted the ICRC to its prisoner-of-war camps and gave them every facility for inspection and reporting on the treatment of prisoners of war. The humane treatment of the prisoners was especially noteworthy in view of the provocative actions of some Communist prisoners, and their repeated efforts to foment disorders. The reports of the ICRC on the conditions in United Nations Command camps have been almost uniformly favorable. In those few instances where the ICRC had criticism to offer, the United Nations Command was prompt to correct the situation.

On the other hand, the Communists, while stating they are abiding by the Convention, have failed to live up to it in virtually every important respect. They have never informed the ICRC of captured personnel, except for a token list of 110 names transmitted to the ICRC in the early days of hostilities. The Communists failed to appoint a protecting power or a benevolent organization such as the ICRC and rejected the efforts of the ICRC to obtain entry into the Communist prisoner-of-war camps; they refused to exchange relief packages and even, until recently on a very limited basis, mail; they have not reported on the health of prisoners of war and have refused to exchange seriously sick and wounded; they have failed to give the accurate location of their prisoner-of-war camps and to mark them properly; and they have situated their camps in positions of danger in proximity to legitimate military targets.

2. Exchange of Prisoners Lists.—When the prisoner-of-war question was first considered, the United Nations Command still had not received any lists of the United Nations and Republic of Korea prisoners in Communist custody, while the Communists had received lists totalling approximately 170,000 names through the ICRC. Subsequently, it was found that during the period of large scale

North Korean surrenders and of mass movements of refugees from the North that some 37,500 persons had erroneously been included on these lists as prisoners of war. These persons were reclassified as civilian internees and later released to their homes in the Republic of Korea. The ICRC was informed of this action. When the Communists finally agreed to exchange lists at Panmunjom the United Nations Command gave the Communist a list containing approximately 132,000 names. At a later date, upon further investigation an additional 11,000 persons were also reclassified as civilian internees and are in process of release. Consequently, the United Nations Command has currently in its custody about 121,000 persons.

The list provided by the Communists contained only some 11,500 United Nations Command and Republic of Korea prisoners, although the Communists had themselves indicated earlier in Pyongyang radio broadcasts on February 9 and April 8, 1951, that they had captured 65,000 persons in just the first nine months of the hostilities. The Communists stated at Pammunjom that large numbers of the captured persons had been "reeducated" and released at the front where many of them joined North Korean forces and that the process was so rapid they had no opportunity to obtain their names.

3. Extent of Agreements on Prisoner of War Exchange.—In subsequent discussions, agreement was reached on a number of points relating to the exchange of prisoners. The two delegations agreed that—

(1) Prisoners of war, when released from custody, will not again be employed in acts of war in the Korean conflict.

(2) Sick and injured prisoners will be repatriated first.

(3) The exchange of prisoners of war will be completed within two months.

(4) A committee of Communist and United Nations Command officers will supervise the exchange of prisoners of war.

(5) This committee will be assisted by joint Red Cross teams composed of representatives of United Nations Red Cross societies and Communist Red Cross societies.

(6) Korean civilians will be permitted to return to their homes on either side of the demarcation line.

(7) Foreign civilians will be permitted to return to their homes.

4. United Nations Command Efforts to Settle Prisoner of War Question.—As increasing numbers of enemy personnel deserted to or were otherwise captured by the United Nations Command, it became evident that a substantial number of the prisoners of war felt that they would suffer death or injury if returned to the Communists. Many prisoners of war, it became clear, would violently resist such return. Therefore, decent respect for the rights of these individuals and the recognized humanitarian principles to which the United Nations is dedicated rendered it unthinkable that United Nations Command forces under the United Nations banner should compel these resisting prisoners of war to return to the other side. Many other governments, particularly those with troops in Korea, indicated that they shared this view. The magnitude of the problem, however, was not fully appreciated by the United Nations Command. It was not until the attitudes of the prisoners of war were examined in April 1952 that it was recognized how many prisoners of war would resist repatriation.

The United Nations Command has made its position frankly and fully known to the Communists. It has indicated that it did not wish to retain a single prisoner of war, or to send any prisoner of war to any particular destination. The United Nations Command stated to the Communists that, consistent with the basic condition that it would not use force to repatriate prisoners of war, it would consider any plan or proposal for settling the prisoner of war question. It has repeatedly invited Communist proposals to this end. Furthermore, the United Nations Command in formulating its proposal has welcomed the valuable assistance and suggestions of various governments, groups, and individuals. It has also welcomed diplomatic efforts undertaken by United Nations members to persuade the Communists to agree to a humanitarian solution of the prisoner of war question.

In early April, the armistice negotiations went temporarily into secret session at the suggestion of the United Nations Command. At that time, the Communists requested a round-number estimate of the prisoners of war whom the United Nations Command would be able to repatriate. The United Nations Command pointed out that this could only be determined by interviewing the individual prisoners of war. It should also be noted that the United Nations Command and presumably the Communists assumed that only a relatively small percentage of the prisoners would violently resist repatriation.

At the suggestion of the United Nations Command, the Communists issued an amnesty statement.[92] The United Nations Command then proceeded to the screening of the prisoners of war in its custody. The interviewing was carried out by carefully selected qualified individuals, most of whom were United States military personnel; the interrogation of Chinese prisoners of war was handled exclusively by United States nationals. The Communist announcement of amnesty of prisoners of war, which the United Nations Command had suggested, was brought to the attention of every prisoner of war. The prisoners of war were warned of the possible effects on their families if they refused to return, and were told that no promises could be made as to their disposition if they refused to return, and that they might be in camps many months after the repatriates had gone home. The United Nations Command presumed in every case that the prisoner of war was prepared to go home, and only those who the interrogators were convinced would violently resist repatriation were excluded from the number available for repatriation. The questioning was stopped if, at any time, the prisoner indicated he desired repatriation.[93]

The United Nations Command screened in early April only those prisoners of war consenting to be interviewed, some 106,000, and, to its surprise, found that only about 70,000 wanted repatriation. No attempt was made to screen the prisoners of war in Communist-dominated camps which refused to cooperate. However, since the Communists pressed for an early reply on a round number, the United Nations Command obtained the 70,000 figure by including all prisoners of war who in interviews indicated that they would not resist repatriation and an estimate covering the prisoners of war who were not screened; in making the latter estimate the United Nations Command assumed that in the camps refusing to be interviewed most prisoners of war would desire repatriation. (It may be noted that out of the camps which were Communist controlled and refused to cooperate in screening more than a thousand individuals sought at the earliest opportunity and at the risk of their lives to escape from the camps and proclaim their resistance to being returned to the Communists. A considerable number of such individuals were murdered by their Communist fellow prisoners in attempting such escapes.)

Subsequently the United Nations Command completed the interviewing of those who were not previously screened. The results indicated that a total of approximately 83,000 (76,600 Koreans and 6,400 Chinese) could be repatriated without the use of force.

When the Communists were informed of the results of the first screening and realized the large numbers of prisoners resisting repatriation, they insisted upon the full repatriation of all prisoners of war and, at the same time, sought to discredit the screening undertaken by the United Nations Command. It was thus during and after the April screening of the prisoners of war that a series of incidents occurred in the prisoner-of-war camps, particularly on Koje island. On investigation it was found that these incidents were deliberately provoked by Communist prisoners at the instigation of the Communist Command in order to intimidate the prisoners who did not desire repatriation and in order to obscure the results of the screening. Subsequently, following these incidents, the compounds on Koje were reorganized and brought under control.

In support of their position, the Communists cited the Geneva Convention. The Communists cited in particular Article 118, which provides: "Prisoners of war shall be released and repatriated without delay after cessation of hostilities." The United Nations Command, however, has pointed out to the Communists that forcible repatriation was inconsistent with the humanitarian basis, and thus the spirit of the Geneva Convention. Furthermore, Article 6 provides: ". . . the High Contracting Parties may conclude other special agreements for all matters concerning which they may deem it suitable to make separate provi-

---

[92] The amnesty statement read as follows:
"The Korean Peoples Army and the Chinese Peoples Volunteers have always held that, following the cessation of active hostilities, both belligerents should speedily release and repatriate all the prisoners of war in their respective custody. This reasonable position of ours definitely will not undergo any change on account of the fact that a number of our captured personnel, during the period of captivity, have had their arms tattooed or have written certain documents or committed other similar acts. We are deeply aware that such acts have certainly not been done out of their own volition and that they should not be held responsible for these acts.
"We wholeheartedly welcome the return of all of our captured personnel to the arms of the Motherland; we have further guaranteed, in an agreement reached with the other side, that all captured personnel shall, after their repatriation, rejoin their families to participate in peaceful construction and live a peaceful life."
[93] The questions asked the prisoners are set forth in the 44th Report of the United Nations Command Operations in Korea (S/2700, July 14, 1952, pp. 4–5).

sion. No special agreement shall adversely affect the situation of prisoners of war, as defined by the present Convention, nor restrict the rights which it confers upon them. . . ." The United Nations Command pointed out to the Communists that a special agreement on nonforcible repatriation protected the rights of the individual prisoner to elect not to be repatriated to his home and was consistent with the Convention.

Following the Communist refusal to agree to an exchange of prisoners on the basis of the 70,000 estimate, the United Nations Command, on April 28, offered a package proposal. The proposal covered the differences on the arrangements for supervising the armistice, namely rehabilitation and construction of military airfields and the composition of the Neutral Nations Supervisory Commission,[94] and the question of repatriation of prisoners of war. The United Nations Command proposed that:

1. There shall not be forced repatriation of prisoners of war.

2. The United Nations Command will not insist on prohibiting reconstruction and rehabilitation of airfields.

3. The United Nations Command agrees to accept Poland and Czechoslovakia as members of the Neutral Nations Supervisory Commission if the Communists agree to accept Sweden and Switzerland (thus withdrawing their demand for the inclusion of the Soviet Union).

In making the above proposal the United Nations Command made it clear that the proposal must be accepted in whole. Accordingly, Communist acceptance of only the second and third points of the proposal in fact constituted a rejection of the proposal. However, this proposal remains open.

During the five months of fruitless negotiation on the prisoner repatriation issue following Communist rejection of the package proposal, the United Nations Command has indicated to the Communist negotiators, that, while it is firm on the issue of nonforcible repatriation, it is prepared to consider any reasonable suggestion for resolving the deadlock.

The United Nations Command negotiators have also assured the Communists of their willingness to consider any reasonable means for an impartial verification of the wishes of the prisoners of war or for implementing the actual exchange of prisoners so as to avoid embarrassment to the Communists.

Specifically, on April 23, the United Nations Command negotiators proposed that joint Red Cross teams from both sides with, or without military observers of both sides be admitted to the prisoner of war camps of both sides to verify the fact that nonrepatriates would forcibly resist return to the side from which they came. It was also proposed that all prisoners of war of both sides be delivered in groups to the demilitarized zone and be given an opportunity to express their preference on repatriation. The verification would be carried out as one or a combination of (a) the ICRC, (b) teams from impartial nations, (c) joint teams of military observers, or (d) Red Cross representatives from each side.

On September 28, the United Nations Command delegation made its broadest proposals in another effort to meet Communist objections to the principle of nonforcible repatriation and Communist allegations that the previous screening was unfair and that the United Nations Command is forcibly restraining and coercing the nonrepatriates. The United Nations Command put forward three alternative proposals:

1. Both sides would agree that as soon as the armistice agreement goes into effect all prisoners of war of each side shall be entitled to release and repatriation, both sides agreeing that the obligation to exchange and repatriate prisoners of war is fulfilled by having them brought to an agreed exchange point in the demilitarized zone where the prisoner of war will be identified and his name checked against the agreed list of prisoners of war. However, both sides would agree that any prisoner of war who at the time of his identification states that he wishes to return to the side by which he had been detained shall immediately be permitted to do so and that that side will transport him from the demilitarized zone and not detain him as a prisoner of war but permit him to regain civilian status.

2. Prisoners not resisting repatriation would be expeditiously exchanged. All prisoners of war who have indicated to the United Nations Command that they would forcibly resist repatriation will be delivered to the demilitarized zone in small groups where they will be entirely freed from the military control of either side and interviewed by representatives of mutually agreed country or

---

[94] See Section E above.

countries not participating in the Korean hostilities and free to go to the side of their choice as indicated by those interviews.

3. Prisoners not resisting repatriation would be expeditiously exchanged. Prisoners of war who have indicated to the United Nations Command that they will forcibly resist repatriation will be delivered in groups to the demilitarized zone and there entirely freed from the military control of either side and without questioning, interviewing, or screening of any kind to be released and free to go to the side of their choice.

The United Nations Command delegation also made it clear that the procedures contained in the three proposals could be carried out in the presence of or under the observation of one or a combination of (a) the ICRC, (b) joint Red Cross teams, or (c) joint teams of military observers of both sides.

These proposals were rejected by the Communists. At that time, the United Nations Command called a recess in the negotiations. No constructive proposals have been forthcoming from the Communists either since this rejection or in the more than 6 months prior to it. The months of meeting have been used for purely propaganda purposes by the Communists.

The United Nations Command does not desire to break off negotiations and is not doing so; it has merely called a recess. The United Nations Command desires to continue to negotiate in good faith. The numerous proposals it has made remain open. When the Communist delegation is ready to accept any one of the proposals or to make a constructive proposal of its own which could lead to an honorable armistice, the United Nations Command delegation is prepared to meet with it again at Panmunjom and make all possible progress toward the armistice. The United Nations Command liaison officers remain available for consultation and for the performance of their customary duties. That is the present situation in the armistice negotiations in Korea. It remains the sincere hope of the United Nations Command that an honarable armistice can be realized.

47. RESOLUTION OF THE GENERAL ASSEMBLY, DECEMBER 3, 1952 (THE INDIAN RESOLUTION) [95]

The General Assembly,

Having received the special report of the United Nations Command of 18 October 1952 on "the present status of the military action and the armistice negotiations in Korea" and other relevant reports relating to Korea,

Noting with approval the considerable progress towards an armistice made by negotiation at Panmunjom and the tentative agreements to end the fighting in Korea and to reach a settlement of the Korean question,

Noting further that disagreement between the parties on one remaining issue, alone, prevents the conclusion of an armistice and that a considerable measure of agreement already exists on the principles on which this remaining issue can be resolved,

Mindful of the continuing and vast loss of life, devastation, and suffering resulting from and accompanying the continuance of the fighting,

Deeply conscious of the need to bring hostilities to a speedy end and of the need for a peaceful settlement of the Korean question,

Anxious to expedite and facilitate the convening of the political conference as provided in article 60 of the draft armistice agreement,

1. *Affirms* that the release and repatriation of prisoners of war shall be effected in accordance with the Geneva Convention relative to the Treatment of Prisoners of War, dated 12 August 1949, the well-established principles and practice and international law, and the relevant provisions of the draft armistice agreement;

---

[95] United Nations, General Assembly, 7th session, Resolution Adopted on the Reports of the First Committee, 610 (VII), pp. 3–4.

2. *Affirms* that force shall not be used against prisoners of war to prevent or effect their return to their homelands, and that they shall at all time be treated humanely in accordance with the specific provisions of the Geneva Convention and with the general spirit of the Convention;

3. *Accordingly requests* the President of the General Assembly to communicate the following proposals to the Central People's Government of the People's Republic of China and to the North Korean authorities as forming a just and reasonable basis for an agreement so that an immediate cease fire would result and be effected; to invite their acceptance of these proposals and to make a report to the General Assembly during its present session and as soon as appropriate:

PROPOSALS

I. In order to facilitate the return to their homelands of all prisoners of war, there shall be established a Repatriation Commission consisting of representatives of Czechoslovakia, Poland, Sweden, and Switzerland, that is, the four States agreed to for the constitution of the Neutral Nations Supervisory Commission and referred to in paragraph 37 of the draft armistice agreement, or constituted, alternately, of representatives of four States not participating in hostilities, two nominated by each side, but excluding representatives of States that are permanent members of the Security Council.

II. The release and repatriation of prisoners of war shall be effected in accordance with the Geneva Convention relative to the Treatment of Prisoners of War, dated 12 August 1949, the well-established principles and practice of International Law and the relevant provisions of the draft armistice agreement.

III. Force shall not be used against the prisoners of war to prevent or effect their return to their homelands and no violence to their persons or affront to their dignity or self-respect shall be permitted in any manner or for any purpose whatsoever. This duty is enjoined on and entrusted to the Repatriation Commission and each of its members. Prisoners of war shall at all times be treated humanely in accordance with the specific provisions of the Geneva Convention and with the general spirit of that Convention.

IV. All prisoners of war shall be released to the Repatriation Commission from military control and from the custody of the detaining side in agreed numbers and at agreed exchange points in agreed demilitarized zones.

V. Classification of prisoners of war according to nationality and domicile as proposed in the letter of 16 October 1952 from General Kim Il Sung, Supreme Cmmander of the Korean People's Army, and General Peng Teh-huai, Commander of the Chinese People's Volunteers, to General Mark W. Clark, Commander-in-Chief, United Nations Command, shall then be carried out immediately.

VI. After classification, prisoners of war shall be free to return to their homelands forthwith, and their speedy return shall be facilitated by all parties concerned.

VII. In accordance with arrangements prescribed for the purpose by the Repatriation Commission, each party to the conflict shall have freedom and facilities to explain to the prisoners of war "depending upon them" their rights and to inform the prisoners of war on any matter relating to their return to their homelands and particularly their full freedom to return.

VIII. Red Cross teams of both sides shall assist the Repatriation Commission in its work and shall have access, in accordance with the terms of the draft armistice agreement, to prisoners of war while they are under the temporary jurisdiction of the Repatriation Commission.

IX. Prisoners of war shall have freedom and facilities to make representations and communications to the Repatriation Commission and to bodies and agencies working under the Repatriation Commission, and to inform any or all such bodies of their desires on any matter concerning themselves, in accordance with arrangements made for the purpose by the Commission.

X. Notwithstanding the provisions of paragraph III above, nothing in this Repatriation Agreement shall be construed as derogating from the authority of the Repatriation Commission (or its authorized representatives) to exercise its legitimate functions and responsibilities for the control of the prisoners under its temporary jurisdiction.

XI. The terms of this Repatriation Agreement and the arrangements arising therefrom shall be made known to all prisoners of war.

XII. The Repatriation Commission is entitled to call upon parties to the conflict, its own member governments, or the Member States of the United Nations for such legitimate assistance as it may require in the carrying out of its duties and tasks and in accordance with the decisions of the Commission in this respect.

XIII. When the two sides have made an agreement for repatriation based on these proposals, the interpretation of that agreement shall rest with the Repatriation Commission. In the event of disagreement in the Commission, majority decision shall prevail. When no majority decision is possible, an umpire agreed upon in accordance with the succeeding paragraph and with article 132 of the Geneva Convention of 1949 shall have the deciding vote.

XIV. The Repatriation Commission shall at its first meeting and prior to an armistice proceed to agree upon and appoint the umpire who shall at all times be available to the Commission and shall act as its Chairman unless otherwise agreed. If agreement on the appointment of the umpire cannot be reached by the Commission within the period of three weeks after the date of the first meeting this matter should be referred to the General Assembly.

XV. The Repatriation Commission shall also arrange after the armistice for officials to function as umpires with inspecting teams or other bodies to which functions are delegated or assigned by the Commission or under the provisions of the draft armistice agreement, so that the completion of the return of prisoners of war to their homelands shall be expedited.

XVI. When the Repatriation Agreement is acceded to by the parties concerned and when an umpire has been appointed under paragraph 14 above, the draft armistice agreement, unless otherwise altered by agreement between the parties, shall be deemed to have been accepted by them. The provisions of the draft armistice agreement shall apply except in so far as they are modified by the Repatriation Agreement. Arrangements for repatriation under this agreement will begin when the armistice agreement is thus concluded.

XVII. At the end of ninety days, after the Armistice Agreement has been signed, the disposition of any prisoners of war whose return to their homelands may not have been effected in accordance with the procedure set out in these proposals or as otherwise agreed, shall be referred with recommendations for their disposition, including a target date for the termination of their detention to the political conference to be called as provided under article 60 of the draft armistice agreement. If at the end of a further thirty days there are any prisoners of war whose return to their homelands has not been effected under the above procedures or whose future has not been provided for by the political conference, the responsibility for their care and maintenance and for their subsequent disposition shall be transferred to the United Nations, which in all matters relating to them shall act strictly in accordance with international law.

399th plenary meeting,
3 December 1952.

48. ADDRESS BY PRESIDENT EISENHOWER TO A JOINT SESSION OF CONGRESS, FEBRUARY 2, 1953 [96]

[Excerpt]

III

In this general discussion of our foreign policy, I must make special mention of the war in Korea.

This war is, for Americans, the most painful phase of Communist aggression throughout the world. It is clearly a part of the same calculated assault that the aggressor is simultaneously pressing in Indo-China and in Malaya, and of the strategic situation that manifestly embraces the island of Formosa and the Chinese Nationalist forces there. The working out of any military solution to the Korean War will inevitably affect all these areas.

The Administration is giving immediate increased attention to the development of additional Republic of Korea forces. The citizens of that country have proved their capacity as fighting men and their eagerness to take a greater share in the defense of their homeland. Organization, equipment, and training will allow them to do so. Increased assistance to Korea for this purpose conforms fully to our global policies.

In June 1950, following the aggressive attack on the Republic of Korea, the United States Seventh Fleet was instructed both to prevent attack upon Formosa and also to insure that Formosa should not be used as a base of operations against the Chinese Communist mainland.

This has meant, in effect, that the United States Navy was required to serve as a defensive arm of Communist China. Regardless of the situation in 1950, since the date of that order the Chinese Communists have invaded Korea to attack the United Nations forces there. They have consistently rejected the proposals of the United Nations Command for an armistice. They recently joined with Soviet Russia in rejecting the armistice proposal sponsored in the United Nations

---

[96] White House press release, February 2, 1953, pp. 3–4.

by the Government of India. This proposal had been accepted by the United States and fifty-three other nations.

Consequently there is no longer any logic or sense in a condition that required the United States Navy to assume defensive responsibilities on behalf of the Chinese Communists, thus permitting those Communists, with greater impunity, to kill our soldiers and those of our United Nations allies, in Korea.

I am, therefore, issuing instructions that the Seventh Fleet no longer be employed to shield Communist China. This order implies no aggressive intent on our part. But we certainly have no obligation to protect a nation fighting us in Korea.

49. AGREEMENT ON THE EXCHANGE OF SICK AND WOUNDED PRISONERS OF WAR, APRIL 11, 1953 [97]

[Unofficial]

The senior member of the United Nations Command liaison group and the senior member of the Korean People's Army and the Chinese People's Volunteers liaison group, in order to effect the repatriation of such and injured captured personnel in accordance with provisions of article 109 of the 1949 Geneva Convention relative to the treatment of prisoners of war, agree to the following:

Repatriation shall be accomplished at Panmunjom.

Repatriation shall commence at Panmunjom not later than 10 days after the signing of this agreement.

a. The Korean People's Army and the Chinese People's Volunteers shall deliver sick and injured captured personnel at the rate of approximately 100 per day until delivery of all sick and injured captured personnel to be repatriated by the Korean People's Army and the Chinese People's Volunteers is completed. The number of persons actually delivered each day shall be contingent upon the ability of the United Nations Command to receive them, but delivery shall in any case be completed prior to the termination date of this agreement.

b. The United Nations Command shall deliver sick and injured captured personnel at the rate of approximately 500 per day until delivery of all sick and injured captured personnel to be repatriated by the United Nations Command is completed.

The number of persons actually delivered each day shall be contingent upon the ability of the Korean People's Army and Chinese People's Volunteers to receive them, but delivery shall in any case be completed prior to the termination of this agreement.

The United Nations Command shall deliver sick and injured captured personnel in groups of approximately twenty-five. Each group shall be accompanied by rosters, prepared by nationality, to include: (*a*) Name, (*b*) rank, (*c*) internment or military serial number.

After each group of sick and injured captured personnel is delivered and received, a representative of the receiving side shall sign the roster of the captured personnel delivered as a receipt and shall return this to the delivering side.

In order to insure that the sick and injured captured personnel of both sides are given maximum protection during the full period of

---

[97] Department of State Bulletin, April 20, 1953, p. 576.

repatriation, both sides agree to guarantee immunity from all attacks to all rail and motor movements carrying sick and injured captured personnel to Kaesong and Munsan-Ni, respectively, and thence through presently established immunity routes to Panmunjom, subject to the following conditions:

a. Movement of motor convoys to Kaesong and Munsan-Ni, respectively, shall be restricted to daylight hours, and each convoy shall consist of not less than five vehicles in close formation: except that north of Panmunjom, because of actual conditions, the latter provisions shall apply only to the route from Pyongyang to Kaesong.

b. Each car in rail movements and each vehicle in motor convoys shall display clearly visible identification markings.

c. Each side, prior to the initial movement, shall provide the liaison group of the other side with a detailed description of the markings utilized to identify motor convoys and rail movements. This shall include color, size, and manner in which the markings will be displayed.

Each side, prior to the initial movement, shall provide the liaison group of the other side with the sites and markings of the bivouac areas and night stop-over locations for motor convoys.

Each side shall inform the liaison group of the other side, twenty-four hours in advance of each movement, of the selected route, number of cars in rail movement or number of vehicles in motor movement, and the estimated time of arrival at Kaesong or Munsan-Ni.

Each side shall notify the liaison group of the other side, by the most expeditious means of communication available, of the location of emergency stop-overs.

During the period while sick and injured captured personnel are being repatriated through the Panmunjom conference site area, the Oct. 22, 1951, agreement between liaison officers, with the exception of the part therein provided for in Paragraph 8 of this agreement, shall continue in effect. Liaison groups of both sides and their parties shall have free access to, and free movement within, the Panmunjom conference site area. The composition of each liaison group and its party shall be as determined by the senior member thereof: however, in order to avoid congestion in the conference site area, the number of personnel of each side in the area, including captured personnel under its control, shall not exceed 300 persons at any one time. Each side shall transfer repatriated personnel out of the Panmunjom conference site area as expeditiously as possible.

During the period while sick and injured captured personnel are being repatriated through the Panmunjom conference site area, the armed military police of each side, who undertake to maintain order within the conference site area, shall be increased from the maximum number of fifteen, as provided in the Oct. 22, 1951, agreement between liaison officers, to thirty.

Other administrative details shall be mutually arranged by officers designated by the senior member of the liaison group of each side.

This agreement is effective when signed and will terminate twenty days after the commencement of repatriation of sick and injured captured personnel at Panmunjom.

Done at Panmunjom, Korea, this eleventh day of April 1953 in the English, Korean, and Chinese languages, all texts being equally authentic.

LEE SANG CHO, *Major General, Korean People's Army, senior member Korean People's Army and Chinese People's Volunteers liaison group.*

J. C. DANIEL, *Rear Admiral, United States Navy, senior member United Nations Command liaison group.*

50. RESOLUTION OF THE GENERAL ASSEMBLY ON THE EXCHANGE OF SICK AND WOUNDED PRISONERS OF WAR, APRIL 18, 1953 [98]

The General Assembly,

REAFFIRMING its unswerving determination to spare no efforts likely to create conditions favourable to the attainment of the purposes of peace and conciliation embodied in the Charter of the United Nations,

NOTING, following the United Nations Command initiative for the exchange of sick and wounded prisoners of war, the communication by the Minister for Foreign Affairs of the Central People's Government of the People's Republic of China dated 31 March 1953 to the President of the General Assembly, and the exchange of communications between the United Nations Command and the Commanders of the Chinese People's Volunteers and the Korean People's Army in regard thereto.

CONFIDENT that a just and honourable armistice in Korea will powerfully contribute to alleviate the present international tension,

1. *Notes* with deep satisfaction that an agreement has been signed in Korea on the exchange of sick and wounded prisoners of war;

2. *Expresses* the hope that the exchange of sick and wounded prisoners of war will be speedily completed and that the further negotiations at Panmunjom will result in achieving an early armistice in Korea, consistent with the United Nations principles and objectives;

3. *Decides* to recess the present session upon completion of the current agenda items, and requests the President of the General Assembly to reconvene the present session to resume consideration of the Korean question (a) upon notification by the Unified Command to the Security Council of the signing of an armistice agreement in Korea; or (b) when in the view of a majority of Members other developments in Korea require consideration of this question.

51. STATEMENT BY THE DEPARTMENT OF STATE ON THE EXCHANGE OF PRISONERS OF WAR, MAY 15, 1953 [99]

There have been many questions, and some misunderstanding, about the present status of the armistice negotiations at Panmunjom. It is appropriate, therefore, to restate our basic position and to make clear where we stand.

---

[98] Department of State Bulletin, May 4, 1953, p. 661.   U. N. doc. A/Resolution 99.
[99] Department of State Press Release No. 269, May 15, 1953.

The Government of the United States, like the Governments of the other United Nations members participating in Korea, has always wanted peace in Korea. We did not start the war in Korea, but we have always been ready to end it on an honorable basis. For almost two years we have patiently and persistently sought to bring an end to the war. Our efforts to bring peace to Korea were ignored by the Communists for the first year of the fighting. When armistice negotiations finally began in July 1951, the United Nations Command made every effort to reach an honorable armistice. We have negotiated in good faith and with great patience. We are continuing to negotiate in that way.

The negotiations have been deadlocked for more than a year on the question of prisoners of war. Members of the free world have affirmed that there can be no force used to compel the unwilling prisoners to return to the Communists. That is the fundamental issue between us and the Communists and the one on which we stand.

Some weeks ago the Communists for the first time gave some basis for hoping that they may be prepared to meet the moral judgment of the nations of the world on the prisoner question. After several false starts they finally came forward with a proposal which, with necessary modifications and clarifications, could form a basis for an honorable agreement. On May 13, the United Nations Command accepted many points of this latest Communist proposal as a basis for negotiation and proposed some modifications to make the plan workable. These suggestions are designed to make the plan for taking custody of the prisoners of war who resist repatriation practicable and fair, to protect the prisoners in question, while at the same time satisfying the Communists and the peoples of the world that the decision of these persons to go home or not to go home is entirely their own. The United Nations Command has sought to reduce the scope of the problem to give maximum protection to all the prisoners, as well as to make the task of the custodial commission manageable.

On one point there can be no question. The principle that force shall not be used to compel resisting prisoners to go home excludes every form of coercion. We cannot, consistently with that principle, create a situation where such persons are offered no alternative to repatriation other than indefinite captivity or custody. The principles for which we have been striving for many months and which have been approved by the United Nations require that the prisoner question should be finally settled, that persons who wish to go home should be allowed to do so and that those who do not shall be released within a reasonable time after the end of hostilities.

The prisoner-of-war question is no technicality but a fundamental point of Free World philosophy on the integrity and rights of the individual. Freemen cannot and will not agree to regard human beings as mere chattels to be held and used as such. The United Nations Command will continue to explore every possibility for an honorable and reasonable solution in Korea, but it will not surrender a fundamental humanitarian principle vital to the whole Free World.

52. STATEMENT BY PRESIDENT EISENHOWER, MAY 26, 1953 [1]

The attention of the free world is focused upon the armistice negotiations at Panmunjom. There, on May 25, the United Nations Command renewed its efforts to bring an honorable peace to Korea and a fair and humane settlement of the POW issue. To speed these negotiations the United Nations Command requested executive, in other words confidential sessions. We are continuing to observe the executive nature of those sessions.

There are, however, certain principles inherent in the United Nations Command position which are basic and not subject to change. No prisoners will be repatriated by force. No prisoners will be coerced or intimidated in any way. And there must be a definite limit to the period of their captivity. The procedures used in handling the prisoners must reflect these principles.

In all this, our allies are in full accord. These principles accord also with the prevailing view of a representative bipartisan group of Senators and Congressmen who have been consulted.

Finally: These principles on which we stand are the same as those which were formerly approved by fifty-four members of the United Nations.

53. EXCHANGE OF LETTERS BETWEEN PRESIDENT SYNGMAN RHEE, AND PRESIDENT EISENHOWER, MAY 30, JUNE 6, AND JUNE 19, 1953

A. President Rhee to President Eisenhower, May 30, 1953 [2]

Dear Mr. President: I have recently had the honor of receiving several messages from Your Excellency, some oral and some written, through General Clark and Ambassador Briggs, and, as a result, come to be fully cognizant of your intention to settle the war in Korea by means of an armistice. I have given them fully study and attention. I earnestly wish I could see my way clear to make a public statement, as requested, pledging to accept any armistice you may deem necessary. But we are fearfully aware, on the other hand, that to accept any armistice arrangement which would allow the Chinese Communists to remain in Korea would mean to the Korean nation, in terms of eventualities, an acceptance of a death sentence without protest. It is a hard thing for a nation to do. Furthermore, even if I personally agree to such an arrangement, it will not help the matter very much, as subsequent developments, I fear, will show.

It seems at once appropriate and opportune for us, therefore, to make a proposal now for the consideration of the United Nations and the Communist negotiators. Communists made their proposals; so did the United Nations. The Government of the Republic of Korea, however, has been patiently waiting all this while for them to discuss the matter fully among themselves. None of these proposals from both sides has proved to be acceptable to all and consequently there has come about a stalemate in negotiation, in addition to this stale-

---

[1] White House press release, May 26, 1953.
[2] Press release, Korean Embassy, May 30, 1953.

mated war. Whatever academic arguments there may be against it, we cannot but feel that rough and rudimental justice calls for Korea making one first and last proposal on its own part.

From our own point of view, the Korean problem which the United Nations started to settle by military means when they sent their armed forces to Korea to fight the Communists and kept on fighting for three years*should be settled by punishing the aggressors, unifying Korea and thus firmly establishing the collective security of all free nations. This would be honorable and just for all concerned and alone would force the war-makers to abandon their ambition to conquer the world. However, we have found, to our great disappointment, the new United Nations proposal to be of such an appeasing nature that it cannot avoid the appearance of surrender and that that, in turn, will lead to a great disaster to all. We are forced, therefore, to propose something which may not be fraught with such a danger.

Meanwhile, I am sure you have been fully informed of it, for I mentioned it to General Clark and Ambassador Briggs the other day, asking them to present my view of the matter to you. I told them further that I would not publicly announce it until I heard from them. I take it for granted, however, that you would not mind if I released it now. I am going to write down here what I orally said to them by way of confirming it. There are, of course, certain detail matters to be worked out satisfactorily in order to safeguard the fruit of our common efforts so far made from dissipation. I submit the following as a rough outline of what we propose as something to be preferred to any arrangement leaving Korea divided and letting the Chinese Communists stay on in Korea.

We propose a simultaneous withdrawal of both the Communist and United Nations forces from Korea, on the condition that a mutual defense pact between our two governments precede it. The Communist puppet regime in north Korea has a military pact, I understand, with Red China, while the latter has another with the Soviet Union. Korea has nothing to counteract the formidable impact of this series of Communist military copulations. We sincerely believe that once when both parties agree to see this primary need and the danger from the absence of its satisfaction, the difficulties, mostly academic in our view, that seem to discourage such a pact will vanish or, at least, can be brushed aside with much reason and wisdom.

The Mutual Defense Pact will, we earnestly hope, cover the following points, among others to be agreed upon by both sides.

The United States will agree to come to our military aid and assistance immediately without any consultation or conference with any nation or nations, if and when an enemy nation or nations resume aggressive activities against the Korean Peninsula.

The Security Pact should include the United States help in the increase of the ROK armed forces. If we come to agree with the Soviets to refrain from building up the defense forces on both sides, our hands will be tied while the Soviets continue to do it anyway.

Adequate supplies of arms, ammunition, and general logistic materials will be given Korea with a view to making it strong enough to defend itself without needing American soldiers to fight in Korea again.

The United States air and naval forces will remain where they are now so as to deter the enemy from attempting another aggression.

In case the idea of simultaneous withdrawal is found unacceptable to either or both of the negotiating parties, I beg of you to allow the Koreans to continue the fighting, for this is the universal preference of the Korean people to any divisive armistice or peace. Our first choice, if we are allowed to make it, is still to have our allies by our side to actively help us fight out our common issue. But, if that is no longer possible, we would rather wish to have the right of self-determination to decide the issue ourselves conclusively one way or the other. Anyway, it is beyond question that we cannot any longer survive a stalemate of division.

Let me assure Your Excellency that the defense of the United States is as dear to us as is that of our own, for the ultimate safety or security of the whole free world hangs upon that of the United States. For this reason, we even resent the so-called unity of the free nations, some of whom do urge the United States to join in their appeasement policy. These nations do not realize where they stand in this global struggle between Democracy and Communism.

Due to the lack of a firm and steady policy on the part of the free world, we have lost already too many nations to the Soviets. The longer this policy continues, the more free nations will be forced to join with the enemy of Democracy. To disappoint the Koreans is to disappoint most of the anti-Communist elements everywhere. The United States will in the end find itself a democratic oasis in a Communist desert. I trust that the people of America will never sell out their freedom and democratic institutions at the price of peace.

Action, not words, will deter the world aggressor.

Our prayers are unwaveringly behind every effort of yours to pull through an effective action against the enemy, in spite of the difficulties that surround you.

Most sincerely yours,
THE PRESIDENT, UNITED STATES OF AMERICA,
White House, Washington, D. C.

B. PRESIDENT EISENHOWER TO PRESIDENT RHEE, JUNE 6, 1953 [3]

DEAR MR. PRESIDENT: I received on June 2 the cabled text of your communication dated May 30. I have given it the careful and sympathetic consideration it deserves.

The Republic of Korea has engaged all of its resources, human and material, in a struggle which will go down in history as one of the epic struggles of all time. You have dedicated your all without reservation to the principle that human liberty and national liberty must survive against Communist aggression, which tramples upon human dignity and which replaces national sovereignty with a humiliating satellite status. The principles for which your nation has fought and for which so many of your youth have died are principles which defend free men and free nations everywhere.

The United States has stood with you, and with you we have fought for those principles, as part of the United Nations Command. The blood of your youth and our youth has been poured out on the altar of common sacrifice. Thereby we have demonstrated not only our dedication to the cause of human freedom and political liberty, but also our dedication to an equally important principle which is that

---

[3] Department of State Bulletin, June 15, 1953, pp. 835–836.

there cannot be independence without interdependence, and there cannot be human liberty except as men recognize that they are bound together by ties of common destiny.

The moment has now come when we must decide whether to carry on by warfare a struggle for the unification of Korea or whether to pursue this goal by political and other methods.

The enemy has proposed an armistice which involves a clear abandonment of the fruits of aggression. The armistice would leave the Republic of Korea in undisputed possession of substantially the territory which the Republic administered prior to the aggression; indeed, this territory will be somewhat enlarged.

The proposed armistice, true to the principle of political asylum, assures that the thousands of North Koreans and Communist Chinese prisoners in our hands, who have seen liberty and who wish to share it, will have the opportunity to do so and will not be forcibly sent back into Communist areas. The principle of political asylum is one which we could not honorably surrender even though we thereby put an earlier end to our own human and material losses. We have suffered together many thousands of casualties in support of this principle.

It is my profound conviction that under these circumstances acceptance of the armistice is required of the United Nations and the Republic of Korea. We would not be justified in prolonging the war with all the misery that it involves in the hope of achieving, by force, the unification of Korea.

The unification of Korea is an end to which the United States is committed, not once but many times, through its World War II declarations and through its acceptance of the principles enunciated in reference to Korea by the United Nations. Korea is unhappily not the only country which remains divided after World War II. We remain determined to play our part in achieving the political union of all countries so divided. But we do not intend to employ war as an instrument to accomplish the worldwide political settlements to which we are dedicated and which we believe to be just. It was indeed a crime that those who attacked from the North invoked violence to unite Korea under their rule. Not only as your official friend but as a personal friend I urge that your country not embark upon a similar course.

There are three major points I would like to make to you:

1. The United States will not renounce its efforts by all peaceful means to effect the unification of Korea. Also, as a member of the United Nations, we shall seek to assure that the United Nations continues steadfast in its determination in this respect. In the political conference which will follow an armistice that will be our central objective. The United States intends to consult with your Government both before and during such a conference and expects the full participation of your Government in that conference.

2. You speak of a mutual defense pact. I am prepared promptly, after the conclusion and acceptance of an armistice, to negotiate with you a mutual defense treaty along the lines of the treaties heretofore made between the United States and the Republic of the Philippines, and the United States and Australia and New Zealand. You may recall that both of these treaties speak of "the development of a more comprehensive system of regional security in the Pacific area." A security pact between the United States and the Republic of Korea

would be a further step in that direction. It would cover the territory now or hereafter brought peacefully under the administration of the ROK. Of course, you realize that under our constitutional system any such treaty would be made only with the advice and consent of the Senate. However, the action which the United States has heretofore taken, and the great investment of blood and treasure which has already been made for the independence of Korea, are certainly clear indications of American temper and intentions not to tolerate a repetition of unprovoked aggression.

3. The United States Government, subject to requisite Congressional appropriations, will be prepared to continue economic aid to the Republic of Korea which will permit in peace a restoration of its devastated land. Homes must be rebuilt. Industries must be reestablished. Agriculture must be made vigorously productive.

The preamble of the Constitution of the United States states the goals of our people, which I believe are equally the goals of the brave people of Korea, namely "to form a more perfect union, establish justice, insure domestic tranquillity, provide for the common defense, promote the general welfare, and secure the blessings of liberty." Manifestly, not all of these conditions now prevail in Korea. Moreover, in existing circumstances they cannot be achieved either by prolongation of the present conflict or by reckless adventure with a new one. Only by peaceful means can these things be achieved.

With the conclusion of an armistice the United States is prepared to join with the Republic of Korea to seek for Korea these ends. We believe that in Korea there should be a more perfect union and, as I say, we shall seek to achieve that union by all peaceful methods. We believe that there should be domestic tranquillity and that can come from the end of fighting. There should be provision for the defense of Korea. That will come from the mutual security treaty which we are prepared to make. The general welfare should be advanced and that will come from your own peacetime efforts and from economic assistance to your war-torn land. Finally, a peaceful settlement will afford the best opportunity to bring to your people the blessings of liberty.

I assure you, Mr. President, that so far as the United States is concerned, it is our desire to go forward in fellowship with the Republic of Korea. Even the thought of a separation at this critical hour would be a tragedy. We must remain united.

Sincerely,

DWIGHT D. EISENHOWER.

C. PRESIDENT RHEE TO PRESIDENT EISENHOWER, JUNE 19, 1953 [4]

DEAR MR. PRESIDENT: First of all, I must apologize for my long delay in answering your good letter of June 6, 1953. To confess the truth, I made more than one draft, but I could not express myself clearly without appearing to be argumentative, which I wanted to avoid. I do hope you will read this letter in the same friendly spirit in which it is written.

From the beginning, we repeatedly tried to make clear to all friendly nations that if an armistice permitting the Chinese aggressors to remain in Korea should be concluded we could not survive. This apprehensiveness has not abated.

---

[4] Department of State Bulletin, July 6, 1953, pp. 13–14.

Evidently our friendly nations seem to take it for granted that the withdrawal of the Chinese Communists from Korea and the subsequent unification of Korea can be accomplished by the political conference scheduled to follow the armistice. I do not wish to enter detailed argument over this point but I feel I must say, at least, that we do not believe in the possibility.

It is true that is a matter of opinion. Our opinion is, however, supported by facts which we can never ignore or forget. The experiences we have gone through ourselves will remain a guiding factor in forming our judgments until something happens which convincingly counter-attacks them.

Now that the United Nations is to conclude a cease-fire agreement with the Communist aggressors regardless of what may happen to Korea, in practical terms we are constantly haunted by the question of how we can survive as a nation at all. The following passages will, I hope, give you some idea of our reactions to the situation.

We desire to remain friendly to the United States to the last, remembering what it has done for us, both militarily and economically in our struggle against aggression.

If the United States forces have to stand by, for some reason, ceasing to participate in any further struggle or to withdraw from Korea altogether as an aftermath of the impending armistice, we have nothing to say against it.

Whenever they find it necessary or desirable to leave Korea they can do so with a friendly feeling toward us just as we are trying to remain their friends. So long as either party does not interfere with the plans of the other, both can maintain the cordial relations between them.

In the first year of this three-year-old war, both the United States and the United Nations alternately and repeatedly announced, as the war objectives, the establishment of a united, independent, and democratic Korea and the punishment of the aggressors. It was at the time of the United Nations drive to the Yalu that they made these announcements so that we naturally took them as their declared war objectives. But later, when the Communist forces proved to be stronger than expected, the United Nations statesmen took to the interpretation that it had never been intended to unify Korea by war. That was an open confession of weakness; very few people took it at its face value. Nowadays we hear no more about the unification of Korea or the punishment of the Communist aggressors, as if either we had achieved these objectives or abandoned them.

All we hear about is an armistice. There is grave doubt that an armistice reached in such an atmosphere of appeasement can lead to a permanent peace acceptable and honorable to us. Personally, I do not believe that the Communists will agree, at a conference table, to what they have never been made to agree to on the battlefield.

Your generous offers of economic aid and an increase of the R. O. K. defense forces are highly appreciated by all Korean people, for they are what we badly need. But when such offers come as a price for our acceptance of the armistice as we know it, they cannot but have little inducement, because, as I have said before, to accept such an armistice is to accept a death warrant.

Nothing would be of much avail to Korea, to say the least, after that fatal blow should have been dealt it.

We do not question the sincerity with which you kindly promised to use your authority to bring about a mutual defense pact between our two nations, after the conclusion of the armistice. As a matter of fact, a mutual defense pact is what we have constantly sought, and we are behind it heart and soul; but if it is tied up with the armistice, its efficacy would be diminished almost to a vanishing point.

Mr. President, you will easily imagine what a hard situation we confront. We committed everything, including our arms and forces, to the United Nations action in Korea, incurring frightful losses in manpower as well as material destruction, in the sole belief that we and our friends had the self-same objectives of unifying sundered Korea and punishing the Communist aggressors. Now the United Nations seems to stop short of its original aims and to come to terms with the aggressors which we cannot accept, not because we have never been consulted but, because those terms would mean sure death for the Korean nation. Moreover, the United Nations is now putting pressure on us in cooperating with it; and is joining hands, it seems, with the enemy in this matter of armistice terms.

We cannot avoid seeing the cold fact that the counsels of appeasers have prevailed in altering the armistice positions of the United States. In our view, this perilous trend, if perpetuated by the conclusion of this fatal armistice, will eventually endanger the remainder of the free world including the United States, which millions of both free and enslaved hope and pray from the bottom of their hearts will lead them in liberation of the peoples in chains behind the Iron Curtain.

At this very moment, the Communist forces are launching a large-scale offensive when the armistice talks have scarcely left anything except the affixing of signatures by the parties concerned. This should be a warning for our immediate future. The terms of the armistice being what they are, the Communist buildup will go on unhampered until it is capable of overwhelming South Korea with one swoop at a moment of the Communists' own choosing. What is to follow for the rest of the Far East? And the rest of Asia? And the rest of the free world?

Still looking to your wise leadership for a remedy in this perilous hour,

Yours very sincerely,

SYNGMAN RHEE.

54. AGREEMENT ON PRISONERS OF WAR, JUNE 8, 1953 [5]

Within two months after the armistice agreement becomes effective both sides shall, without offering any hindrance, directly repatriate and hand over in groups all those prisoners of war in its custody who insist on repatriation to the side to which they belonged at the time of capture. Repatriation shall be accomplished in accordance with the related provisions of Article III of the draft armistice agreement. In order to expedite the repatriation process of such personnel, each side shall, prior to the signing of the armistice agreement, exchange the total numbers, by nationalities, of personnel to be repatriated direct. Each group delivered to the other side shall be accompanied by rosters, prepared by nationality, to include name, rank (if any), and internment or military serial number.

---

[5] Department of State Bulletin, June 22, 1953, pp. 866–868. This is also a part of the official armistice agreement. See pp. 114–118.

Both sides agree to hand over all those remaining prisoners of war who are not directly repatriated to the Neutral Nations Repatriation Commission for disposition in accordance with the following provisions:

TERMS OF REFERENCE FOR NEUTRAL NATIONS REPATRIATION COMMISSION

I. General

1. In order to ensure that all prisoners of war have the opportunity to exercise their right to be repatriated following an armistice, Sweden, Switzerland, Poland, Czechoslovakia, and India shall each be requested by both sides to appoint a member to a Neutral Nations Repatriation Commission which shall be established to take custody in Korea of those prisoners of war who, while in the custody of the detaining powers, have not exercised their right to be repatriated. The Neutral Nations Repatriation Commission shall establish its headquarters within the demilitarized zone in the vicinity of Panmunjom, and shall station subordinate bodies of the same composition as the Neutral Nations Repatriation Commission at those locations at which the repatriation commission assumes custody of prisoners of war. Representatives of both sides shall be permitted to observe the operations of the repatriation commission and its subordinate bodies to include explanations and interviews.

2. Sufficient armed forces and any other operating personnel required to assist the Neutral Nations Repatriation Commission in carrying out its functions and responsibilities shall be provided exclusively by India, whose representative shall be the umpire in accordance with the provisions of Article 132 of the Geneva Convention, and shall also be chairman and executive agent of the Neutral Nations Repatriation Commission. Representatives from each of the other 4 powers shall be allowed staff assistants in equal number not to exceed fifty (50) each. When any of the representatives of the neutral nations is absent for some reason, that representative shall designate an alternate representative of his own nationality to exercise his functions and authority. The arms of all personnel provided for in this paragraph shall be limited to military police type small arms.

3. No force or threat of force shall be used against the prisoners of war specified in paragraph 1 above to prevent or effect their repatriation, and no violence to their persons or affront to their dignity or self-respect shall be permitted in any manner for any purpose whatsoever (but see paragraph 7 below). This duty is enjoined on and entrusted to the Neutral Nations Repatriation Commission. This commission shall ensure that prisoners of war shall at all times be treated humanely in accordance with the specific provisions of the Geneva Convention, and with the general spirit of that convention.

II. Custody of prisoners of war

4. All prisoners of war who have not exercised their right of repatriation following the effective date of the armistice agreement shall be released from the military control and from the custody of the detaining side as soon as practicable and, in all cases, within sixty (60) days subsequent to the effective date of the armistice agreement to the neutral nations repatriation commission at locations in Korea to be designated by the detaining side.

5. At the time the neutral nations repatriation commission assumes control of the prisoner of war installations, the military forces of the detaining side shall be withdrawn therefrom, so that the locations specified in the preceding paragraph shall be taken over completely by the armed forces of India.

6. Notwithstanding the provisions of paragraph 5 above, the detaining side shall have the responsibility for maintaining and ensuring security and order in the areas around the locations where the prisoners of war are in custody and for preventing and restraining any armed forces (including irregular armed forces) in the area under its control from any acts of disturbance and intrusion against the locations where the prisoners of war are in custody.

7. Notwithstanding the provisions of paragraph 3 above, nothing in this agreement shall be construed as derogating from the authority of the neutral nations repatriation commission to exercise its legitimate functions and responsibilities for the control of the prisoners of war under its temporary jurisdiction.

III, Explanation

8. The Neutral Nations Repatriation Commission, after having received and taken into custody all those prisoners of war who have not exercised their right to be repatriated, shall immediately make arrangements so that within ninety (90) days after the Neutral Nations Repatriation Commission takes over the custody, the nations to which the prisoners of war belong shall have freedom and facilities to send representatives to the location where such prisoners of war are in custody to explain to all the prisoners of war depending upon these nations their rights and to inform them of any matters relating to their return to their homelands, particularly of their full freedom to return home to lead a peaceful life, under the following provisions:

A. The number of such explaining representatives shall not exceed seven (7) per thousand prisoners of war held in custody by the Neutral Nations Repatriation Commission; and the minimum authorized shall not be less than a total of five (5).

B. The hours during which the explaining representatives shall have access to the prisoners shall be as determined by the Neutral Nations Repatriation Commission, and generally in accord with Article 53 of the Geneva Convention relative to the treatment of prisoners of war.

C. All explanations and interviews shall be conducted in the presence of a representative of each member nation of the Neutral Nations Repatriation Commission and a representative from the detaining side;

D. Additional provisions governing the explanation work shall be prescribed by the Neutral Nations Repatriation Commission, and will be designed to employ the principles enumerated in paragraph 3 above and in this paragraph;

E. The explaining representatives, while engaging in their work, shall be allowed to bring with them necessary facilities and personnel for wireless communications. The number of communications personnel shall be limited to one team per location at which explaining representatives are in residence, except in the event that all prisoners of war are concentrated in one location, in which case, two (2) teams shall be permitted.   Each team shall consist of not more than six (6) communications personnel.

9. Prisoners of war in its custody shall have freedom and facilities to make representations and communications to the Neutral Nations Repatriation Commission and to representatives and subordinate bodies of the Neutral Nations Repatriation Commission and to inform them of their desires on any matter concerning the prisoners of war themselves, in accordance with arrangements made for the purpose by the Neutral Nations Repatriation Commission.

IV, Disposition of prisoners of war

10. Any prisoner of war who, while in the custody of the Neutral Nations Repatriation Commission, decides to exercise the right of repatriation, shall make an application requesting repatriation to a body consisting of a representative of each member nation of the Neutral Nations Repatriation Commission.   Once such an application is made, it shall be considered immediately by the Neutral Nations Repatriation Commission or one of its subordinate bodies so as to determine immediately by majority vote the validity of such application.   Once such an application is made to and validated by the Commission or one of its subordinate bodies, the prisoner of war concerned shall immediately be transferred to and accommodated in the tents set up for those who are ready to be repatriated.   Thereafter, he shall, while still in the custody of the Neutral Nations Repatriation Commission, be delivered forthwith to the prisoner of war exchange point at Panmunjom for repatriation under the procedure prescribed in the armistice agreement.

11. At the expiration of ninety (90) days after the transfer of custody of the prisoners of war to the Neutral Nations Repatriation Commission, access of representatives to captured personnel as provided for in paragraph 8 above, shall terminate, and the question of disposition of the prisoners of war who have not exercised their right to be repatriated shall be submitted to the political conference recommended to be convened in paragraph 60, draft armistice agreement, which shall endeavor to settle this question within thirty (30) days, during which period the Neutral Nations Repatriation Commission shall continue to retain custody of those prisoners of war.   The Neutral Nations Repatriation Commission shall declare the relief from the prisoner of war status to civilian status of any prisoners of war who have not excerised their right to be repatriated and for whom no other disposition has been agreed to by the political conference within one hundred and twenty (120) days after the Neutral Nations Repatriation Commission has assumed their custody.   Thereafter, according to the application of each individual, those who choose to go to Neutral Nations shall be assisted by the Neutral Nations Repatriation Commission and the Red Cross Society of India. This operation shall be completed within thirty (30) days, and upon its completion, the Neutral Nations Repatriation Commission shall immediately cease its functions and declare its dissolution. After the dissolution of the Neutral Nations Repatriation Commission, whenever and wherever any of those above-mentioned civilians who have been relieved from the prisoner-of-war status desire to return

to their fatherlands, the authorities of the localities where they are shall be responsible for assisting them in returning to their fatherlands.

V, Red Cross visitation

12. Essential Red Cross service for prisoners of war in custody of the Neutral Nations Repatriation Commission shall be provided by India in accordance with regulations issued by the Neutral Nations Repatriation Commission.

VI, Press coverage

13. The Neutral Nations Repatriation Commission shall insure freedom of the press and other news media in observing the entire operation as enumerated herein, in accordance with procedures to be established by the Neutral Nations Repatriation Commission.

VII, Logistical support for prisoners of war

14. Each side shall provide logistical support for the prisoners of war in the area under its military control, delivering required support to the Neutral Nations Repatriation Commission at an agreed delivery point in the vicinity of each prisoner of war installation.

15. The cost of repatriating prisoners of war to the exchange point at Panmunjom shall be borne by the detaining side and the cost from the exchange point by the side on which said prisoners depend, in accordance with Article 118 of the Geneva Convention.

16. The Red Cross Society of India shall be responsible for providing such general service personnel in the prisoner-of-war installations as required by the Neutral Nations Repatriation Commission.

17. The Neutral Nations Repatriation Commission shall provide medical support for the prisoners of war as may be practicable. The detaining side shall provide medical support as practicable upon the request of the Neutral Nations Repatriation Commission and specifically for those cases requiring extensive treatment or hospitalization.

The Neutral Nations Repatriation Commission shall maintain custody of prisoners of war during such hospitalization. The detaining side shall facilitate such custody. Upon completion of treatment, prisoners of war shall be returned to a prisoner of war installation as specified in paragraph 4 above.

18. The Neutral Nations Repatriation Commission is entitled to obtain from both sides such legitimate assistance as it may require in carrying out its duties and tasks, but both sides shall not under any name and in any form interfere or exert influence.

VIII, Logistical support for the Neutral Nations Repatriation Commission

19. Each side shall be responsible for providing logistical support for the personnel of the Neutral Nations Repatriation Commission stationed in the area under its military control, and both sides shall contribute on an equal basis to such support within the demilitarized zone. The precise arrangements shall be subject to determination between the Neutral Nations Repatriation Commission and the detaining side in each case.

20. Each of the detaining sides shall be responsible for protecting the explaining representatives from the other side while in transit over lines of communication within its area, as set forth in paragraph 23 for the Neutral Nations Repatriation Commission, to a place of

residence and while in residence in the vicinity of but not within each of the locations where the prisoners of war are in custody. The Neutral Nations Repatriation Commission shall be responsible for the security of such representatives within the actual limits of the locations where the prisoners of war are in custody.

21. Each of the detaining sides shall provide transportation, housing, communication, and other agreed logistical support to the explaining representatives of the other side while they are in the area under its military control. Such services shall be provided on a reimbursable basis.

IX, Publication

22. After the armistice agreement becomes effective, the terms of this agreement shall be made known to all prisoners of war who, while in the custody of the detaining side, have not exercised their right to bet repatriated.

X, Movement

23. The movement of the personnel of the Neutral Nations Repatriation Commission and repatriated prisoners of war shall be over lines of communication as determined by the command(s) of the opposing side and the Neutral Nations Repatriation Commission. A map showing these lines of communication shall be furnished the command of the opposing side and the Neutral Nations Repatriation Commission. Movement of such personnel, except within locations as designated in paragraph 4 above, shall be under the control of, and escorted by, personnel of the side in whose area the travel is being undertaken; however, such movement shall not be subject to obstruction and coercion.

XI, Procedural matters

24. The interpretation of this agreement shall rest with the Neutral Nations Repatriation Commission. The Neutral Nations Repatriation Commission, and/or any subordinate bodies to which functions are delegated or assigned by the Neutral Nations Repatriation Commission, shall operate on the basis of majority vote.

25. The Neutral Nations Repatriation Commission shall submit a weekly report to the opposing commanders on the status of prisoners of war in its custody, indicating the numbers repatriated and remaining at the end of each week.

26. When this agreement has been acceded to by both sides and by the 5 powers herein, it shall become effective upon the date the armistice becomes effective.

27. Done at Panmunjom, Korea, at 1400 hours on the 8th day of June 1953, in English, Korean, and Chinese, all texts being equally authentic.

Signed NAM IL, *General, Korean People's Army senior delegate, delegation of the Korean People's Army and the Chinese People's Volunteers.*

Signed WILLIAM K. HARRISON, JR., *Lieutenant General, United States Army senior delegate, United Nations Command Delegation.*

55. UNIFIED COMMAND STATEMENT ON THE RELEASE OF ANTI-COMMUNIST PRISONERS OF WAR BY SOUTH KOREA, JUNE 18, 1953 [6]

Between midnight and dawn today, approximately 25,000 militantly anti-Communist North Korean prisoners of war broke out of United Nations Command prisoner-of-war camps at Pusan, Masan, Nonsan, and Sang Mu Dai, Korea.

Statements attributed to high officials of the Republic of Korea now make it clear that the action had been secretly planned and carefully coordinated at top levels in the Korean Government and that outside assistance was furnished the P. O. W.'s in their mass breakout. R. O. K. security units assigned as guards at the P. O. W. camps did little to prevent the breakouts and there is every evidence of actual collusion between the R. O. K. guards and the prisoners.

During the past year, these R. O. K. security guard units have been especially trained for their duties at P. O. W. camps, in order that more than 13,000 United States and R. O. K. Army combat troops, which would otherwise be required as security personnel, might be made available for frontline duty. The R. O. K. security guards were considered especially suitable for the camps containing anti-Communist Korean prisoners in view of the previous cooperative attitude of these P. O. W.'s.

United States personnel at these nonrepatriate camps, limited in each case to the camp commander and a few administrative personnel, exerted every effort to prevent today's mass breakouts, but in the face of collusion between the R. O. K. guards and the prisoners, their efforts were largely unavailing. The large quantities of nontoxic irritants (tear gas and other nonpoisonous gases) employed proved ineffective because of the great number of prisoners involved in the nighttime breakouts. Nine prisoners were killed and sixteen injured by rifle fire. There were no casualties among United States personnel.

As of 1 o'clock this afternoon, 971 escaped P. O. W.'s had been recovered.

R. O. K. security guard units which have left their posts and nonrepatriate camps are being replaced by United States troops.

56. EXCHANGE ON THE RESUMPTION OF ARMISTICE NEGOTIATIONS BETWEEN GENERAL CLARK, COMMANDER IN CHIEF, UNITED NATIONS COMMAND, AND THE COMMUNISTS, JUNE 29 AND JULY 8, 1953

A. GENERAL CLARK, COMMANDER IN CHIEF, UNITED NATIONS COMMAND, TO THE COMMUNISTS, JUNE 29, 1953 [7]

Marshal KIM IL SUNG,
   Commander of the Korean People's Army
General PENG TEH-HUAI,
   Commander of the Chinese People's Volunteers

The United Nations Command agrees, of course, that the escape of about 25,000 captured personnel of the Korean People's Army is

---

[6] Department of State Bulletin, June 29, 1953, p. 905.
[7] Department of State Bulletin, July 13, 1953, pp. 46–47.

a serious incident and unfortunately has not been conducive to the early armistice for which both sides have been earnestly striving. The United Nations Command, by means of General Harrison's letter of 18 June 1953, immediately informed you of the facts regarding the loss of these prisoners.

We felt that you deserved to have this information at the earliest possible time. However, in your letter of 19 June I note that for one reason or another you fail to accept the realities of the situation which we accurately reported to you, and you have made several inaccurate statements of fact. In an earnest endeavor to achieve an early armistice, I shall further clarify these facts.

Despite our voluntary and accurate presentation of these facts you still seem to consider that the "escape" of the prisoners and their "release" by order of the Republic of Korea Government are contradictory terms. The fact is, as you are well aware by this time, that the prisoners "escaped" by breaking through the prison fences and barricades and, except for those who were captured, disappeared into the civil population. They were "released" in that the Republic of Korea Government, without the knowledge of, and contrary to the intent of, the United Nations Command, planned and arranged the breakout, and the Republic of Korea Army security guards made little real effort to prevent the escape.

In replying to the questions which you asked in your letter, I believe that you realize the armistice which both of us seek is a military armistice between the military commanders of both sides. The United Nations Command is a military command and, contrary to the opinion indicated in your letter of 19 June, does not exercise authority over the Republic of Korea, which is an independent sovereign state whose government is the product of the self-determination of its millions of people. The Republic of Korea Army was placed by its Government under the control of the United Nations Command in order to more effectively repel the armed aggression against the Republic of Korea. I believe it should be clear to you that the United Nations Command, as the result of a commitment made by the Republic of Korea, does not command the Republic of Korea Army. In this incident that Government violated its commitment, issuing orders which were unknown to me, through other than recognized military channels to certain Korean army units, which permitted the prisoners of war to escape.

You also asked whether the armistice in Korea included the Republic of Korea as represented by President Syngman Rhee; another question, which is closely related, expressed your interest in knowing what assurances there may be for the implementation of the armistice agreement on the part of South Korea. It is necessary here to reiterate that the armistice which we seek is a military armistice between the commanders of both sides and involving the forces available to the commanders of both sides.

It is recognized that certain provisions of the armistice agreement require the cooperation of the authorities of the Republic of Korea. You are assured that the United Nations Command and the interested governments concerned will make every effort to obtain the cooperation of the Government of the Republic of Korea. Where necessary the United Nations Command will, to the limits of its ability, establish military safeguards to insure that the armistice terms are observed.

Our willingness to do this should be apparent to you by the con-currence which we have given to those portions of the terms of refer-ence which require the United Nations Command to take certain action to insure the safety and security of the Neutral Nations Repatriation Commission and its personnel.

It is regrettable that you choose to allege that the United Nations Command connived in the escape of the prisoners.   Besides being con-trary to the obvious facts, such accusation tends to obstruct rather than to facilitate an armistice agreement.   The United Nations Command is continuing its efforts to recover the prisoners of war who have escaped.   It would be unrealistic, however, and misleading to imply that an appreciable number of these prisoners could be recovered now that they have disappeared among the population, which is disposed to shelter and protect them.   You undoubtedly realize that the recov-ery of all these prisoners would be as impossible for us as it would be for your side to recover the 50,000 South Korean prisoners "released" by your side during the course of hostilities.   You, of course, under-stand that the cessation of hostilities will facilitate the return of the escaped prisoners of war to your side if they are not opposed to such return.   Under the provisions of Paragraph 59 of the draft armistice agreement, the escaped prisoners of war can proceed to your side if they so desire after the armistice becomes effective.

Following the signing of an armistice, the exchange of those pris-oners of war who desire repatriation will involve the 12,000 of our personnel reported by you in April 1952, plus the additional ones captured since that date and now in your hands, as compared with about 74,000 of your personnel, including approximately 69,000 Ko-reans, now in our hands, whom we are prepared to return to you.

This letter is an earnest effort by the United Nations Command to acquaint you with the facts.   It is suggested that the delegations meet immediately to exchange information as to the time at which respec-tive components of the neutral nations supervisory commission can be prepared to function in order that an effective date for the armistice may be established and, on receipt of that information, the armistice argreement as has been developed by our respective delegations be signed.

MARK W. CLARK,
General, United States Army, Commander in Chief, United
Nations Command.

B. COMMUNISTS TO GENERAL CLARK, COMMANDER IN CHIEF, UNITED NATIONS COMMAND, JULY 8, 1953 [8]

In your letter of reply dated June 29, 1953, you admit that the incident of coercing the captured personnel of the Korean People's Army into leaving the prisoner-of-war camps and of forcible retention of them by the Syngman Rhee clique is a serious and unfortunate inci-dent.   It is right that you do so.   However, your explanation and handling of this incident are not satisfactory.

Every obvious fact proves that the United Nations Command can-not completely evade the responsibility for this incident.   Your side was aware of the premeditated scheme of the South Korean Govern

<hr>

[8] Department of State Bulletin, July 20, 1953, pp. 73–74.

ment and Army for this incident, of which there had been indications long ago, but your side did not take any preventive measures.

Following the occurrence of the incident, your side not only failed to apply any effective sanctions against the acts of coercing the prisoners of war into leaving prisoner-of-war camps in violation of the prisoner-of-war agreement on the part of the South Korean security units who were under the control of the United Nations Command, but even after our side, by our letter of June 19, called for the full attention of your side, you still allowed the South Korean security units to continue to coerce the prisoners of war into leaving the camps so that the total of prisoners of war retained forcibly by the Syngman Rhee clique has amounted to more than 27,000, in which are included more than fifty captured personnel of the Chinese People's volunteers.

Both General Harrison, senior delegate of your side, in his letter on June 18, and in your letter of reply of June 29, indicate that efforts are being made to recover the "escaped" prisoners of war; however, you assert at the same time that it is impossible to recover all those prisoners of war.   In actuality, your military police are instructed not to interfere with any prisoners of war who "escape," but to allow them to be forced to report to the military training centers run by Syngman Rhee.

The attitude taken by the United Nations Command during this period has connived, at least in fact, at the Syngman Rhee clique in carrying out unscruplously its activities of violating the prisoner-of-war agreement and obstructing the realization of an armistice.

Your side also attempts to compare the humanitarian action of our side of releasing prisoners of war in the battlefield prior to the armistice negotiations with the disruptive action taken by the South Korean security units of coercing prisoners into leaving the camps after the signing of the prisoner-of-war agreement.   This is totally improper. Your side bears at all times the responsibility for recovering all the "escaped" prisoners of war.

It must be warned that the Syngman Rhee clique now is still clamoring for the continued "release," that is forcible retention, of the more than 8,500 remaining captured personnel of the Korean's People's Army not to be directly repatriated, and is attempting, in league with the special agents of Chiang Kai-Shek, to coerce the captured personnel of the Chinese People's Volunteers into leaving the prisoner-of-war camps, in an attempt to violate thoroughly the prisoner-of-war agreement which is already signed by both sides.

We hold that, regarding this, your side must shoulder the absolute responsibility for insuring that no such incidents will occur again.

In your letter, you give assurance that the United Nations Command will, to the limit of its ability, establish military safeguards, where necessary, to insure that the armistice terms are observed.   We consider that this is necessary.   However, your side indicates that it is not yet definitely sure of a guarantee that the South Korean Government and Army will abide by the armistice agreement reached by the delegations of both sides.   Moreover, the Syngman Rhee clique has been and still is clamoring for unification of Korea by force; this is sufficient in itself to prove from which side the aggression was launched three years ago.

Now, should the United Nations Command continue to connive at the Syngman Rhee clique and permit it to lay out various premeditated schemes for undermining the possibilities of a peaceful settlement of the Korean question, armed aggression against the Korean Democratic People's Republic might break out again at any time, even if the Korean armistice agreement were signed.

Therefore, our side holds that your side must take effective steps regarding the observance of the South Korean Government and Army of the armistice agreement and all other related agreements; it is only thus that the Korean armistice can be safeguarded against disruption.

To sum up, although our side is not entirely satisfied with the reply of your side, yet in view of the indication of the desire of your side to strive for an early armistice and in view of the assurances given by your side, our side agrees that the delegations of both sides meet at an appointed time to discuss the question of implementation of the armistice agreement and the various preparations prior to the signing of the armistice agreement.

The date for the meeting will be discussed and decided by the senior delegates of both sides through the liaison officers.

KIM IL SUNG,
Marshal, Supreme Commander of the Korean People's Army.

PENG TEH-HUAI,
Commander of the Chinese People's Volunteers.

57. STATEMENT BY ASSISTANT SECRETARY OF STATE ROBERTSON AND PRESIDENT RHEE, JULY 11, 1953 [9]

During the past 2 weeks we have had many frank and cordial exchanges of views which have emphasized the deep friendship existing between the Republic of Korea and the United States and have gone far toward achieving mutual understanding of the troubled questions which have arisen in connection with arrangements for an armistice, the exchange of prisoners, and the forthcoming political conference.

These discussions have cemented our determination to continue and extend in the postarmistice period the close collaboration for our common objectives, marking our relations since the Communist aggression commenced 3 years ago.

In respect to the prisoners of war, we have reaffirmed our determination that no prisoners shall be subject to coercion and that, at the end of the specified period, all prisoners desiring to avoid returning to Communist jurisdiction shall be set free in South Korea, or, in the case of the non-Communist Chinese, to proceed to a destination chosen by them.

Our two Governments are in agreement in respect to entering into a mutual-defense pact, negotiations for which are under way.

We have likewise discussed collaboration along political, economic, and defense lines, and our conversations have disclosed a wide area of agreement concerning these matters.

---

[9] Department of State Bulletin, July 20, 1953, pp. 72–73.

In particular, we wish to emphasize our determination to work together for the realization within the shortest practical time of our common objective; namely, a free, independent, and unified Korea.

We are confident that the spirit of accord in which our talks have progressed, and the large areas of agreement which have resulted, will be followed by continuing mutual consideration and by the spirit of mutual accommodation which will lead most certainly to our broad objective of a secure and lasting peace in the Far East.

58. KOREAN ARMISTICE AGREEMENT, JULY 27, 1953 [10]

Agreement between the Commander-in-Chief, United Nations Command, on the one hand, and the Supreme Commander of the Korean People's Army and the Commander of the Chinese People's Volunteers, on the other hand, concerning a military armistice in Korea.

PREAMBLE

The undersigned, the commander-in-chief, United Nations Command, on the one hand, and the Supreme Commander of the Korean People's Army and the Commander of the Chinese People's Volunteers, on the other hand, in the interest of stopping the Korean conflict, with its great toll of suffering and bloodshed on both sides, and with the objective of establishing an armistice which will insure a complete cessation of hostilities and of all acts of armed forces in Korea until a final peaceful settlement is achieved, do individually, collectively, and mutually, agree to accept and to be bound and governed by the conditions and terms of armistice set forth in the following articles and paragraphs, which said conditions and terms are intended to be purely military in character and to pertain solely to the belligerents in Korea.

ARTICLE I

MILITARY DEMARCATION LINE AND DEMILITARIZED ZONE [11]

1. A military demarcation line shall be fixed and both sides shall withdraw two (2) kilometers from this line so as to establish a demilitarized zone between the opposing forces. A demilitarized zone shall be established as a buffer zone to prevent the occurrence of incidents which might lead to a resumption of hostilities.

2. The military demarcation line is located as indicated on the attached map (Map 1).

3. This demilitarized zone is defined by a northern and a southern boundary as indicated on the attached map (Map 1).

4. The Military Demarcation Line shall be plainly marked as directed by the Military Armistice Commission hereinafter established. The Commanders of the opposing sides shall have suitable markers erected along the boundary between the Demilitarized Zone and their respective areas. The Military Armistice Commission shall supervise

---

[10] Department of State press release, July 26, 1953.
[11] The maps referred to below are not included in the present document.

the erection of all markers placed along the Military Demarcation Line and along the boundaries of the Demilitarized Zone.

5. The waters of the Han River Estuary shall be open to civil shipping of both sides wherever one bank is controlled by one side and the other bank is controlled by the other side. The Military Armistice Commission shall prescribe rules for the shipping in that part of the Han River Estuary indicated on the attached map (Map 2). Civil shipping of each side shall have unrestricted access to the land under the military control of that side.

6. Neither side shall execute any hostile act within, from, or against the Demilitarized Zone.

7. No person, military or civilian, shall be permitted to cross the Military Demarcation Line unless specifically authorized to do so by the Military Armistice Commission.

8. No person, military or civilian, in the Demilitarized Zone shall be permitted to enter the territory under the military control of either side unless specifically authorized to do so by the Commander into whose territory entry is sought.

9. No person, military or civilian, shall be permitted to enter the Demilitarized Zone except persons concerned with the conduct of civil administration and relief and persons specifically authorized to enter by the Military Armistice Commission.

10. Civil administration and relief in that part of the Demilitarized Zone which is south of the Military Demarcation Line shall be the responsibility of the Commander-in-Chief, United Nations Command; and civil administration and relief in that part of the Demilitarized Zone which is north of the Military Demarcation Line shall be the joint responsibility of the Supreme Commander of the Korean People's Army and the Commander of the Chinese People's Volunteers. The number of persons, military or civilian, from each side who are permitted to enter the Demilitarized Zone for the conduct of civil administration and relief shall be as determined by the respective Commanders, but in no case shall the total number authorized by either side exceed one thousand (1,000) persons at any one time. The number of civil police and the arms to be carried by them shall be as prescribed by the Military Armistice Commission. Other personnel shall not carry arms unless specifically authorized to do so by the Military Armistice Commission.

11. Nothing contained in this article shall be construed to prevent the complete freedom of movement to, from, and within the Demilitarized Zone by the Military Armistice Commission, its assistants, its Joint Observer Teams with their assistants, the Neutral Nations Supervisory Commission hereinafter established, its assistants, its Neutral Nations Inspection Teams with their assistants, and of any other persons, materials, and equipment specifically authorized to enter the Demilitarized Zone by the Military Armistice Commission. Convenience of movement shall be permitted through the territory under the military control of either side over any route necessary to move between points within the Demilitarized Zone where such points are not connected by roads lying completely within the Demilitarized Zone.

Article II

CONCRETE ARRANGEMENTS FOR CEASE-FIRE AND ARMISTICE

A. *General*

12. The Commanders of the opposing sides shall order and enforce a complete cessation of all hostilities in Korea by all armed forces under their control, including all units and personnel of the ground, naval, and air forces, effective twelve (12) hours after this Armistice Agreement is signed. (See paragraph 63 hereof for effective date and hours of the remaining provisions of this Armistice agreement.)

13. In order to insure the stability of the Military Armistice so as to facilitate the attainment of a peaceful settlement through the holding by both sides of a political conference of a higher level, the Commanders of the opposing sides shall:

(a) Within 72 hours after this armistice agreement becomes effective, withdraw all of their military forces, supplies, and equipment from the demilitarized zone except as otherwise provided herein. All demolitions, minefields wire entanglements, and other hazards to the safe movement of personnel of the Military Armistice Commission or its joint observer teams, known to exist within the demilitarized zone after the withdrawal of military forces therefrom, together with lanes known to be free of all such hazards, shall be reported to the Military Armistice Commission by the commander of the side whose forces emplaced such hazards. Subsequently, additional safe lanes shall be cleared, and eventually, within 45 days after the termination of the 72-hour period, all such hazards shall be removed from the demilitarized zone as directed by and under the supervision of the Military Armistice Commission. At the termination of the 72-hour period, except for unarmed troops authorized a 45-day period to complete salvage operations under Military Armistice Commission supervision, such units of a police nature as may be specifically requested by the Military Armistice Commission and agreed to by the commanders of the opposing sides, and personnel authorized under paragraphs 10 and 11 hereof, no personnel of either side shall be permitted to enter the demilitarized zone.

(b) Within ten (10) days after this Armistice Agreement becomes effective, withdraw all of their military forces, supplies, and equipment from the rear and the coastal islands and waters of Korea of the other side. If such military forces are not withdrawn within the stated time limit, and there is no mutually agreed and valid reason for the delay, the other side shall have the right to take any action which it deems necessary for the maintenance of security and order. The term "coastal islands" as used above, refers to those islands which, though occupied by one side at the time when this Armistice Agreement becomes effective, were controlled by the other side on 24 June 1950; provided, however, that all the islands lying to the north and west of the provincial boundary line between HWANGHAE-DO and KYONGGI-DO shall be under the military control of the Supreme Commander of the Korean People's Army and the Commander of the Chinese People's Volunteers, except the island groups of PAENGYONG-DO (37°58′N, 124°40′E), TAECHONG-DO (37°50′N, 124°42′E), SOCHONG-DO (37°46′N, 124°46′E), YONPYONG-DO (37°38′N, 12°40′E) and U-DO (37°36′N, 125°58′E) which shall remain under the military control of the Commander-in-Chief, United Nations Command. All the islands on the west coast of Korea lying south of the above mentioned boundary line shall remain under the military control of the Commander-in-Chief, United Nations Command. (See Map 3).

(c) Cease the introduction into Korea of reinforcing military personnel provided, however, that the rotation of units and personnel, the arrival in Korea of personnel on a temporary duty basis, and the return to Korea of personnel after short periods of leave or temporary duty outside of Korea shall be pemitted within the scope prescribed below:

"Rotation" is defined as the replacement of units or personnel by other units or personnel who are commencing a tour of duty in Korea. Rotation personnel shall be introduced into and evacuated from Korea only through the ports of entry enumerated in paragraph 43 hereof. Rotation shall be conducted on a man-for-man basis; provided, however, that no more than 35,000 persons in the military service shall be admitted into Korea by either side in any calendar month under the rotation policy. No military personnel of either side shall be introduced into Korea if the introduction of such personnel will cause the aggregate of the military personnel of that side admitted into Korea since the effective date of this armistice agreement to exceed the cumulative total of the military personnel of that side who have departed from Korea since that date. Reports concerning arrivals in and departures from Korea of military personnel shall be made daily to the Military Armistice Commission and the Neutral Nations Supervisory Commission; such reports shall include places of arrival and departure and the number of persons arriving at or departing from each such place. The Neutral Nations Supervisory Commission, through its Neutral Nations Inspection Teams, shall conduct supervision and inspection of the rotation of units and personnel authorized above, at the ports of entry enumerated in paragraph 43 hereof.

(d) Cease the introduction into Korea of reinforcing combat aircraft, armored vehicles, weapons, and ammunition; provided, however, that combat aircraft, armored vehicles, weapons, and ammunition which are destroyed, damaged, worn out, or used up during the period of the armistice may be replaced on the basis of piece-for-piece of the same effectiveness and the same type. Such combat aircraft, armored vehicles, weapons, and ammunition shall be introduced into Korea only through the ports of entry enumerated in paragraph 43 hereof. In order to justify the requirements for combat aircraft, armored vehicles, weapons, and ammunition to be introduced into Korea for replacement purposes, reports concerning every incoming shipment of these items shall be made to the Military Armistice Commission and the Neutral Nations Supervisory Commission; such reports shall include statements regarding the disposition of the items being replaced. Items to be replaced which are removed from Korea shall be removed only through the ports of entry enumerated in paragraph 43 hereof. The Neutral Nations Supervisory Commission, through its Neutral Nations Inspection Teams, shall conduct supervision and inspection of the replacement of combat aircraft, armored vehicles, weapons, and ammunition authorized above, at the ports of entry enumerated in paragraph 43 hereof.

(e) Insure that personnel of their respective commands who violate any of the provisions of this Armistice Agreement are adequately punished.

(f) In those cases where places of burial are a matter of record and graves are actually found to exist, permit graves registration personnel of the other side to enter, within a definite time limit after this Armistice Agreement becomes effective, the territory of Korea under their military control, for the purpose of proceeding to such graves to recover and evacuate the bodies of the deceased military personnel of that side, including deceased prisoners of war. The specific procedures and the time limit for the performance of the above task shall be determined by the Military Armistice Commission. The Commanders of the opposing sides shall furnish to the other side all available information pertaining to the places of burial of the deceased military personnel of the other side.

(g) Afford full protection and all possible assistance and cooperation to the Military Armistice Commission, its Joint Observer Teams, the Neutral Nations Supervisory Commission, and its Neutral Nations Inspection Teams, in the carrying out of their functions and responsibilities hereinafter assigned; and accord to the Neutral Nations Supervisory Commission, and to its Neutral Nations Inspection Teams, full convenience of movement between the headquarters of the Neutral Nations Supervisory Commission and the ports of entry enumerated in paragraph 43 hereof over main lines of communication agreed upon by both sides (See Map 4), and between the headquarters of the Neutral Nations Supervisory Commission and the places where violations of this Armistice Agreement have been reported to have occurred. In order to prevent unnecessary delays, the use of alternate routes and means of transportation will be permitted whenever the main lines of communication are closed or impassable.

(h) Provide such logistic support, including communications and transportation facilities, as may be required by the Military Armistice Commission and the Neutral Nations Supervisory Commission and their Teams.

(i) Each construct, operate, and maintain a suitable airfield in their respective parts of the demilitarized zone in the vicinity of the headquarters of the Military Armistice Commission, for such uses as the Commission may determine.

(j) Insure that all members and other personnel of the Neutral Nations Supervisory Commission and of the Neutral Nations Repatriation Commission hereinafter established shall enjoy the freedom and facilities necessary for the proper exercise of their functions, including privileges, treatment, and immunities equivalent to those ordinarily enjoyed by accredited diplomatic personnel under international usage.

14. This Armistice Agreement shall apply to all opposing ground forces under the military control of either side, which ground forces shall respect the Demilitarized Zone and the area of Korea under the military control of the opposing side.

15. This Armistice Agreement shall apply to all opposing naval forces, which naval forces shall respect the waters contiguous to the Demilitarized Zone and to the land area of Korea under the military control of the opposing side, and shall not engage in blockade of any kind of Korea.

16. This Armistice Agreement shall apply to all opposing air forces, which air forces shall respect the air space over the Demilitarized Zone and over the area of Korea under the military control of the opposing side, and over the waters contiguous to both.

17. Responsibility for compliance with and enforcement of the terms and provisions of this Armistice Agreement is that of the signatories hereto and their successors in command. The Commanders of the opposing sides shall establish within their respective commands all measures and procedures necessary to insure complete compliance with all of the provisions hereof by all elements of their commands. They shall actively cooperate with one another and with the Military Armistice Commission and the Neutral Nations Supervisory Commission in requiring observance of both the letter and the spirit of all of the provisions of this Armistice Agreement.

18. The costs of the operations of the Military Armistice Commission and of the Neutral Nations Supervisory Commission and of their Teams shall be shared equally by the two opposing sides.

B. Military Armistice Commission

1. Composition

19. A Military Armistice Commission is hereby established.

20. The Military Armistice Commission shall be composed of ten (10) senior officers, five (5) of whom shall be appointed by the Commander in Chief, United Nations Command, and five (5) of whom shall be appointed jointly by the Supreme Commander of the Korean People's Army and the Commander of the Chinese People's Volunteers. Of the ten members, three (3) from each side shall be of general or flag rank. The two (2) remaining members on each side may be major generals, brigadier generals, colonels, or their equivalent.

21. Members of the Military Armistice Commission shall be permitted to use staff assistants as required.

22. The Military Armistice Commission shall be provided with the necessary administrative personnel to establish a Secretariat charged with assisting the Commission by performing record-keeping, secretarial, interpreting, and such other functions as the Commission may assign to it. Each side shall appoint to the Secretariat a Secretary and an Assistant Secretary and such clerical and specialized personnel as required by the Secretariat. Records shall be kept in English, Korean, and Chinese, all of which shall be equally authentic.

23. (a) The Military Armistice Commission shall be initially provided with and assisted by ten (10) Joint Observer Teams, which number may be reduced by agreement of the senior members of both sides on the Military Armistice Commission.

(b) Each Joint Observer Team shall be composed of not less than four (4) nor more than six (6) officers of field grade, half of whom shall be appointed by the Commander-in-Chief, United Nations Command, and half of whom shall be appointed jointly by the Supreme Commander of the Korean People's Army and the Commander of the Chinese People's Volunteers. Additional personnel such as drivers, clerks, and interpreters shall be furnished by each side as required for the functioning of the Joint Observer Teams.

2. Functions and Authority

24. The general mission of the Military Armistice Commission shall be to supervise the implementation of this Armistice Agreement and to settle through negotiations any violations of this Armistice Agreement.

25. The Military Armistice Commission shall:

(a) Locate its headquarters in the vicinity of PANMUNJOM (37°57:29 N, 126°40'00'' E). The Military Armistice Commission may relocate its headquarters at another point within the Demilitarized Zone by agreement of the senior members of both sides on the Commission.

(b) Operate as a joint organization without a chairman.

(c) Adopt such rules of procedure as it may, from time to time, deem necessary.

(d) Supervise the carrying out of the provisions of this Armistice Agreement pertaining to the Demilitarized Zone and to the Han River Estuary.

(e) Direct the operations of the Joint Observer Teams.

(f) Settle through negotiations any violations of this Armistice Agreement.

(g) Transmit immediately to the Commanders of the opposing sides all reports of investigations of violations of this Armistice Agreement and all other reports and records of proceedings received from the Neutral Nations Supervisory Commission.

(h) Give general supervision and direction to the activities of the Committee for Repatriation of Prisoners of War and the Committee for Assisting the Return of Displaced Civilians, hereinafter established.

(i) Act as an intermediary in transmitting communications between the Commanders of the opposing sides; provided, however, that the foregoing shall not be construed to preclude the Commanders of both sides from communicating with each other by any other means which they may desire to employ.

(j) Provide credentials and distinctive insignia for its staff and its Joint Observer Teams, and a distinctive marking for all vehicles, aircraft, and vessels used in the performance of its mission.

26. The mission of the Joint Observer Teams shall be to assist the Military Armistice Commission in supervising the carrying out of the provisions of this Armistice Agreement pertaining to the Demilitarzed Zone and to the Han River Estuary.

27. The Military Armistice Commission, or the senior member of either side thereof, is authorized to dispatch Joint Observer Teams to investigate violations of this Armistice Agreement reported to have occurred in the Demilitarized Zone or in the Han River Estuary; provided, however, that not more than one-half of the Joint Observer Teams which have not been dispatched by the Military Armistice Commission may be dispatched at any one time by the senior member of either side on the Commission.

28. The Military Armistice Commission, or the senior member of either side thereof, is authorized to request the Neutral Nations Supervisory Commission to conduct special observations and inspections at places outside the Demilitarized Zone where violations of this Armistice Agreement have been reported to have occurred.

29. When the Military Armistice Commission determines that a violation of this Armistice Agreement has occurred, it shall immediately report such violation to the Commanders of the opposing sides.

30. When the Military Armistice Commission determines that a violation of this Armistice Agreement has been corrected to its satisfaction, it shall so report to the Commanders of the opposing sides.

3. General

31. The Military Armistice Commission shall meet daily. Recesses of not to exceed seven (7) days may be agreed upon by the senior members of both sides; provided, that such recesses may be terminated on twenty-four (24) hour notice by the senior member of either side.

32. Copies of the record of the proceedings of all meetings of the Military Armistice Commission shall be forwarded to the Commanders of the opposing sides as soon as possible after each meeting.

33. The Joint Observer Teams shall make periodic reports to the Military Armistice Commission as required by the Commission and, in addition, shall make such special reports as may be deemed necessary by them or as may be required by the Commission.

34. The Military Armistice Commission shall maintain duplicate files of the reports and records of proceedings required by this Armistice Agreement. The Commission is authorized to maintain duplicate files of such other reports, records, etc., as may be necessary in the conduct of its business. Upon eventual dissolution of the Commission, one set of the above files shall be turned over to each side.

35. The Military Armistice Commission may make recommendations to the Commanders of the opposing sides with respect to amendments or additions to this Armistice Agreement. Such recommended changes should generally be those designed to insure a more effective armistice.

C. Neutral Nations Supervisory Commission

1. Composition

36. A Neutral Nations Supervisory Commission is hereby established.

37. The Neutral Nations Supervisory Commission shall be composed of four (4) senior officers, two (2) of whom shall be appointed by neutral nations nominated by the Commander-in-Chief, United Nations Command, namely, SWEDEN and SWITZERLAND, and two (2) of whom shall be appointed by neutral nations nominated jointly by the Supreme Commander of the Korean People's Army and the Commander of the Chinese People's Volunteers, namely, POLAND and CZECHOSLOVAKIA. The term "neutral Nations" as herein used is defined as those nations whose combatant forces have not participated in the hostilities in Korea. Members appointed to the Commission may be from the armed forces of the appointing nations. Each member shall designate an alterate member to attend those meetings which for any reason the principal member is unable to attend. Such alternate members shall be of the same nationality as their principals. The Neutral Nations Supervisory Commission may take action whenever the number of members present from the neutral nations nominated by one side is equal to the number of members present from the neutral nations nominated by the other side.

38. Members of the Neutral Nations Supervisory Commission shall be permitted to use staff assistants furnished by the neutral nations as required.   These staff assistants may be appointed as alternate members of the Commission.

39. The neutral nations shall be requested to furnish the Neutral Nations Supervisory Commission with the necessary administrative personnel to establish a Secretariat charged with assisting the Commission by performing necessary record-keeping, secretarial, interpreting, and such other functions as the Commission may assign to it.

40. (a) The Neutral Nations Supervisory Commission shall be initially provided with, and assisted by, twenty (20) Neutral Nations Inspection Teams, which number may be reduced by agreement of the senior members of both sides on the Military Armistice Commission. The Neutral Nations Inspection Teams shall be responsible to, shall report to, and shall be subject to the direction of, the Neutral Nations Supervisory Commission only.

(b) Each Neutral Nations Inspection Team shall be composed of not less than four (4) officers, preferably of field grade, half of whom shall be from the neutral nations nominated by the Commander-in-Chief, United Nations Command, and half of whom shall be from the neutral nations nominated jointly by the Supreme Commander of the Korean People's Army and the Commander of the Chinese People's Volunteers. Members appointed to the Neutral Nations Inspection Teams may be from the armed forces of the appointing nations.   In order to facilitate the functioning of the Teams, sub-teams composed of not less than two (2) members, one of whom shall be from a neutral nation nominated by the Commander-in-Chief, United Nations Command, and one of whom shall be from a neutral nation nominated jointly by the Supreme Commander of the Korean People's Army and the Commander of the Chinese People's Volunteers, may be formed as circumstances require. Additional personnel such as drivers, clerks, interpreters, and communications personnel, and such equipment as may be required by the Teams to perform their missions, shall be furnished by the Commander of each side, as required, in the Demilitarized Zone and in the territory under his military control. The Neutral Nations Supervisory Commission may provide itself and the Neutral Nations Inspection Teams with such of the above personnel and equipment of its own as it may desire; provided, however, that such personnel shall be personnel of the same neutral nations of which the Neutral Nations Supervisory Commission is composed.

2. Functions and Authority

41. The mission of the Neutral Nations Supervisory Commission shall be to carry out the functions of supervision, observation, inspection, and investigation, as stipulated in sub-paragraphs 13 (c) and 13 (d) and paragraph 28 hereof, and to report the results of such supervision, observation, inspection, and investigation to the Military Armistice Commission.

42. The Neutral Nations Supervisory Commission shall:

(a) Locate its headquarters in proximity to the headquarters of the Military Armistice Commission.

(b) Adopt such rules of procedure as it may, from time to time, deem necessary.

(c) Conduct, through its members and its Neutral Nations Inspection Teams, the supervision and inspection provided for in subparagraphs 13 (c) and 13 (d) of this Armistice Agreement at the ports of entry enumerated in paragraph 43 hereof, and the special observations and inspections provided for in paragraph 28 hereof at those places where violations of this Armistice Agreement have been reported to have occurred. The inspection of combat aircraft, armored vehicles, weapons, and ammunition by the Neutral Nations Inspection Teams shall be such as to enable them to properly insure that reinforcing combat aircraft, armored vehicles, weapons, and ammunition are not being introduced into Korea; but this shall not be construed as authorizing inspections or examinations of any secret designs or characteristics of any combat aircraft, armored vehicle, weapon, or ammunition.

(d) Direct and supervise the operations of the Neutral Nations Inspection Teams.

(e) Station five (5) Neutral Nations Inspection Teams at the ports of entry enumerated in paragraph 43 hereof located in the territory under the military control of the Commander in Chief, United Nations Command; and five (5) Neutral Nations Inspection Teams at the ports of entry enumerated in paragraph 43 hereof located in the territory under the military control of the Supreme Commander of the Korean People's Army and the Commander of the Chinese People's Volunteers; and establish initially ten (10) mobile Neutral Nations Inspection Teams in reserve, stationed in the general vicinity of the headquarters of the Neutral Nations Supervisory Commission, which number may be reduced by agreement of the senior members of both sides on the Military Armistice Commission. Not more than half of the mobile Neutral Nations Inspection Teams shall be dispatched at any one time in accordance with requests of the senior member of either side on the Military Armistice Commission.

(f) Subject to the provisions of the preceding subparagraphs, conduct without delay investigations of reported violations of this Armistice Agreement, including such investigations of reported violations of this Armistice Agreement as may be requested by the Military Armistice Commission or by the senior member of either side on the Commission.

(g) Provide credentials and distinctive insignia for its staff and its Neutral Nations Inspection Teams, and a distinctive marking for all vehicles, aircraft, and vessels used in the performance of its mission.

43. Neutral Nations Inspection Teams shall be stationed at the following ports of entry:

Territory under the military control of the United Nations Command	Territory under the military control of the Korean People's Army and the Chinese People's Volunteers
INCHON (37°28′ N., 126°38′ E.)	
TAEGU (35°52′ N., 128°36′ E.)	SINUIJU (40°06′ N., 124°24′ E.)
PUSAN (35°06′ N., 129°02′ E.)	CHONGJIN (41°46′ N., 129°49′ E.)
KANGNUNG (37°45′ N., 128°54′ E.)	HUNGNAM (39°50′ N., 127°37′ E.)
KUNSAN (35°59′ N., 126°45′ E.)	MANPO (41°09′ N., 126°18′ E.)
	SINANJU (39°36′ N., 125°36′ E.)

These Neutral Nations Inspection Teams shall be accorded full convenience of movement within the areas and over the routes of communication set forth on the attached map (Map 5).

3. General

44. The Neutral Nations Supervisory Commission shall meet daily. Recesses of not to exceed seven (7) days may be agreed upon by the members of the Neutral Nations Supervisory Commission; provided, that such recesses may be terminated on twenty-four (24) hour notice by any member.

45. Copies of the record of the proceedings of all meetings of the Neutral Nations Supervisory Commission shall be forwarded to the Military Armistice Commission as soon as possible after each meeting. Records shall be kept in English, Korean, and Chinese.

46. The Neutral Nations Inspection Teams shall make periodic reports concerning the results of their supervision, observations, inspections, and investigations to the Neutral Nations Supervisory Commission as required by the Commission and, in addition, shall make such special reports as may be deemed necessary by them, or as may be required by the Commission. Reports shall be submitted by a Team as a whole, but may also be submitted by one or more individual members thereof; provided, that the reports submitted by one or more individual members thereof shall be considered as informational only.

47. Copies of the reports made by the Neutral Nations Inspection Teams shall be forwarded to the Military Armistice Commission by the Neutral Nations Supervisory Commission without delay and in the language in which received. They shall not be delayed by the process of translation or evaluation. The Neutral Nations Supervisory Commission shall evaluate such reports at the earliest practicable time and shall forward their findings to the Military Armistice Commission as a matter of priority. The Military Armistice Commission shall not take final action with regard to any such report until the evalution thereof has been received from the Neutral Nations Supervisory Commission. Members of the Neutral Nations Supervisory Commission and of its Team shall be subject to appearance before the Military Armistice Commission, at the request of the senior member of either side on the Military Armistice Commission, for clarification of any report submitted.

48. The Neutral Nations Supervisory Commission shall maintain duplicate files of the reports and records of proceedings required by this Armistice Agreement. The Commission is authorized to maintain duplicate files of such other reports, records, etc., as may be necessary in the conduct of its business. Upon eventual dissolution of the Commission, one set of the above files shall be turned over to each side.

49. The Neutral Nations Supervisory Commission may make recommendations to the Military Armistice Commission with respect to amendments or additions to this Armistice Agreement. Such recommended changes should generally be those designed to insure a more effective armistice.

50. The Neutral Nations Supervisory Commission, or any member thereof, shall be authorized to communicate with any member of the Military Armistice Commission.

ARTICLE III

ARRANGEMENTS RELATING TO PRISONERS OF WAR

51. The release and repatriation of all prisoners of war held in the custody of each side at the time this Armistice Agreement becomes effective shall be effected in conformity with the following provisions agreed upon by both sides prior to the signing of this armistice agreement.

(a) Within sixty (60) days after this Armistice Agreement becomes effective, each side shall, without offering any hindrance, directly repatriate and hand over in groups all those prisoners of war in its custody who insist on repatriation to the side to which they belonged at the time of capture. Repatriation shall be accomplished in accordance with the related provisions of this article. In order to expedite the repatriation process of such personnel, each side shall, prior to the signing of the armistice agreement, exchange the total numbers, by nationalities, of personnel to be directly repatriated. Each group of prisoners of war delivered to the other side shall be accompanied by rosters, prepared by nationality to include, name, rank (if any), and internment of military serial number.

(b) Each side shall release all those remaining prisoners of war, who are not directly repatriated, from its military control and from its custody and hand them over to the Neutral Nations Repatriation Commission for disposition in accordance with the provisions in the annex hereto: "Terms of Reference for Neutral Nations Repatriation Commission."

(c) So that there may be no misunderstanding owing to the equal use of three languages, the act of delivery of a prisoner of war by one side to the other shall, for the purposes of this Armistice Agreement, be called "repatriation" in English, "Song Hwan" in Korean, and "Ch'ien Fan" in Chinese, notwithstanding the nationality or place of residence of such prisoner of war.

52. Each side insures that it will not employ in acts of war in the Korean conflict any prisoner of war released and repatriated incident to the coming into effect of this Armistice Agreement.

53. All the sick and injured prisoners of war who insist upon repatriation shall be repatriated with priority. Insofar as possible, there shall be captured medical personnel repatriated concurrently with the sick and injured prisoners of war, so as to provide medical care and attendance en route.

54. The repatriation of all of the prisoners of war required by subparagraph 51 (a) hereof shall be completed within a time limit of 60 days after this Armistice Agreement becomes effective. Within this time limit each side undertakes to complete the repatriation of the above-mentioned prisoners of war in its custody at the earliest practicable time.

55. PANMUNJOM is designated as the place where prisoners of war will be delivered and received by both sides. Additional place(s) of delivery and reception of prisoners of war in the Demilitarized Zone may be designated, if necessary, by the Committee for Repatriation of Prisoners of War.

56. A. A committee for repatriation of prisoners of war is hereby established. It shall be composed of six (6) officers of field grade, three (3) of whom shall be appointed by the Commander in Chief, United Nations Command, and three (3) of whom shall be appointed jointly by the Supreme Commander of the Korean Peoples Army and the Commander of the Chinese Peoples Volunteers. This committee shall, under the general supervision and direction of the Military Armistice Commission, be responsible for coordinating the specific plans of both sides for the repatriation of prisoners of war and for supervising the execution by both sides of all of the provisions of this Armistice Agreement relating to the repatriation of prisoners of war. It shall be the duty of this committee to coordinate the timing of the arrival of prisoners of war at the place(s) of delivery and reception of prisoners of war from the prisoners of war camps of both sides; to make, when necessary, such special arrangements as may be required with regard to the transportation and welfare of sick and injured prisoners of war; to coordinate the work of the Joint Red Cross teams, established in paragraph 57 hereof, in assisting in the repatriation of prisoners of war; to supervise the implementation of the arrangements for the actual repatriation of prisoners of war stipulated in paragraphs 53 and 54 hereof; to select, when necessary, additional place(s) of delivery and reception of prisoners of war; to arrange for security at the place(s) of delivery and reception of prisoners of war; and to carry out such other related functions as are required for the repatriation of prisoners of war.

B. When unable to reach agreement on any matter relating to its responsibilities, the Committee for Repatriation of Prisoners of War shall immediately refer such matter to the Military Armistice Commission for decision. The Committee for Repatriation of Prisoners of War shall maintain its headquarters in proximity to the headquarters of the Military Armistice Commission.

C. The Committee for Repatriation of Prisoners of War shall be dissolved by the Military Armistice Commission upon completion of the program of repatriation of prisoners of war.

57. A. Immediately after this armistice agreement becomes effective, Joint Red Cross teams composed of representatives of the National Red Cross Societies of the countries contributing forces to the United Nations Command on the one hand, and representatives of the Red Cross Society of the Democratic Peoples Republic of Korea and representatives of the Red Cross Society of the People's Republic of China on the other hand, shall be established. The Joint Red Cross teams shall assist in the execution by both sides of those provisions of this Armistice Agreement relating to the repatriation of all the prisoners of war specified in subparagraph 51 A. hereof, who insist upon repatriation, by the performance of such humanitarian services as are necessary and desirable for the welfare of the prisoners of war. To accomplish this task, the Joint Red Cross teams shall provide assistance in the delivering and receiving of prisoners of war by both sides at the place(s) of delivery and reception of prisoners of war, and shall visit the prisoner-of-war camps of both sides to comfort the prisoners of war and to bring in and distribute gift articles for the comfort and welfare of the prisoners of war. The Joint Red Cross teams may provide services to prisoners of war while en route from

prisoner-of-war camps to the place(s) of delivery and reception of prisoners of war.

B. The Joint Red Cross teams shall be organized as set forth below:

(1) One team shall be composed of twenty (20) members, namely, ten (10) representatives from the national Red Cross societies of each side, to assist in the delivering and receiving of prisoners of war by both sides at the place(s) of delivery and reception of prisoners of war. The chairmanship of this team shall alternate daily between representatives from the Red Cross societies of the two sides. The work and services of this team shall be coordinated by the Committee for Repatriation of Prisoners of War.

(2) One team shall be composed of sixty (60) members, namely, thirty (30) representatives from the national Red Cross societies of each side, to visit the prisoner-of-war camps under the administration of the Korean People's Army and the Chinese People's Volunteers. This team may provide services to prisoners of war while en route from the prisoner-of-war camps to the place(s) of delivery and reception of prisoners of war. A representative of the Red Cross Society of the Democratic People's Republic of Korea or of the Red Cross Society of the People's Republic of China shall serve as chairman of this team.

(3) One team shall be composed of sixty (60) members, namely, thirty (30) representatives from the national Red Cross societies of each side, to visit the prisoner-of-war camps under the administration of the United Nations Command. This team may provide services to prisoners of war while en route from the prisoner-of-war camps to the place(s) of delivery and reception of prisoners of war. A representative of a Red Cross Society of a nation contributing forces to the United Nations Command shall serve as chairman of this team.

(4) In order to facilitate the functioning of each joint Red Cross team, subteams composed of not less than two (2) members from the team, with an equal number of representatives from each side, may be formed as circumstances require.

(5) Additional personnel such as drivers, clerks, and interpreters, and such equipment as may be required by the joint Red Cross teams to perform their missions, shall be furnished by the Commander of each side to the team operating in the territory under his military control.

(6) Whenever jointly agreed upon by the representatives of both sides on any joint Red Cross team, the size of such team may be increased or decreased, subject to confirmation by the Committee for Repatriation of Prisoners of War.

C. The Commander of each side shall cooperate fully with the joint Red Cross teams in the performance of their functions, and undertakes to insure the security of the personnel of the joint Red Cross team in the area under his military control. The Commander of each side shall provide such logistic, administrative, and communications facilities as may be required by the team operating in the territory under his military control.

D. The Joint Red Cross teams shall be dissolved upon completion of the program of repatriation of all the prisoners of war specified in subparagraph 51A hereof, who insist upon repatriation.

58. A. The Commander of each side shall furnish to the Commander of the other side as soon as practicable, but not later than ten (10) days

after this Armistice Agreement becomes effective, the following information concerning prisoners of war:

(1) Complete data pertaining to the prisoners of war who escaped since the effective date of the data last exchanged.

(2) Insofar as practicable, information regarding name, nationality, rank, and other identification data, date and cause of death, and place of burial, of those prisoners of war who died while in his custody.

B. If any prisoners of war escape or die after the effective date of the supplementary information specified above, the detaining side shall furnish to the other side, through the Committee for Repatriation of Prisoners of War, the data pertaining thereto in accordance with the provisions of subparagraph 58A hereof. Such data shall be furnished at 10-day intervals until the completion of the program of delivery and reception of prisoners of war.

C. Any escaped prisoner of war who returns to the custody of the detaining side after the completion of the program of delivery and reception of prisoners of war shall be delivered to the Military Armistice Commission for disposition.

59. A. All civilians who, at the time this Armistice Agreement becomes effective, are in territory under the military control of the Commander in Chief, United Nations Command, and who, on 24 June 1950, resided north of the military demarcation line established in this Armistice Agreement shall, if they desire to return home, be permitted and assisted by the Commander in Chief, United Nations Command, to return to the area north of the military demarcation line and all civilians who, at the time this Armistice Agreement becomes effective, are in territory under the military control of the Supreme Commander of the Korean Peoples Army and the Commander of the Chinese Peoples Volunteers, and who, on 24 June 1950, resided south of the military demarcation line established in this Armistice Agreement shall, if they desire to return home, be permitted and assisted by the Supreme Commander of the Korean Peoples Army and the Commander of the Chinese Peoples Volunteers to return to the area south of the military demarcation line. The commander of each side shall be responsible for publicizing widely throughout territory under his military control the contents of the provisions of this subparagraph, and for calling upon the appropriate civil authorities to give necessary guidance and assistance to all such civilians who desire to return home.

B. All civilians of foreign nationality who, at the time this Armistice Agreement becomes effective, are in territory under the military control of the Supreme Commander of the Korean Peoples Army and the Commander of the Chinese Peoples Volunteers shall, if they desire to proceed to territory under the military control of the Commander in Chief, United Nations Command, be permitted and assisted to do so; all civilians of foreign nationality who, at the time this Armistice Agreement becomes effective, are in territory under the military control of the Commander in Chief, United Nations Command, shall, if they desire to proceed to territory under the military control of the Supreme Commander of the Korean Peoples Army and the Commander of the Chinese Peoples Volunteers, be permitted and assisted to do so. The Commander of each side shall be responsible for publicizing widely throughout the territory under his military control the contents of the provisions of this subparagraph, and for calling upon the appropriate civil authorities to give necessary guidance and assistance to all such civilians of foreign nationality who desire to proceed to territory under the military control of the commander of the other side.

C. Measures to assist in the return of civilians provided for in subparagraph 59 A. hereof and the movement of civilians provided for in subparagraph 59B, hereof shall be commenced by both sides as soon as possible after this Armistice Agreement becomes effective.

D. (1) A committee for assisting the return of displaced civilians is hereby established. It shall be composed of four (4) officers of field grade, two (2) of whom shall be appointed by the Commander in Chief, United Nations Command, and two (2) of whom shall be appointed jointly by the Supreme Commander of the Korean Peoples Army and the Commander of the Chinese Peoples Volunteers. This committee shall, under the general supervision and direction of the Military Armistice Commission, be responsible for coordinating the specific plans of both sides for assistance to the return of the above-mentioned civilians, and for supervising the execution by both sides of all the provisions of the Armistice Agreement relating to the return of the above-mentioned civilians. It shall be the duty of this committee to make necessary arrangements, including those of transportation, for expediting and coordinating the movement of the above-mentioned civilians; to select the crossing point through which the above-mentioned civilians will cross the military demarcation line; to arrange for security at the crossing point; and to carry out such other functions as are required to accomplish the return of the above-mentioned civilians.

(2) When unable to reach agreement on any matter relating to its responsibilities, the Committee for Assisting the Return of Displaced Civilians shall immediately refer such matter to the Military Armistice Commission for decision. The Committee for Assisting the Return of Displaced Civilians shall maintain its headquarters in proximity to the headquarters of the Military Armistice Commission.

(3) The Committee for Assisting the Return of Displaced Civilians shall be dissolved by the Military Armistice Commission upon fulfillment of its mission.

ARTICLE IV

RECOMMENDATION TO THE GOVERNMENTS CONCERNED ON BOTH SIDES

60. In order to insure the peaceful settlement of the Korean question, the military commanders of both sides hereby recommend to the governments of the countries concerned on both sides, that, within three (3) months after the Armistice Agreement is signed and becomes effective, a political conference of a higher level of both sides be held by representatives appointed respectively to settle through negotiation the questions of the withdrawal of all foreign forces from Korea, the peaceful settlement of the Korean question, etc.

ARTICLE V

MISCELLANEOUS

61. Amendments and additions to this Armistice Agreement must be mutually agreed to by the Commanders of the opposing sides.

62. The articles and paragraphs of this Armistice Agreement shall remain in effect until expressly superseded either by mutually acceptable amendments and additions or by provision in an appropriate agreement for a peaceful settlement at a political level between both sides.

63. All of the provisions of this Armistice Agreement, other than paragraph 12, shall become effective at 2200 hours on 27 July 1953.

Done at PANMUNJOM, Korea, at 1000 hours on the 27th day of July, 1953, in English, Korean, and Chinese, all texts being equally authentic.

KIM IL SUNG,
Marshal, Democratic People's Republic of Korea,
Supreme Commander, Korean People's Army.
PENG TEH-HUAI,
Commander of the Chinese People's Volunteers.
MARK W. CLARK,
General, United States Army,
Commander in Chief, United Nations Command.

PRESENT:

NAM IL,
General, Korean People's Army. Senior Delegate. Delegation of the Korean People's Army and Chinese People's Volunteers
WILLIAM K. HARRISON, JR.,
Major General, United States Army,
Senior Delegate, United Nations Command Delegation.

ANNEX

TERMS OF REFERENCE FOR NEUTRAL NATIONS REPATRIATION COMMISSION

(See Subparagraph 51b)

I. GENERAL

1. In order to ensure that all prisoners of war have the opportunity to exercise their right to be repatriated following an armistice, Sweden, Switzerland, Poland, Czechoslovakia and India shall each be requested by both sides to appoint a member to a Neutral Nations Repatriation Commission which shall be established to take custody in Korea of those prisoners of war who, while in the custody of the detaining powers, have not exercised their right to be repatriated. The Neutral Nations Repatriation Commission shall establish its headquarters within the Demilitarized Zone in the vicinity of Panmunjom, and shall station subordinate bodies of the same composition as the Neutral Nations Repatriation Commission at those locations at which the Repatriation Commission assumes custody of prisoners of war. Representatives of both sides shall be permitted to observe the operations of the Repatriation Commission and its subordinate bodies to include explanations and interviews.

2. Sufficient armed forces and any other operating personnel required to assist the Neutral Nations Repatriation Commission in carrying out its functions and responsibilities shall be provided exclusively by India, whose representative shall be the umpire in accordance with the provisions of Article 132 of the Geneva Convention, and shall also be chairman and executive agent of the Neutral Nations Repatriation Commission. Representatives from each of the other four powers shall be allowed staff assistants in equal number not to exceed fifty (50) each. When any of the representatives of the neutral nations is absent for some reason, that representative shall designate an alternate representative of his own nationality to exercise his functions and authority. The arms of all personnel provided for in this Paragraph shall be limited to military police type small arms.

3. No force or threat of force shall be used against the prisoners of war specified in Paragraph 1 above to prevent or effect their repatriation, and no violence

to their persons or affront to their dignity or self-respect shall be permitted in any manner for any purpose whatsoever (but see Paragraph 7 below). This duty is enjoined on and entrusted to the Neutral Nations Repatriation Commission. This Commission shall ensure that prisoners of war shall at all times be treated humanely in accordance with the specific provisions of the Geneva Convention, and with the general spirit of that Convention.

II. CUSTODY OF PRISONERS OF WAR

4. All prisoners of war who have not exercised their right of repatriation following the effective date of the Armistice Agreement shall be released from the military control and from the custody of the detaining side as soon as practicable, and, in all cases, within sixty (60) days subsequent to the effective date of the Armistice Agreement to the Neutral Nations Repatriation Commission at locations in Korea to be designated by the detaining side.

5. At the time the Neutral Nations Repatriation Commission assumes control of the prisoner of war installations, the military forces of the detaining side shall be withdrawn therefrom, so that the locations specified in the preceding Paragraph shall be taken over completely by the armed forces of India.

6. Notwithstanding the provisions of Paragraph 5 above, the detaining side shall have the responsibility for maintaining and ensuring securty and order in the areas around the locations where the prisoners of war are in custody and for preventing and restraining any armed forces (including irregular armed forces) in the area under its control from any acts of disturbance and intrusion against the locations where the prisoners of war are in custody.

7. Notwithstanding the provisions of Paragraph 3 above, nothing in this agreement shall be construed as derogating from the authority of the Neutral Nations Repatriation Commission to exercise its legitimate functions and responsibilities for the control of the prisoners of war under its temporary jurisdiction.

III. EXPLANATION

8. The Neutral Nations Repatriation Commission, after having received and taken into custody all those prisoners of war who have not exercised their right to be repatriated, shall immediately make arrangements so that within ninety (90) days after the Neutral Nations Repatriation Commission takes over the custody, the nations to which prisoners of war belong shall have freedom and facilities to send representatives to the locations where such prisoners of war are in custody to explain to all the prisoners of war depending upon these nations their rights and to inform them of any matters relating to their return to their homelands, particularly of their full freedom to return home to lead a peaceful life, under the following provisions:

(*a*) The number of such explaining representatives shall not exceed seven (7) per thousand prisoners of war held in custody by the Neutral Nations Repatriation Commission; and the minimum authorized shall not be less than a total of five (5):

(*b*) The hours during which the explaining representatives shall have access to the prisoners shall be as determined by the Neutral Nations Repatriation Commission, and generally in accord with Article 53 of the Geneva Convention Relative to the Treatment of Prisoners of War:

(*c*) All explanations and interviews shall be conducted in the presence of a representative of each member nation of the Neutral Nations Repatriation Commission and a representative from the detaining side;

(*d*) Additional provisions governing the explanation work shall be prescribed by the Neutral Nations Repatriation Commission, and will be designed to employ the principles enumerated in Paragraph 3 above and in this Paragraph;

(*e*) The explaining representatives, while engaging in their work, shall be allowed to bring with them necessary facilities and personnel for wireless communications. The number of communications personnel shall be limited to one team per location at which explaining representatives are in residence, except in the event all prisoners of war are concentrated in one location, in which case, two (2) teams shall be permitted. Each team shall consist of not more than six (6) communications personnel.

9. Prisoners of war in its custody shall have freedom and facilities to make representations and communications to the Neutral Nations Repatriation Commission and to representatives and subordinate bodies of the Neutral Nations Repatriation Commission and to inform them of their desires on any matter concerning the prisoners of war themselves, in accordance with arrangement made for the purpose by the Neutral Nations Repatriation Commission.

IV. DISPOSITION OF PRISONERS OF WAR

10. Any prisoner of war who, while in the custody of the Neutral Nations Repatriation Commission, decides to exercise the right of repatriation, shall make an application requesting repatriation to a body consisting of a representative of each member nation of the Neutral Nations Repatriation Commission. Once such an application is made, it shall be considered immediately by the Neutral Nations Repatriation Commission or one of its subordinate bodies so as to determine immediately by majority vote the validity of such application. Once such an application is made to and validated by the Commission or one of its subordinate bodies, the prisoner of war concerned shall immediately be transfered to and accommodated in the tents set up for those who are ready to be repatriated. Thereafter, he shall, while still in the custody of the Neutral Nations Repatriation Commission, be delivered forthwith to the prisoner of war exchange point at Panmunjom for repatriation under the procedure prescribed in the Armistice Agreement.

11. At the expiration of ninety (90) days after the transfer of custody of the prisoners of war to the Neutral Nations Repatriation Commission, access of representatives to captured personnel as provided for in Paragraph 8 above, shall terminate, and the question of disposition of the prisoners of war who have not exercised their right to be repatriated shall be submitted to the Political Conference recommended to be convened in Paragraph 60, Draft Armistice Agreement, which shall endeavor to settle this question within thirty (30) days, during which period the Neutral Nations Repatriation Commission shall continue to retain custody of those prisoners of war. The Neutral Nations Repatriation Commission shall declare the relief from the prisoner of war status to civilian status of any prisoners of war who have not exercised their right to be repatriated and for whom no other disposition has been agreed to by the Political Conference within one hundred and twenty (120) days after the Neutral Nations Repatriation Commission has assumed their custody. Thereafter, according to the application of each individual, those who choose to go to neutral nations shall be assisted by the Neutral Nations Repatriation Commission and the Red Cross Society of India. This operation shall be completed within thirty (30) days, and upon its completion, the Neutral Nations Repatriation Commission shall immediately cease its functions and declare its dissolution. After the dissolution of the Neutral Nations Repatriation Commission, whenever and wherever any of those above-mentioned civilians who have been relieved from the prisoner of war status desire to return to their fatherlands, the authorities of the localities where they are shall be responsible for assisting them in returning to their fatherlands.

V. RED CROSS VISITATION

12. Essential Red Cross service for prisoners of war in custody of the Neutral Nations Repatriation Commission shall be provided by India in accordance with regulations issued by the Neutral Nations Repatriation Commission.

VI. PRESS COVERAGE

13. The Neutral Nations Repatriation Commission shall insure freedom of the press and other news media in observing the entire operation as enumerated herein, in accordance with procedures to be established by the Neutral Nations Repatriation Commission.

VII. LOGISTICAL SUPPORT FOR PRISONERS OF WAR

14. Each side shall provide logistical support for the prisoners of war in the area under its military control, delivering required support to the Neutral Nations Repatriation Commission at an agreed delivery point in the vicinity of each prisoner of war installation.

15. The cost of repatriating prisoners of war to the exchange point at Panmunjom shall be borne by the detaining side and the cost from the exchange point by the side on which said prisoners depend, in accordance with Article 118 of the Geneva Convention.

16. The Red Cross Society of India shall be responsible for providing such general service personnel in the prisoner of war installations as required by the Neutral Nations Repatriation Commission.

17. The Neutral Nations Repatriation Commission shall provide medical support for the prisoners of war as may be practicable. The detaining side shall provide medical support as practical upon the request of the Neutral Nations Repatriation Commission and specifically for those cases requiring extensive treatment or hospitalization. The Neutral Nations Repatriation Commission shall maintain custody of prisoners of war during such hospitalization. The detaining side shall facilitate such custody. Upon completion of treatment, prisoners of war shall be returned to a prisoner of war installation as specified in Paragraph 4 above.

18. The Neutral Nations Repatriation Commission is entitled to obtain from both sides such legitimate assistance as it may require in carrying out its duties and tasks, but both sides shall not under any name and in any form interfere or exert influence.

VIII. LOGISTICAL SUPPORT FOR THE NEUTRAL NATIONS REPATRIATION COMMISSION

19. Each side shall be responsible for providing logistical support for the personnel of the Neutral Nations Repatriation Commission stationed in the area under its military control, and both sides shall contribute on an equal basis to such support within the Demilitarized Zone. The precise arrangements shall be subject to determination between the Neutral Nations Repatriation Commission and the detaining side in each case.

20. Each of the detaining sides shall be responsible for protecting the explaining representatives from the other side while in transit over lines of communication within its area, as set forth in Paragraph 23 for the Neutral Nations Repatriation Commission, to a place of residence and while in residence in the vicinity of but not within each of the locations where the prisoners of war are in custody. The Neutral Nations Repatriation Commission shall be responsible for the security of such representatives within the actual limits of the locations where the prisoners of war are in custody.

21. Each of the detaining sides shall provide transportation, housing, communication, and other agreed logistical support to the explaining representatives of the other side while they are in the area under its military control. Such services shall be provided on a reimbursable basis.

IX. PUBLICATION

22. After the Armistice Agreement becomes effective, the terms of this agreement shall be made known to all prisoners of war who, while in the custody of the detaining side, have not exercised their right to be repatriated.

X. MOVEMENT

23. The movement of the personnel of the Neutral Nations Repatriation Commission and repatriated prisoners of war shall be over lines of communication as determined by the command(s) of the opposing side and the Neutral Nations Repatriation Commission. A map showing these lines of communication shall be furnished the command of the opposing side and the Neutral Nations Repatriation Commission. Movement of such personnel, except within locations as designated in Paragraph 4 above, shall be under the control of, and escorted by, personnel of the side in whose area the travel is being undertaken; however, such movement shall not be subject to any obstruction and coercion.

XI. PROCEDURAL MATTERS

24. The interpretation of this agreement shall rest with the Neutral Nations Repatriation Commission. The Neutral Nations Repatriation Commission, and/or any subordinate bodies to which functions are delegated or assigned by the Neutral Nations Repatriation Commission, shall operate on the basis of majority vote.

25. The Neutral Nations Repatriation Commission shall submit a weekly report to the opposing Commanders on the status of prisoners of war in its custody, indicating the numbers repatriated and remaining at the end of each week.

26. When this agreement has been acceded to by both sides and by the five powers named herein, it shall become effective upon the date the Armistice becomes effective.

Done at Panmunjom, Korea, at 1400 hours on the 8th day of June 1953, in English, Korean, and Chinese, all texts being equally authentic.

NAM IL,
General, Korean People's Army; Senior Delegate,
Delegation of the Korean People's Army
and the Chinese People's Volunteers.

WILLIAM K. HARRISON, Jr.,
Lieutenant General, United States Army;
Senior Delegate,
United Nations Command Delegation.

59. SUPPLEMENTARY AGREEMENT ON PRISONERS OF WAR, JULY 27, 1953 [12]

In order to meet the requirements of the disposition of the prisoners of war not for direct repatriation in accordance with the provisions of the terms of reference for Neutral Nations Repatriation Commission, the Supreme Commander of the Korean People's Army and the Commander of the Chinese People's Volunteers, on the one hand, and the Commander in Chief, United Nations Command, on the other hand, in pursuance of the provisions in Paragraph 61, Article 5, of the agreement concerning a military armistice in Korea, agree to conclude the following temporary agreement suplementary to the armistice agreement:

1. Under the provisions of Paragraphs 4 and 5, Article II, of the terms of reference for Neutral Nations Repatriation Commission, the United Nations Command has the right to designate the area between the military demarcation line and the eastern and southern boundaries of the demilitarized zone between the Imjin River on the south and the road leading south from Okum-Ni on the northeast (the main road leading southeast from Panmunjom not included), as the area within which the United Nations Command will turn over the prisoners of war, who are not directly repatriated and whom the United Nations Command has the responsibility for keeping under its custody, to the Neutral Nations Repatriation Commission and the armed forces of India for custody. The United Nations Command shall, prior to the signing of the armistice agreement, inform the side of the Korean People's Army and the Chinese People's Volunteers of the approximate figures by nationality of such prisoners of war held in its custody.

2. If there are prisoners of war under their custody who request not to be directly repatriated, the Korean People's Army and the Chinese People's Volunteers have the right to designate the area in the vicinity of Panmunjom between the military demarcation line and the western and northern boundaries of the demilitarized zone, as the area within which such prisoners of war will be turned over to the Neutral Nations Repatriation Commission and the armed forces of India for custody. After knowing that there are prisoners of war under their custody who request not to be directly repatriated, the Korean People's Army and the Chinese People's Volunteers shall inform the United Nations Command side of the approximate figures by nationality of such prisoners of war.

3. In accordance with Paragraphs 8, 9 and 10, Article I, of the armistice agreement, the following paragraphs are hereby provided:

a. After the cease-fire comes into effect, unarmed personnel of each side shall be specifically authorized by the Military Armistice Com-

---

mission to enter the above-mentioned area designated by their own side to perform necessary construction operations.   None of such personnel shall remain in the above-mentioned areas upon the completion of the construction operations.

b. A definite number of prisoners of war as decided upon by both sides, who are in the respective custody of both sides and who are not directly repatriated, shall be specifically authorized by the Military Armistice Commission to be escorted respectively by a certain number of armed forces of the detaining sides to the above-mentioned areas of custody designated respectively by both sides to be turned over to the Neutral Nations Repatriation Commission and the armed forces of India for custody.   After the prisoners of war have been taken over, the armed forces of the detaining sides shall be withdrawn immediately from the areas of custody to the area under the control of their own side.

c. The personnel of the Neutral Nations Repatriation Commission and its subordinate bodies, the armed forces of India, the Red Cross Society of India, the explaining representatives and observation representatives of both sides, as well as the required material and equipment, for exercising the function provided for in the terms of reference for Neutral Nations Repatriation Commission shall be specifically authorized by the Military Armistice Commission to have the complete freedom of movement to, from, and within the above-mentioned areas designated respectively by both sides for the custody of prisoners of war.

4. The provisions of subparagraph 3C of this agreement shall not be construed as derogating from the privileges enjoyed by those personnel mentioned above under Paragraph 11, Article I, of the armistice agreement.

5. This agreement shall be abrogated upon the completion of the mission provided for in the terms of reference for Neutral Nations Repatriation Commission.

Done at Panmunjom, Korea, at 1000 hours on the 27th day of July 1953, in Korean, Chinese, and English, all texts being equally authentic.

60. STATEMENT BY PRESIDENT EISENHOWER TO THE NATION, JULY 26, 1953 [13]

My fellow citizens: Tonight we greet, with prayers of Thanksgiving, the official news that an armistice was signed almost an hour ago in Korea. It will quickly bring to an end the fighting between the United forces and the Communist armies. For this Nation the cost of repelling aggression has been high. In thousands of homes it has been incalculable. It has been paid in terms of tragedy.

With special feeling of sorrow—and of solemn gratitude—we think of those who were called upon to lay down their lives in that far-off land to prove once again that only courage and sacrifice can keep freedom alive upon the earth. To the widows and orphans of this war, and to those veterans who bear disabling wounds, America renews tonight her pledge of lasting devotion and care.

Our thoughts turn also to those other Americans wearied by many months of imprisonment behind the enemy lines. The swift return of all of them will bring joy to thousands of families. It will be evi-

---

dence of good faith on the part of those with whom we have signed this armistice.

Soldiers, sailors, and airmen of sixteen different countries have stood as partners beside us throughout these long and bitter months. America's thanks go to each. In this struggle we have seen the United Nations meet the challege of aggression—not with pathetic words of protest, but with deeds of decisive purpose. It is proper that we salute particularly the valorous armies of the Republic of Korea, for they have done even more than prove their right to freedom. Inspired by President Syngman Rhee, they have given an example of courage and patriotism which again demonstrates that men of the West and men of the East can fight and work and live together side by side in pursuit of a just and noble cause.

And so at long last the carnage of war is to cease and the negotiations of the conference table is to begin. On this Sabbath evening each of us devoutly prays that all nations may come to see the wisdom of composing differences in this fashion before, rather than after, there is resort to brutal and futile battle.

Now as we strive to bring about that wisdom, there is, in this moment of sober satisfaction, one thought that must discipline our emotions and steady our resolution. It is this: We have won an armistice on a single battleground—not peace in the world. We may not now relax our guard nor cease our quest.

Throughout the coming months, during the period of prisoner screening and exchange, and during the possibly longer period of the political conference which looks toward the unification of Korea, we and our United Nations Allies must be vigilant against the posssibility of untoward developments.

And as we do so, we shall fervently strive to insure that this armistice will, in fact, bring free peoples one step nearer to their goal of a world at peace.

My friends, almost ninety years ago, Abraham Lincoln at the end of a war delivered his Second Inaugural Address. At the end of that speech he spoke some words that I think more nearly express the true feeling of America tonight than would any other words ever spoken or written. You will recall them:

"With malice toward none; with charity for all; with firmness in the right as God gives us to see the right, let us strive on to finish the work we are in * * * to do all which may achieve and cherish a just and a lasting peace, among ourselves, with all nations."

This is our resolve and our dedication.

61. MESSAGE FROM PRESIDENT EISENHOWER TO THE CONGRESS, JULY 27, 1953, REQUESTING APPROPRIATIONS FOR REHABILITATION AND ECONOMIC SUPPORT OF THE REPUBLIC OF KOREA [14]

To the Congress of the United States:

The signing of the truce in Korea makes it imperative that the United States immediately initate a program of expanded aid to the Republic of Korea to assist in its rehabilitation and economic support. Such a program, affecting the whole future of the Republic of Korea, must extend over several years, and I shall make further recommendations concerning that program to the Congress at its next session.

---

[14] H. Doc. 215, 83d Cong.

At this time I urge upon the Congress the passage of interim legislation which will authorize the President to use, for the rehabilitation and economic support of the Republic of Korea, a sum up to $200 million from the savings in expenditures in the Department of Defense that result from the cessation of hostilities.

The need for this action can quickly and accurately be measured in two ways: One is the critical need of Korea at the end of 3 years of tragic and devastating warfare. The second is the opportunity which this occasion presents the free world to prove its will and capacity to do constructive good in the cause of freedom and peace.

The extent of devastation suffered by the people and the economy of Korea is staggering. Since the outbreak of war in 1950, 1 million South Koreans have been killed; more than 2½ million have become homeless refugees; 5 million depend in whole or in part upon relief to stay alive. Property destruction exceeds $1 billion. This colossal economic disaster has made all the more remarkable the courage and magnitude of the Republic of Korea's military effort.

This Government has been constantly aware that all that has been won by this valiant struggle could be imperiled and lost by an economic collapse. Poverty and despair could inflict wounds beyond the power of enemy guns. Knowing this, we and our allies, throughout the period of hostilities, took necessary measures to keep the Korean economy from buckling under the strain. We were able, through "Defense" appropriations, to meet minimum relief needs and to contain the threats of disease and unrest. We contributed important support to the program of the United Nations Korean Reconstruction Agency. We provided important incidental benefits to the Korean economy through payments to the Republic of Korea for local currency requirements of our military forces.

But these measures cannot suffice. They were necessarily designed to meet the immediate exigencies of fighting a war. They cannot be expected either to meet the huge total cost of this effort or to set the foundation for a healthy peacetime economy.

The facing of these needs has been the subject of the most careful study. I directed that a firsthand survey of them be undertaken in Korea more than 3 months ago. The completed survey has been reviewed by the National Security Council. On the basis of its analysis and recommendation, I am convinced that the security interests of the United States clearly indicate the need to act promptly not only to meet immediate relief needs but also to begin the long-range work of restoring the Korean economy to health and strength.

While this program is geared to meeting simply indispensable needs, its precise shape in the future must to some extent be governed by future events. It must take account of the fact that our objectives in Korea are not completely attained so long as Korea remains divided; and the assistance now proposed is carefully designed to avoid projects which would prove valueless in a united country. The implementation of the program will depend upon the continued cooperation of the Government of the Republic of Korea with the United States and the United Nations Command.

There is, as I have said, a second fact beyond the desperate need of Korea which, I believe, must govern our action at this time. It is the chance—and the need—for the free peoples to give clear and tangible testimony to their awareness that true peace means more than the simple absence of war. It means moral and material health. It means political order and economic progress. It means the living hope, in the hearts of all peoples, that tomorrow can bring a more just, a more free, a more productive life than today.

No people on earth has proved more valiantly than the people of Korea their right to hold and cherish this hope. Ours is the task to help and nourish this hope—for the sake of one brave people, and for the sake of all peoples who wait and watch to see if free men can be as wise in the ways of peace as they have proved courageous in the ways of war.

DWIGHT D. EISENHOWER.

THE WHITE HOUSE, *July 27, 1953.*

JOINT RESOLUTION Making appropriations for relief and rehabilitation in Korea, and for other purposes

Resolved by the Senate and House of Representatives of the United States of America in Congress assembled, That there are hereby appropriated, out of funds available to the Department of Defense for the fiscal year 1954 and certified by the Secretary of Defense to be saved as a result of the armistice in Korea, not to exceed $200,000,000 to be available, under such terms and conditions as the President may specify and through such officers or agencies as he may designate, for relief and rehabilitation in Korea: *Provided,* That funds appropriated hereunder shall be used only in such parts of Korea as the President deems to be not under Communist control.

62. DECLARATION OF THE SIXTEEN NATIONS RELATING TO THE ARMISTICE, JULY 27, 1953 [14a]

"We the United Nations Members whose military forces are participating in the Korean action support the decision of the Commander-in-Chief of the United Nations Command to conclude an armistice agreement. We hereby affirm our determination fully and faithfully to carry out the terms of that armistice. We expect that the other parties to the agreement will likewise scrupulously observe its terms.

"The task ahead is not an easy one. We will support the efforts of the United Nations to bring about an equitable settlement in Korea based on the principles which have long been established by the United Nations, and which call for a united, independent and democratic Korea. We will support the United Nations in its efforts to assist the people of Korea in repairing the ravages of war.

"We declare again our faith in the principles and purposes of the United Nations, our consciousness of our continuing responsibilities in Korea, and our determination in good faith to seek a settlement of the Korean problem. We affirm, in the interests of world peace, that if there is a renewal of the armed attack, challenging again the principles of the United Nations, we should again be united and prompt to resist. The consequences of such a breach of the armistice would be so grave that, in all probability, it would not be possible to confine hostilities within the frontiers of Korea.

"Finally, we are of the opinion that the armistice must not result in jeopardizing the restoration or the safeguarding of peace in any other part of Asia."

[14a] U. N. Document S/3079, August 7, 1953, made public August 7, 1953. See also p. 130.

63. STATEMENTS BY SECRETARY OF STATE DULLES, JULY 28, 1953

A. Meetings With President Syngman Rhee [15]

During the course of the negotiations and discussions which preceded the conclusion of the Korean armistice, I indicated to President Rhee that I would be disposed upon the conclusion of an armistice, promptly to meet with him to discuss a number of matters of common concern which will come up during the armistice period.

I received yesterday a very cordial invitation from President Rhee to come to Korea, and I expect to leave probably on next Sunday morning.

There will be three major problems which we have to discuss.

The first will be the development of the political conference and the effort to work out common positions between ourselves and the Republic of Korea with reference to the conduct of that political conference, which has as its two identified goals the withdrawal of foreign forces from Korea and the peaceful settlement of the Korean question, which is interpreted to mean the unification of Korea. Those were the two items specifically mentioned in the armistice terms.

Secondly, there will be the problem of working out the program of economic rehabilitation for the Republic of Korea, for which certain sums are now available, and for which the President yesterday requested from Congress an additional appropriation of $200,000,000. The problem of administration of that rehabilitation program is something to be discussed.

Thirdly, there is the negotiation of a security pact, which we told President Rhee we would be prepared to negotiate with him upon the conclusion of an armistice. In view of the problem of negotiating that treaty and of the constitutional role of the Senate in relation to it, that such treaties shall be made with the advice and consent of the Senate, I am asking Senators on a bipartisan basis to accompany me. I hope that Senator William F. Knowland and Senator H. Alexander Smith on the Republican side, and Senator Lyndon B. Johnson and Senator Richard Russell on the Democratic side will accompany me to Korea for the purpose of participating in the negotiation of the proposed security pact.

I look forward to going back to Korea. I was there, as you perhaps recall, a few days before this war began; I was there while the war was going on, and it will be a pleasure to be there again after the war has come to an end—at least the fighting has stopped, and particularly to see again my very good friend, President Rhee. Our trip will probably be a short trip, I hope to get back here within about a week.

B. Conditions Under Which the United States Would Withdraw From the Korean Political Conference [16]

I think that what there is to say has already been said, but I will be glad to try to make it clearer. We have agreed through Assistant Secretary Robertson that if after 90 days it seems that the conference is a sham and unproductive and is being availed of by the Communists

---

[15] Department of State Press Release 402, July 28, 1953.
[16] Department of State Press Release 403, July 28, 1953.

as a cover for carrying on subversive activities in Korea, we would join with President Rhee in walking out of the Political Conference.

We will make our own decision on this as the conference progresses.

We have made it clear to President Rhee, however, that we would not automatically resume war at that time. It was made clear to him that the question of what, if anything, we would do would be a matter for discussion and agreement at that time in the light of the surrounding circumstances.

C. Unification of Korea [17]

I have not only the hope, but I have the faith and belief that it is possible to detach satellite areas. I don't proceed on the theory that the only areas that get detached from their present orbit are free world countries. I think it can work both ways, and I think some of the things that are going on in the satellite areas of Europe—in the Soviet sector of Berlin and in the Soviet Zone of Germany and Czechoslovakia—all indicate that there can be an attraction of those areas to the Western world so strong that it will not seem worthwhile for the Soviet masters to try to keep them under their rule.

As far as I personally am concerned, I think I have made it clear I would not be prepared on behalf of the United States to try to buy the unity of Korea at the price of a concession which would involve bringing Communist China into the United Nations and, above all, into the Security Council.

64. STATEMENT BY SECRETARY OF STATE DULLES UPON DEPARTURE FOR KOREA [18]

Three years of fighting in Korea has now been brought to an end. And we go on to the second phase of our task, the search for a peace with justice. This, of course, raises many new and difficult problems. But at least they are problems to be solved by peaceful means and not by stopping bullets with the bodies of our boys.

I promised President Syngman Rhee of the Republic of Korea, a personal friend, that if there was an armistice in which he cooperated, I would go out to meet him so that we could develop common attitudes in relation to the political conference to follow the armistice. I am now fulfilling that promise.

The fact that President Rhee and I are meeting does not mean that our two Governments exclude the viewpoint of other interested Governments. We, with all our allies, agree that Korea should be unified. Thus, it is clearly appropriate that there should be a preliminary exchange of views with the Government of the Republic of Korea, which was the victim of the Communist aggression and which contributed so mightily to stopping that aggression. But the United States will not finally determine its position in relation to the Political conference and its procedures until we have had the benefit of wider consultation.

I was in Korea the week when the Communist aggression began. I was there while the fighting was under way. And it is now a great pleasure for me to return when the Republic of Korea, with the help of the United Nations, is gallantly emerging from its great trial.

[17] Department of State Press Release 404, July 28, 1953.
[18] Department of State Press Release 416, August 2, 1953.

I hope and believe that the future of our two countries which have been so close in war will now be transferred to an even closer friendship in peace.

I regret that the bipartisan group of Senators—William F. Knowland, H. Alexander Smith, Lyndon B. Johnson, Richard B. Russell—will be unable to accompany me. There is still a chance, though I fear this morning a rather slight chance, that they might join me later. The reason I leave today, without waiting for the Congress to adjourn, is that the United Nations General Assembly will meet August 17 and it is important for us to be back before that time.

65. STATEMENT BY SECRETARY OF STATE DULLES AND PRESIDENT RHEE, AUGUST 7, 1953 [19]

Our friendly and understanding consultations demonstrate clearly the determination of the United States and the Republic of Korea to stand together in cordial cooperation to achieve our common objectives, including the reunification of Korea.

We have today initialed a draft of a mutual-defense treaty. That treaty is designed to unit our nations in common action to meet common danger and it will cement the ties which have brought us together to combat in Korea the menace of Communist aggression.

Our two governments will actively proceed with the constitutional processes necessary to bring this treaty into full force and effect. These constitutional processes, in the case of the United States, require that the United States Senate consent to the ratification. The United States Senate, having adjourned this week, will not again be in regular session until next January. However, United States Senate leaders have been kept fully informed of the exchange of views which have led to the action we have taken today and it is our sincere hope that this will lead to prompt and favorable United States Senate action.

Between now and the date when the Mutual Defense Treaty can be expected to come into force and effect, our armed forces in Korea will be subject to the United Nations Command which will comply with the armistice terms. If, during this period, there should occur unprovoked armed attack by the Communist forces against the Republic of Korea in violation of the armistice, the UNC, including the Republic of Korea forces, would at once and automatically react, as such an unprovoked attack would be an attack upon and a threat to the UNC itself and to the forces under its command. Such reaction to an unprovoked armed attack would not be a new war but rather a resumption by the Communist forces of the active belligerency which the armistice has halted. The UNC will be constantly alert against such an attack.

Our Governments will promptly negotiate agreements to cover the status of such forces as the United States may elect to maintain in Korea after the mutual-defense treaty comes into force and effect, and the availability to them of Korean facilities and services needed for the discharge of our common task. In the meantime, the Republic of Korea will continue to cooperate with the UNC and the status of UNC forces in Korea and the availability to them of Korean facilities and services will continue as at present.

---

[19] Department of State Press Release 424, August 7, 1953.

The armistice contemplates that a political conference will be convened within three months, that is, prior to October 27, 1953. At that conference the United States delegation, in cooperation with the ROK delegation and other delegations from the UNC side, will seek to achieve the peaceful unification of historic Korea as a free and independent nation. We and our advisers have already had a full and satisfactory exchange of views which we hope and trust will establish a preparatory foundation for coordinated effort at the political conference.

If, after the political conference has been in session for 90 days, it becomes clear to each of our governments that all attempts to achieve these objectives have been fruitless and that the conference is being exploited by the Communist delegates mainly to infiltrate, propagandize or otherwise embarrass the Republic of Korea, we shall then be prepared to make a concurrent withdrawal from the conference. We will then consult further regarding the attainment of a unified, free and independent Korea which is the postwar goal the United States set itself during World War II, which has been accepted by the United Nations as its goal and whch will continue to be an object of concern of United States foreign policy.

We recognize that the Republic of Korea possesses the inherent right of sovereignty to deal with its problems, but it has agreed to take no unilateral action to unite Korea by military means for the agreed duration of the political conference.

We contemplate that the projected three to four year program for the rehabilitation of the war ruined Korean economy shall be coordinated through the combined economic board, under the joint chairmanship of the Korean and American representatives. This program contemplates the expenditure of approximately one billion dollars of funds, subject to appropriations thereof by the United States Congress. Two hundred million dollars has already been authorized, out of prospective defense savings.

We have exchanged preliminary views with respect to various problems involving the maintenance and development of ROK land, air and sea forces.

We feel confident that the relationship thus established between our two governments marks an important contribution to the developing of independence and freedom in the Far East. With unshaking faith in the principle of collective security, and with loyal adherence to the Charter of the United Nations, we intend to move forward together toward the achievement of our common objective—the restoration of a unified, democratic and independent Korean nation.

There are no other agreements or understandings stated or implied resulting from these consultations other than those herein contained.

66. DRAFT OF REPUBLIC OF KOREA-UNITED STATES MUTUAL DEFENSE TREATY, AUGUST 8, 1953 [20]

The Parties to this Treaty, reaffirming their desire to live in peace with all peoples and all governments, and desiring to strengthen the fabric of peace in the Pacific Area, desiring to declare publicly and formally their common determination to defend themselves against external armed attack so that no potential aggressor could be under

---

[20] Department of State Press Release 426, August 7, 1953.

the illusion that either of them stands alone in the Pacific Area, de-siring further to strengthen their efforts for collective defense for the preservation of peace and security pending the development of a more comprehensive and effective system of regional security in the Pacific Area have agreed as follows:

Article I. The Parties undertake to settle any international dis-putes in which they may be involved by peaceful means in such a manner that international peace and security and justice are not en-dangered and to refrain in their international relations from the threat or use of force in any manner inconsistent with the purposes of the United Nations, or obligations assumed by any Party toward the United Nations.

Article II. The Parties will consult together whenever, in the opin-ion of either of them, the political independence, or security of either of the Parties is threatened by external armed attack. Separately and jointly, by self help and mutual aid, the Parties will maintain and develop appropriate means to deter armed attack and will take suitable measures in consultation and agreement to implement this Treaty and to further its purposes.

Article III. Each Party recognizes that an armed attack in the Pacific Area on either of the Parties in territories now under their respective administrative control, or hereafter recognized by one of the Parties as lawfully brought under the administrative control of the other, would be dangerous to its own peace and safety and declares that it would act to meet the common danger in accordance with its constitutional processes.

Article IV. The Republic of Korea grants, and the United States of America accepts, the right to dispose United States land, air and sea forces in and about the territory of the Republic of Korea as determined by mutual agreement.

Article V. This Treaty shall be ratified by the Republic of Korea and the United States of America in accordance with their respective constitutional processes and will come into force when instruments of ratification thereof have been exchanged by them at _____________.

Article VI. This Treaty shall remain in force indefinitely. Either Party may terminate it one year after notice has been given to the other Party.

In witness whereof the undersigned plenipotentiaries have signed this Treaty.

Done in duplicate at Seoul this 8th day of August.

For the United States of America: John Foster Dulles.

For the Republic of Korea: Syngman Rhee.

67. STATEMENT BY DEPARTMENT OF STATE [21]

The State Department is gravely concerned by reports that the Communists may not intend to return all of our prisoners now in their custody. It has long been believed on good authority that the Soviet Union still holds an unknown number of World War II pris-oners of different nationalities, and it was with this in mind that we insisted on a clause in the armistice agreement which provided that any United Nations personnel who are said not to desire repatriation must nevertheless be transferred to the custody of the Repatriation

---

[21] Department of State Press Release 428, August 8, 1953.

Commission where United Nations and United States officials will have access to them. This would include any prisoners alleged to have been given "jail sentences." None is exempt.

We must avoid action which might jeopardize the safety or liberty of our prisoners now in Communist hands. The progress of the prisoner exchange is being watched closely and appropriate action will be taken just as soon as definite facts are established.

68. REPORT OF THE UNIFIED COMMAND ON THE ARMISTICE IN KOREA [22]

LETTER DATED 7 AUGUST 1953 FROM THE ACTING UNITED STATES REPRESENTATIVE TO THE UNITED NATIONS, ADDRESSED TO THE SECRETARY-GENERAL, TRANSMITTING A SPECIAL REPORT OF THE UNIFIED COMMAND ON THE ARMISTICE IN KOREA IN ACCORDANCE WITH THE SECURITY COUNCIL RESOLUTION OF 7 JULY 1950 (S/1588)

I have the honor to refer to paragraph 6 of the resolution of the Security Council of 7 July 1950, requesting the United States to provide the Security Council with reports, as appropriate, on the course of action taken under the United Nations Command.

In compliance with this resolution, there is enclosed herewith, for circulation to the members of the Security Council, a special report of the Unified Command on the armistice in Korea. With this report the Unified Command is submitting the official text of the Armistice Agreement entered into in Korea on 27 July 1953.

I would be grateful if you also would circulate copies of this special report and the Armistice Agreement to the Members of the General Assembly for their information.[22]

(*Signed*)   JAMES J. WADSWORTH,
Acting United States Representative to the United Nations.

SPECIAL REPORT OF THE UNIFIED COMMAND ON THE ARMISTICE IN KOREA

I. FOREWORD

The Government of the United States, as the Unified Command, transmits herewith a special report on the United Nations action against aggression in Korea, together with a copy of the official text of the Armistice Agreement concluded by the Commander-in-Chief, United Nations Command, the Supreme Commander of the Korean People's Army, and the Commander of the Chinese People's Volunteers.

The agreement was signed by Lt. General William K. Harrison, Senior Delegate, United Nations Command Delegation, and by General Nam Il, Senior Delegate, Delegation of the Korean People's Army and Chinese People's Volunteers, at 10.00 a. m., 27 July 1953. It was subsequently signed by Mark W. Clark, Commander-in-Chief, United Nations Command, and by Peng Teh-Huai, Commander of the Chinese People's Volunteers, and Kim Il Sung, Marshal, Democratic People's Republic of Korea, Supreme Commander, Korean People's Army. In accordance with the terms of the Armistice Agreement, hostilities ceased at 2200 hours on 27 July 1953, and the Armistice Agreement became effective at that time.

The Armistice Agreement is a military agreement between military commanders. It is intended to make possible a final peaceful settlement and assumes that this end will, in good faith, be pursued. The authority of the Unified Command under the resolutions of the Security Council of 27 June and 7 July 1950 to conduct military operations in Korea against aggression included also the authority to negotiate a military armistice to end the fighting on a basis con-

___
[22] U. N. Document S/3079, August 7, 1953.

sistent with United Nations objectives and principles. The authority of the Unified Command to conclude an armistice and the desirability of an armistice generally along the lines finally incorporated in the Armistice Agreement of 27 July 1953 were in effect affirmed by the General Assembly in its resolution of 3 December 1952.

The Armistice Agreement has brought about a cessation of hostilities in Korea after more than thirty-seven months of bloodshed and destruction resulting from the Communist aggression. The armistice was signed more than twenty-five months after the first indications that, due to the achievements of United Nations forces in Korea and the determination of the United Nations to bring an honourable end to the fighting in Korea, the Communist aggressors were prepared to consider ending hostilities. During these twenty-five months the representatives of the United Nations Command negotiated in good faith and made every effort to achieve an armistice. It was not until the spring of 1953 that the Communists appeared ready to settle the outstanding issues on an honourable basis. The intransigence of the aggressors was responsible for the continued loss of life and destruction and for the long delay in bringing the armistice negotiations to a successful conclusion.

In negotiating this Armistice Agreement, the United Nations Command has been guided by the basic objectives of the United Nations military action in Korea—to repel the aggression against the Republic of Korea and to restore international peace and security in the area. The Agreement leaves the forces of the Republic of Korea and of the United Nations in strong defensive positions and contains provisions offering reasonable assurances against renewal of the aggression.

As safeguards against resumption of hostilities there are provisions for a Demilitarized Zone, with a Military Armistice Commission composed of representatives of both sides responsible for supervising the implementation of the Armistice and for settling any violations of the Agreement. There are also provisions prohibiting the introduction into Korea of reinforcing military personnel, combat aircraft, armored vehicles, weapons and ammunition, together with arrangements for supervision and inspection to observe compliance with these prohibitions.

The armistice is in full accord with the humanitarian principles of the United Nations. A separate Agreement entered into on 8 June 1953, supplemented by an Agreement of 27 July attached to and incorporated by reference in the Armistice Agreement, provides for the exchange of captured personnel on a basis consistent with the principles of the United Nations resolution (VII) of 3 December 1952. It satisfies in particular the provision in that resolution that "force shall not be used against the prisoners of war to prevent or effect their return to their homelands . . . ."

Attention is called to paragraph 60 of the Armistice Agreement, which recommends to the governments of the countries concerned on both sides that within three months after the signature of the armistice a political conference be held to settle through negotiation "the questions of the withdrawal of all foreign forces from Korea, the peaceful settlement of the Korean question, etc." This recommendation has also been communicated to the governments of the other fifteen Members of the United Nations whose armed forces are participating in the Korean action and to the Government of the Republic of Korea.

The United Nations Command will do its utmost to ensure fulfilment of the terms of the Armistice Agreement. There can, of course, be no certain guarantee that the Communists will abide by its terms. The armistice, moreover, does not contain all the assurances against the renewal of aggression that might be desired. It became clear at the end of 1951 that it would not be possible to obtain all the arrangements behind enemy lines which the United Nations Command might have considered desirable. Moreover, while the safeguards achieved in the armistice are important, basically maximum assurance against the renewal of attack by the Communist lies in their knowledge that such unprovoked attack would meet with prompt reaction by the United Nations forces. The Unified Command, therefore, agreed to waive certain safeguards (e. g., in regard to the construction and rehabilitation of military airfields in North Korea) but asked that governments with forces under the Command should make clear in a Declaration to be issued after the signature of an armistice that if there was an unprovoked renewal of the armed attack by the Communists the sixteen governments would again be united and prompt to resist. This arrangement was agreed upon in January 1952, by the sixteen Members of the United Nations whose armed forces were participating in the Korean action. The Declaration signed by representatives of the sixteen participating nations in Washington on 27 July 1953, shortly after the signature of the Armistice Agreement, provides:

"We the United Nations Members whose military forces are participating in the Korean action support the decision of the Commander-in-Chief of the United Nations Command to conclude an armistice agreement. We hereby affirm our determination fully and faithfully to carry out the terms of that armistice. We expect that the other parties to the agreement will likewise scrupulously observe its terms.

"The task ahead is not an easy one. We will support the efforts of the United Nations to bring about an equitable settlement in Korea based on the principles which have long been established by the United Nations, and which call for a united, independent and democratic Korea. We will support the United Nations in its efforts to assist the people of Korea in repairing the ravages of war.

"We declare again our faith in the principles and purposes of the United Nations, our consciousness of our continuing responsibilities in Korea, and our determination in good faith to seek a settlement of the Korean problem. We affirm, in the interests of world peace, that if there is a renewal of the armed attack, challenging again the principles of the United Nations, we should again be united and prompt to resist. The consequences of such a breach of the armistice would be so grave that, in all probability, it would not be possible to confine hostilities within the frontiers of Korea.

"Finally, we are of the opinion that the armistice must not result in jeopardizing the restoration or the safeguarding of peace in any other part of Asia."

The achievement in Korea is a collective achievement. The people of Korea and the people of the world are indebted to the men of many countries, namely, Australia, Belgium, Colombia, Canada, Ethiopia, France, Greece, Luxembourg, the Philippines, the Netherlands, New Zealand, Thailand, Turkey, Union of South Africa, the United Kingdom and the United States, who fought side by side with the forces of the Republic of Korea that aggression should not succeed. They were given assistance by the hospital units of Denmark, India, Italy, Norway, and Sweden. Many other nations which made supporting contributions of other kinds also deserve the appreciation of the United Nations.

11. MILITARY ACTION

The course of military action during most of the fighting was described in the special report of the Unified Command of 18 October 1952 (A/2228). The United Nations forces, after being compelled to withdraw southward by the intervention of massive Chinese Communist forces, took the initiative in early 1951 and by March succeeded in advancing to a line across central Korea. The Communist armies were compelled by consistent pressure from United Nations forces to withdraw slowly northward, and by June 1951 United Nations forces occupied positions generally north of the 38th parallel.

After the opening of armistice negotiations, neither the United Nations forces nor the Communists undertook sustained offensive action. There was, however, consistent and often heavy military contact resulting in serious personnel casualties. During the last stages of negotiations, the Communists, on the night of 13–14 July, launched their heaviest offensive in over two years, resulting in limited advances by the Communist forces and heavy casualties to the United Nations forces, as well as appalling losses for the Communist attackers.

The operations of the United Nations Command were conducted solely for the purpose of achieving the military objective of the United Nations in Korea, i. e., repelling the aggression and restoring peace and security in Korea. For its part, the United Nations Command has sought in every way to minimize the loss of lives, and to conduct the action with the maximum respect for humanitarian considerations. The United Nations Command has never, as falsely charged in Communist propaganda, attacked any territory outside of Korea or used bacteriological weapons or poison gas. It has always been prepared for, and has been willing to accept, inspection to verify these facts.

The forces of the United Nations Command suffered many casualties during the thirty-seven months of fighting. The number of killed, wounded, and missing from the Armed Forces of the Republic of Korea exceeded 300,000. The total casualties of the United States Armed Forces were approximately 141,000, and of the Armed Forces of the other fifteen Members of the United Nations approximately 14,000. At the same time, United Nations forces inflicted on the enemy a far greater number of casualties. Enemy casualties are estimated at between

1½ to 2 million. It is impossible to estimate the number of civilians who lost their lives or were injured, or the damage to property as a result of hostilities. Millions of Koreans were forced by hostilities to leave their homes, and there was a mass movement of refugees constantly southward toward the areas beyond Communist control.

III. ARMISTICE NEGOTIATIONS

A. *In general*

The history of the continuing efforts of the Unified Command and of the United Nations at all times to bring an end to the fighting in Korea on an honourable basis is set forth in various documents of the United Nations. The Unified Command took numerous steps to this end on its own initiative and cooperated fully with proposals of others for bringing about peace on a basis consistent with United Nations objectives in Korea.

In July 1951, it appeared from statements made by Communist spokesmen that the aggressor forces were willing to cease hostilities. However, the hopes of the Unified Command for quickly concluding an agreement that would stop the fighting soon proved illusory. Time after time the Communists stalled, injected extraneous issues, endeavoured to use the negotiations for propaganda purposes, and otherwise indicated a lack of good faith. Despite these obstacles the United Nations negotiators consistently evinced a willingness to reach agreement.

The United Nations Command was determined that the Armistice Agreement must contribute to the achievement of the basic purposes of the United Nations military action in Korea—to repel the aggression against the Republic of Korea and to restore peace and security in the area. The United Nations Command therefore insisted on the following requirements :

(1) A line of demarcation based upon military realities and affording defensible positions for the opposing forces, consistent with the United Nations objective of repelling aggression ;

(2) Other provisions offering maximum reasonable assurance against a renewal of the aggression ;

(3) Appropriate arrangements for an exchange of prisoners of war on a basis that would ensure the return of United Nations Command prisoners of war and the disposition of prisoners safeguarding the right of asylum, consistent with international law, the Geneva Convention, and humanitarian principles.

So long as the Communists refused to agree to an armistice on this basis, the United Nations Command was compelled to insist on the continuation of the fighting in accordance with the resolutions of the Security Council and the General Assembly, so as to compel the enemy to accept an honourable end to the fighting.

B. *Early obstacles to agreement*

(1) *The agenda and the conference site.*—At the very beginning of negotiations the Communists raised issues calculated to delay them. They sought adoption of an agenda that would prejudice in their favour the substance of the items to be discussed. The Communists sought, for example, to obtain agreement on language in the agenda recognizing the 38th parallel as the line of demarcation for the cease-fire. The Communists also proposed an agenda item on the withdrawal of foreign forces from Korea. The United Nations Command insisted on an objective agenda, and one was finally adopted. The question of the withdrawal of foreign troops was rejected as beyond the scope of military negotiations.

Delay was also occasioned by Communist violations of the neutrality of the conference area and failure to provide equal treatment to both delegations as originally promised. Fabricated charges by the Communists that the United Nations Command had violated the neutrality of the conference area led to suspension of the talks for two months from August to October 1951.

(2) *Arrangements for implementing the armistice.*—The armistice, of course, had to contain provisions for putting an end to the fighting. The United Nations Command delegation also sought arrangements which would make renewal of the hostilities less likely. The negotiations on these matters were extended and painstaking. The United Nations Command delegation wanted the broadest possible access to all parts of Korea for a supervisory body to ensure against violations of the armistice. It was quite willing to have such inspection behind its own lines. The Communists, however, for some time resisted all proposals for inspection and finally agreed to it only on a limited scale. At one point, the United Nations Command proposed inspection of the implementation of the armistice by joint teams to operate throughout Korea. Following Communist rejec-

tion of this proposal, agreement was reached on arrangements for inspection by observers drawn from countries not participating in the Korean action and acceptable to both sides. But the Communists further delayed the negotiations by nominating the Soviet Union as a "neutral"; this was of course unacceptable to the United Nations Command.

The United Nations Command proposed a ban, applicable to both sides, on the construction of new military airfields and a ceiling on the number of civilian airfields that could be rehabilitated. Such a prohibition would have made resumption of the aggression more difficult and less likely. The Communists adamantly refused to agree to such a limitation.

(3) *Prisoners of war.*—The issue that, in appearance at least, contributed most to the delay in achieving an armistice involved the repatriation of prisoners of war. From the outset the United Nations Command made it clear that, while it was prepared to repatriate all the prisoners of war in its custody, it would not agree to use force against prisoners resisting return to the Communists. The Communists stubbornly insisted, however, that all prisoners of war must be returned, by force if necessary.

In an extraordinary effort to break the long continuing deadlock on this issue the United Nations Command, on 28 April 1952, offered a "package proposal" providing that (a) there shall not be forced repatriation of prisoners of war; (b) that the United Nations Command will not insist on prohibiting reconstruction and rehabilitation of airfields; and (c) the United Nations Command agrees to accept Poland and Czechoslovakia as members of the Neutral Nations Supervisory Commission if the Communists agree to accept Sweden and Switzerland (thus withdrawing their demand for the inclusion of the Soviet Union).

The United Nations Command made it clear that this proposal must be accepted as a unit. The Communists, however, purported to accept the second and third points only, remaining adamant on prisoners of war. As a result of their rejection, the armistice was delayed and the fighting continued for fifteen additional months. They persisted in this inhumane attitude for many months, contrary to international law and in the face of preponderant world opinion, even after the principle of nonforcible repatriation was approved by fifty-four Members of the United Nations who supported the General Assembly resolution of 3 December 1952. Communist intransigence, and Communist failure to bargain in good faith on this issue, compelled the United Nations Command to recess the plenary negotiations on 8 October 1952. They were not resumed until 26 April 1953, when the Communists finally indicated that they were prepared to consider a solution for the prisoner of war question consistent with humanitarian principles and the principles of the General Assembly resolution.

C. The agreements finally reached

All the agreements between the United Nations Command Delegation and the Communist Delegation are set forth in the attached Armistice Agreement and the Prisoner of War Agreement with the Supplementary Agreement of 27 July attached to it. In some cases, as the record of the negotiations indicates, the United Nations Command recorded its understanding as to the meaning of phrases in the Armistice Agreement that might otherwise be ambiguous.

(1) *The Military Demarcation line.*—The Communists delayed negotiations for some time by insisting that the demarcation line between both sides should be the 38th parallel. Finally, however, they recognized the merit of the United Nations Command position that the line should be determined strictly on military grounds and should correspond to the actual line of contact between the opposing forces. The objective of the United Nations Command in insisting on such a line was to provide maximum defensive safeguards against a possible renewal of the aggression.

The line of demarcation was first marked out on 27 November 1951, on the basis of the line of contact as of that time. It was then agreed that this should be the final demarcation line, provided an armistice was achieved within thirty days; otherwise the line should be redrawn on the basis of the line of contact at the time of the armistice. In fact, tentative agreement was reached on a new line in June 1953, when it seemed that an armistice could be signed within a very few days, but the Communists insisted that it be redrawn again to take account of the results of the offensive they launched on 13–14 July 1953. The Demarcation Line was finally agreed on the basis indicated in the map attached to the Armistice Agreement. The Demilitarized Zone was established in accordance with the agreement, each side withdrawing its forces two kilometres north and south of the Demarcation Line respectively.

(2) *Arrangements for implementing the armistice.*—With the exception of the continuing disagreement on the rehabilitation of airfields, the arrangements for implementing the armistice were virtually completed by March 1952. The United Nations Command finally gave up its insistence on the limitation of airfields when it signed the armistice. The agreements on this subject may be summarized as follows:

1. There will be a cease-fire within twelve hours of the signing of an armistice.

2. Both sides will withdraw their forces from the Demilitarized Zone within seventy-two hours after the signing of an armistice.

3. All military forces will be withdrawn from rear areas and the coastal islands and waters of Korean within five days after the signing of an armistice.

4. Both sides shall cease the introduction into Korea of reinforcing military personnel. However, the rotation of 35,000 military personnel a month shall be permitted. Rotated personnel shall enter Korea only through designated ports of entry, under the supervision and inspection of the teams of the Neutral Nations Supervisory Commission.

5. Both sides shall cease the introduction into Korea of reinforcing combat aircraft, amoured vehicles, weapons and ammunition. However, the replacement of destroyed, damaged, worn-out or used up equipment on the basis of piece-for-piece of the same effectiveness and the same type is permitted. Such replacement shall take place only through designated ports of entry, under the supervision and inspection of teams of the Neutral Nations Supervisory Commission.

6. A Military Armistice Commission, with headquarters at Panmunjom composed of military officers of the United Nations Command and the Communist forces and aided by Joint Observer Teams will:

(a) Supervise the implementation of the Armistice Agreement;

(b) Deal with alleged armistice violations and settle through negotiations any such violations;

(c) Report all violations of the Armistice Agreement to the Commanders of the opposing sides.

7. A Neutral Nations Supervisory Commission, with headquarters in proximity to those of the Military Armistice Commission, composed of four senior officers, two of whom shall be appointed by neutral nations nominated by the United Nations Command and two of whom shall be appointed by neutral nations nominated jointly by the Supreme Commander of the Korean People's Army and the Commander of the Chinese People's Volunteers will supervise, observe, inspect, and investigate adherence to the terms of the armistice agreement relative to the introduction into Korea of reinforcing military personnel and equipment. At the request of the Military Armistice Commission or senior member of either side, it can conduct special observation and inspection at places outside the demilitarized zone where violations have been reported. Twenty inspection teams, ten of which will be located at the designated ports of entry, five in North Korea and five in South Korea, with ten mobile teams in reserve, will assist the Commission.

(3) *The political conference following an armistice.*—In order to counter the constant efforts of the Communists to inject political questions into the Korean armistice negotiations, and to prevent such extraneous issues from delaying armistice negotiations, the United Nations Command agreed to dispose of political questions by recommending their consideration at a political conference following an armistice. The United Nations Command Delegation accepted a revised Communist proposal now contained in article 60 of the Armistice Agreement, which provides:

"In order to insure the peaceful settlement of the Korean question, the military Commanders of both sides hereby recommend to the governments of the countries concerned on both sides that, within three (3) months after the Armistice Agreement is signed and becomes effective, a political conference of a higher level of both sides be held by representatives appointed respectively to settle through negotiation the questions of the withdrawal of all foreign forces from Korea, the peaceful settlement of the Korean question, etc.".

(4) *Prisoners of war.*—The background of this question, and the position of the United Nations Command was outlined in the Special Unified Command report of 18 October 1952 (A/2228). As indicated at that time, the only issue preventing agreement was Communist insistence that all prisoners of war must be repatriated, even if the use of force should be necessary to effect their return, and United Nations Command refusal to use force against such unwilling

prisoners. When the Communists insisted that there were in fact no prisoners who refused to be repatriated, but that the United Nations Command was detaining them against their will, the United Nations Command made numerous proposals for impartial determination of the true attitudes of the prisoners of war. The Communists refused to submit this question to the test and thus further delayed achievement of an armistice.

On 8 October 1952, the United Nations Command Delegation recessed the negotiations. In doing so, it made clear that the numerous proposals which it had made for an honourable solution of the prisoner question remained open. Whenever the Communists were prepared to negotiate in good faith, to accept any one of the United Nations Command proposals, or to make a constructive proposal of their own on the prisoner issue, the United Nations Command Delegation would be prepared to meet again.

At this juncture the Korean question came before the General Assembly, and the United States Government, as the Unified Command, reported on the state of the negotiations. It urged the Assembly to approve the principle of nonforcible repatriation and to call upon the Communists to accept an armistice on this basis. A definite plan for the solution of the prisoner-of-war question was proposed by India and discussed in the hope of gaining Communist approval, and on 3 December 1952, by a majority of 54 votes in favour, with only the Soviet bloc in opposition, the General Assembly adpoted resolution 610 (VII). This resolution specified that force should not be used against prisoners to prevent or effect their return, and it set forth a detailed series of proposals which the Assembly believed would form a just and reasonable basis for an agreement on the prisoner issue. The Communists rejected this plan, and hopes for an armistice in the foreseeable future appeared dim.

Nevertheless, the United Command continued to examine every possibility for solving the prisoner question. Seizing the opportunity offered by a resolution adopted by the Executive Committee of the League of Red Cross Societies on 13 December 1952, which appealed to the parties, as a gesture of good will, to implement the humanitarian principles of the Geneva Convention by repatriating sick and wounded prisoners of war, the Commander-in-Chief of the United Nations Command, on 22 February 1953, addressed a letter to the Communist commanders stating that the United Nations Command still remained ready to implement, immediately, the repatriation of the sick and wounded, and asking if the Communists were prepared to proceed with the repatriation of sick and wounded prisoners in their custody. The United Nations Command had made this same proposal to the Communists on a number of previous occasions during the armistice negotiations, but they had failed to respond. It was hoped that the Communists would at last agree to such an exchange, that it would bring about the return of at least some of the United Nations Command prisoners of war, and this first step might pave the way for the solution of the prisoner issue as a whole. The hopes of the United Nations Command in this regard proved not unwarranted. On 28 March the Communists agreed to the principle of the exchange of sick and wounded, which they stated "should be made to lead to the smooth settlement of the entire question of prisoners of war," and arrangements for the exchange were initiated through the respective liaison officers on 6 April.

The Communist acceptance was followed on 30 March by a statement by Chou En-lai, Foreign Minister of the Communist People's Government of the People's Republic of China, subsequently endorsed by the Prime Minister of the North Korean regime, indicating a desire to resume negotiations on the entire prisoner question and a readiness to take a more constructive and humane attitude on the question of forcible repatriation.

Sick and wounded prisoners of war were in fact exchanged between 20 April and 3 May 1953 pursuant to an agreement reached on 11 April 1953.

Negotiations by the plenary armistice delegations on the prisoner-of-war question as a whole resumed on 26 April. At the outset, the Communist submitted a proposal for sending all prisoners not directly repatriated to an agreed neutral State where for six months after their arrival representatives of the States to which they belonged would "explain" to them matters related to their return; if after this period any nonrepatriates remained, their disposition would be referred to the political conference. Discussion subsequently centered upon the questions of what neutral State should be nominated, of whether nonrepatriates should be removed from Korea, and how long the nonrepatriates would remain in neutral custody.

On 7 May, the Communists put forward a new proposal providing for establishment of a Neutral Nations Repatriation Commission to be composed of the four States already nominated for membership on the Neutral Nations Supervisory Commission, namely, Czechoslovakia, Poland, Sweden, and Switzerland, and India as agreed upon by both sides. This Commission was to take custody of the prisoners in Korea. The United Nations Command on 13 May presented a counterproposal shortening the period of time in which the non-repatriates would remain in neutral custody, providing for the release of Korean nonrepatriates immediately after the armistice, and proposing that only Indian forces take actual custody of the non-repatriates. The Communists rejected this proposal.

On 25 May, the United Nations Command, in another effort to obtain Communist agreement on an equitable solution of the prisoner issue, submitted a new proposal providing for the transfer of both Korean and Chinese nonrepatriates to neutral custody and for consideration of the disposition of any remaining nonrepatriates by the political conference for a limited period, after which they might either be released to civilian status or the question of their disposition referred to the General Assembly. On 4 June, the Communists offered a counterproposal in effect based upon the mechanics of General Assembly resolution 610 (VII), also closely paralleling the United Nations Command 25 May proposal, but vague on the basic principle of nonforcible repatriation. The United Nations Command succeeded in reaching agreement with the Communists on elaboration of the Neutral Nations Repatriation Commission's terms of reference to insure that there could be no abuse and that the principle approved by the General Assembly that force should not be used to compel or to prevent repatriation of any prisoner of war would be fully observed.

On 8 June, the Senior Delegates for the United Nations Command and for the Communists signed the Prisoner-of-War Agreement which is attached to and incorporated by reference in the Armistice Agreement. The delegations then proceeded to the final arrangements looking toward an early signature of the armistice.

As a result of discussions with the Republic of Korea, described in the succeeding section, a Supplementary Agreement on Prisoners of War was signed on 27 July 1953, which permits the United Nations Command (and the Communists if applicable), to transport the nonrepatriates to the Demilitarized Zone where the Neutral Nations Repatriation Commission will take custody of them.

D. *The Attitude of the Republic of Korea*

On 18 June an incident occurred which further delayed the achievement of an armistice at a time when the conclusion of hostilities seemed imminent. On that date, officials of the Republic of Korea brought about a breakout from prisoner-of-war camps of some 27,000 Korean prisoners of war who had previously indicated they would resist repatriation to North Korea. This action by the Republic of Korea was inconsistent with the 8 June Agreement on Prisoners of War which the United Nations Command had entered into on behalf of all the forces under its command. The United Nations Command at once protested the action of the Republic of Korea Government. It immediately informed the Communists of the event and told them that, while efforts would be made to recover as many of the escapees as possible, there was not much hope that many of these could be recaptured since they had melted into the South Korean population.

This incident led to immediate discussions with the Republic of Korea by representatives of the Unified Command. After prolonged conversations, the Republic of Korea gave assurances that it would not obstruct the implementation of the terms of the Armistice Agreement.

The incident, however, gave the Communists an excuse for delaying still further the conclusion of the armistice. They demanded assurances that the United Nations Command would live up to the Armistice Agreement, that the Republic of Korea and its forces would also abide by it, and that the released prisoners would be recaptured. The United Nations Command reply to the Communists stressed that the armistice was a military agreement between military commanders and that it was being entered into by the United Nations Command, as Commander of all the forces under its command, including those of the Republic of Korea. The United Nations Command Delegation also told the Communists that so far as recovering the released prisoners of war, as they had already been informed, this would be impossible; they were assured, however, that the remaining nonrepatriate prisoners would be turned over to the Neutral Nations Repatriation Commission, as provided by the agreement on prisoners of war. The Communists were assured that the United Nations Command forces (including those of the Republic of Korea) would observe the armistice. The United Nations Command informed the Communists, however, that it would not undertake to use force against the Republic of Korea forces to ensure compliance with the armistice by the Republic of Korea.

Despite these comprehensive assurances by the United Nations Command, the Communists continued to delay negotiations and in the meanwhile launched the biggest offensive in more than two years, an offensive which obviously took much planning and preparation and caused heavy casualties. Finally, however, on 19 July, the Communists stated their readiness to proceed with the final work on the Armistice Agreement leading to its signature.

The armistice was finally signed on 27 July 1953, at 10 a. m. Korean time.

IV. CONCLUSION

The fighting and bloodshed in Korea have been halted. After having caused millions of casualties, untold civilian suffering and death, economic devastation, and destruction of property, the Communist aggressors have been driven back to and beyond the point from which they started their initial attack. The heavy price of their aggression is evident.

As a result of prompt and sustained collective action of the United Nations against aggression, an armistice has been effected on a basis that promises to maintain the integrity of the Republic of Korea against further aggression and that constitutes a major step toward the establishment of peace and security for that war-torn country. These achievements have been made possible by the heroic sacrifices of the troops of the United Nations and of the Republic of Korea.

The United States stands ready to participate and cooperate fully in political discussions leading to an enduring solution of the Korean problem on the basis of the objectives of the United Nations—the achievement by peaceful means of a unified, independent, and democratic Korea. If the Communists abide by the armistice and negotiate in good faith, a true and lasting peace may yet come to the brave and long-suffering people of Korea

69. RESOLUTIONS OF THE GENERAL ASSEMBLY, AUGUST 28, 1953, ON THE CONVENING OF THE POLITICAL CONFERENCE PURSUANT TO THE KOREAN ARMISTICE AGREEMENT [23]

A

IMPLEMENTATION OF PARAGRAPH 60 OF THE KOREAN ARMISTICE AGREEMENT

The General Assembly

1. *Notes with approval* the Armistice Agreement concluded in Korea on 27 July 1953, the fact that the fighting has ceased, and that a major step has thus been taken towards the full restoration of international peace and security in the area;

2. *Reaffirms* that the objectives of the United Nations remain the achievement by peaceful means of a unified, independent and democratic Korea under a representative form of government and the full restoration of international peace and security in the area;

3. *Notes* the recommendation contained in the Armistice Agreement that "In order to ensure the peaceful settlement of the Korean question, the military Commanders of both sides hereby recommend to the governments of the countries concerned on both sides that, within three (3) months after the Armistice Agreement is signed and becomes effective, a political conference of a higher level of both sides be held by representatives appointed respectively to settle through negotiation the questions of the withdrawal of all foreign forces from Korea, the peaceful settlement of the Korean question, etc.";

---

[23] U. N. Document A/Resolution/102, August 31, 1953.

4. *Welcomes* the holding of such a conference;

5. *Recommends* that:

(a) The side contributing armed forces under the Unified Command in Korea shall have as participants in the conference those among the Member States contributing armed forces pursuant to the call of the United Nations which desire to be represented, together with the Republic of Korea. The participating governments shall act independently at the conference with full freedom of action and shall be bound only by decisions or agreements to which they adhere;

(b) The United States Government, after consultation with the other participating countries referred to in sub-paragraph (a) above, shall arrange with the other side for the political conference to be held as soon as possible, but not later than 28 October 1953, at a place and on a date satisfactory to both sides;

(c) The Secretary-General of the United Nations shall, if this is agreeable to both sides, provide the political conference with such services and facilities as may be feasible;

(d) The Member States participating pursuant to sub-paragraph (a) above shall inform the United Nations when agreement is reached at the conference and keep the United Nations informed at other appropriate times;

6. *Reaffirms* its intention to carry out its programme for relief and rehabilitation in Korea, and appeals to the governments of all Member States to contribute to this task.

B

The General Assembly,

Having adopted the resolution entitled "Implementation of paragraph 60 of the Korean Armistice Agreement",

Recommends that the Union of Soviet Socialist Republics participate in the Korean political conference provided the other side desires it.

C

The General Assembly

Requests the Secretary-General to communicate the proposals on the Korean question submitted to the resumed meetings of the seventh session and recommended by the Assembly, together with the records of the relevant proceedings of the General Assembly, to the Central People's Government of the People's Republic of China and to the Government of the People's Democratic Republic of Korea and to report as appropriate.

70. RESOLUTION OF THE GENERAL ASSEMBLY, AUGUST 28, 1953, GIVING TRIBUTE TO THE ARMED FORCES WHO HAVE FOUGHT IN KOREA TO RESIST AGGRESSION [24]

The General Assembly

Recalling the resolutions of the Security Council of 25 June, 27 June and 7 July 1950 and the resolutions of the General Assembly of 7 October 1950, 1 December 1950, 1 February 1951, 18 May 1951 and 3 December 1952,

---

[24] U. N. Document A/Resolution/103, August 31, 1953.

Having received the report of the Unified Command dated 7 August 1953,

Noting with profound satisfaction that fighting has now ceased in Korea on the basis of an honourable armistice,

1. *Salutes* the heroic soldiers of the Republic of Korea and of all those countries which sent armed forces to its assistance;

2. *Pays tribute* to all those who died in resisting aggression and thus in upholding the cause of freedom and peace;

3. *Expresses its satisfaction* that the first efforts pursuant to the call of the United Nations to repel armed aggression by collective military measures have been successful, and expresses its firm conviction that this proof of the effectiveness of collective security under the United Nations Charter will contribute to the maintenance of international peace and security.

APPENDIX

I. KOREA: A CHRONOLOGY OF EVENTS

(The following chronology was prepared by J. Clement Lapp, Foreign Affairs Division, Legislative Reference Service, Library of Congress, for the use of the Committee.)

1943

December 1_____________ At the Cairo conference the United States, the United Kingdom, and China agree that "in due course Korea shall become free and independent."

1945

July 26________________ In the Potsdam Declaration the United States, United Kingdom, and China reaffirm the pledge made at the Cairo conference; (subscribed to by the U. S. S. R. on August 8).

September 8____________ United States troops enter Korea.

December 27____________ In the Moscow agreement the United States, the United Kingdom, and the Union of Soviet Socialist Republics (and, later, China) agree to establish a trusteeship over Korea, and to form a Korean provisional government through the activities of a Joint United States-U. S. S. R. Commission.

1947

May 17_________________ South Korean interim government is established by Ordinance No. 141 of the United States Army Military Government in Korea.

September 23___________ The U. N. General Assembly places the Korean problem on its agenda.

November 14____________ The U. N. General Assembly passes a resolution creating a Temporary Commission on Korea and stating that the Korean people themselves should create a provisional government through free and secret election of representatives with subsequent withdrawal of troops.

1948

January 8_______________ The U. N. Temporary Commission on Korea arrives in Seoul.

February 19____________ U. N. Commission is instructed to observe the election in the areas accessible to it.

March 22_______________ United States Army Military Government Ordinance No. 173 provides for redistribution of former Japanese-owned farmlands in South Korea.

May 10_________________ Election is held in the southern zone, under the observation of the U. N. Temporary Commission on Korea.

June 25________________ The U. N. Temporary Commission on Korea adopts a resolution stating that the election held in the southern zone on May 10 was a "valid expression of the free will of the electorate in those parts of Korea which were accessible to the Commission and in which the inhabitants constituted approximately two-thirds of the people of all Korea."

July 20________________ Syngman Rhee is elected President of the Republic of Korea, and Si Yung Lee, Vice President.

August 15______________ The Government of the Republic of Korea is inaugurated and Army Military Government in Korea is terminated.

1948

September 9____________ The Supreme People's Council in North Korea formally declares the establishment of a "Democratic People's Republic of Korea" claiming jurisdiction over the entire country.

1949

January 1____________ The United States extends full recognition to the Republic of Korea.

January 18____________ The United Kingdom recognizes the Republic of Korea.

February 6____________ The United Nations Commission on Korea (UNCOK) assumes its duties in Korea.

February 16____________ U. N. Security Council refuses to act on the application of North Korea for membership.

February 18____________ Syngman Rhee, President of South Korea, opposes U. N. attempts to negotiate with Government of North Korea, calling any such move a tacit recognition of Communist government as well as an affront to his own Government in the South.

April 8____________ Soviet veto blocks Korean Republic's admission to U. N.

April 20____________ Syngman Rhee receives John J. Muccio as first United States Ambassador to Republic of Korea.

July 1____________ United States Army discloses that the withdrawal of American occupation forces is completed. Only a small contingent of some 500 officers and men for training Korean forces is left.

July 6____________ North Korean regime announces it will sponsor nationwide elections September 15 to create a "unified legislature" that, in turn, will establish an all-Korean Government.

July 27____________ Intermittent artillery fire is reported between North and South Korean forces across the 38th parallel at Kaesong.

August 26____________ UNCOK says real progress toward union of North and South Korea is impossible unless United States and Russia attempt to settle their differences.

September 8____________ Report of UNCOK criticizes both sides and says Korea faces a serious danger of a "most barbarous civil war."

October 21____________ U. N. Korean Commission is continued by a vote of 48 to 6 in the General Assembly and is instructed to observe developments that might lead to civil conflict.

1950

January 26____________ United States and Korea sign a mutual defense assistance pact.

April 27____________ South Korean Army claims complete defeat of the 600 Communists who raided South Korean territory on March 27.

May 30____________ Korean election returns only 31 old members of the 210 representatives of the National Assembly.

June 19____________ John Foster Dulles assures Korea of continued United States support and predicts Communists will lose grip on North Korea eventually.

June 25____________ Between 4 and 5 o'clock in the morning (Korean time) North Korean Communist forces attack South Korean defense positions south of the 38th parallel.
At 5:45 p. m. the Security Council adopts a resolution (9–0, Yugoslavia abstaining, U. S. S. R. absent) calling for an immediate cease-fire and the withdrawal of the North Korean forces to the 38th parallel. All members are requested to "render every assistance to the United Nations in the execution of this resolution and to refrain from giving assistance to the North Korean forces."

1950

December 1___________ General MacArthur states that orders forbidding him to strike across the Korean border at Chinese Communists were putting the U. N. forces under "an enormous handicap, without precedent in military history."

December 5___________ U. N. forces withdraw from North Korean capital of Pyongyang.

Thirteen Far Eastern and Middle Eastern U. N. members send appeal to Communist China to stop their troops at the 38th parallel.

December 22___________ Communist China's Premier and Foreign Minister Chou En-lai rejects the proposal of the U. N. Cease-Fire Committee, stating the committee is unlawful because Communist China had not participated in creating it. He demands the withdrawal of all foreign troops from Korea, the withdrawal of the United States from Formosa, and the admission of Communist China to the United Nations.

1951

January 1___________ Communist offensive south of the 38th parallel begins.

January 4___________ Seoul is evacuated by U. N. forces and the South Korean Government.

January 14___________ United Nations forces establish a firm line and begin counterattack.

January 19___________ United States House of Representatives passes resolution calling on the United Nations to act immediately and declare the Chinese Communist regime an aggressor in Korea.

January 23___________ United States Senate unanimously adopts a resolution calling on the United Nations "to immediately declare Communist China an aggressor in Korea."

February 1___________ The United States resolution introduced January 20, as amended, which would declare the Chinese Communist government to be engaged in aggression and establish a Good Offices Commission, is adopted 44–7 with 9 abstentions. The amendment, submitted by Lebanon, had the effect of withholding any recommendations for sanctions if the proposed Good Offices Committee reported satisfactory progress."

February 15___________ President Truman states that it is up to General MacArthur to decide whether United Nations troops again cross the 38th parallel, that the United Nations directive of October which gave MacArthur the authority to pacify the Korean area and pave the way for free elections throughout the peninsula was still in effect.

February 26___________ British Government announces agreement with the United States that General MacArthur may allow small excursions over the 38th parallel but no "substantial crossing" without consulting the United Nations Allies.

March 7___________ United Nations forces recapture Seoul.

March 24___________ General MacArthur asserts he is ready at any time to confer in the field with the commander of the Chinese and North Korean forces to end the war and "find any military means whereby the realization of the political objectives of the United Nations in Korea, to which no nation may justly take exceptions, might be accomplished without further bloodshed." He added that a decision of the United Nations to depart from its effort to contain the war in Korea would "doom Red China to the risk of imminent military collapse."

The State Department subsequently issues a statement that "the political issues, which General MacArthur has stated are beyond his responsibility as a field commander, are being dealt with in the United Nations and by intergovernmental consultations."

1951

April 5_________________ A letter written March 20 by General MacArthur is made public in which the general endorses the use of Chinese Nationalist forces to open a second front against the Communists in Asia.

April 11______________ President Truman relieves General MacArthur of his Far Eastern commands and appoints Gen. Matthew B. Ridgway as his successor.

April 19______________ General MacArthur, speaking before joint meeting of United States Senate and House of Representatives, says United States policy in Asia is 'blind to reality" and reiterates his ideas for winning Korean war.

May 3________________ Hearings on the military situation in the Far East before the joint Senate Committee on Armed Services and Foreign Relations begin in Washington with General MacArthur as first witness.

May 18_______________ United Nations General Assembly adopts resolution calling for an embargo of arms and strategic materials to Communist China.

May 26_______________ South Korean Government announces that it will continue war alone if any truce were agreed upon which did not provide for unification of Korea.

June 23______________ In a recorded radio broadcast at New York, Jacob Malik, Soviet Deputy Foreign Minister, states that peaceful settlement of the Korean conflict can be achieved and recommends, as a first step, cease-fire and armistice discussions.

June 24______________ U. N. Secretary General Trygve Lie urges that negotiations based on the Soviet proposals should begin at once.

June 27______________ Representatives of 16 nations who have armed forces in Korea meet at State Department in Washington to discuss the truce proposal.

June 29______________ General Ridgway, acting under instructions from Washington, offers to meet the representative of the "commander in chief, Communist forces in Korea" for the purpose of discussing an armistice and cessation of hostilities in Korea.

July 1_______________ In statement broadcast from Peking, Gen. Kim Il Sung, commander of North Korean forces, and Gen. Peng Teh-huai, commander of "Chinese people's volunteers" agree to a meeting of their representatives with those of the United Nations.

July 3_______________ President Rhee, of South Korea, sends telegram to President Truman expressing confidence that American people would never allow Communist aggressors to divide Korea again.

July 10______________ United Nations military representatives, headed by Vice Adm. Charles Turner Joy, arrive at Kaesong to begin armistice discussions with Communist leaders.

July 26______________ Agreement on an agenda for armistice talks is reached at Kaesong.

The agenda included : (1) The adoption of agenda, (2) fixing of a demarcation line between the forces in order to establish a demilitarized zone, (3) concrete arrangements for a cease-fire and armistice, (4) arrangements regarding prisoners of war, and (5) recommendations to be made to the Governments of both sides.

August 23____________ Communist leaders announce "suspension" of armistice talks after alleging provocative military incidents in neutral zone.

1951

October 25______________ Cease-fire negotiations resume at Panmunjom after 2
months of suspension.

     During this period there were Communist allega-
tions of U. N. violations of neutral zones and
U. N. insistence that Kaesong was impractica-
ble as a conference site. Agreements which
would permit resumption of talks were reached
in a series of meetings of liaison officers of the
two delegations.

February 19______________ Agreement is reached by truce delegations on item 5
of agenda concerning recommendations to the Gov-
ernments of both sides.

     The delegations agreed to recommend that a po-
litical conference be held within 90 days after
the signing of an armistice, at which "the
withdrawal of all foreign forces from Korea
and the peaceful settlement of the Korean question * * *" would be discussed.

February 22______________ General Ridgway's headquarters announces that a
riot occurred at a civilian internment camp on Koje
Island on February 18.

February 27______________ General Ridgway's headquarters issue statement declaring Communist allegations concerning germ
warfare to be false and to have been made to dis-
tract attention from Communist obstruction at
truce-talks and to conceal their inadequacies in
dealing with seasonal epidemics.

March 26______________ Secretary Acheson denies use of bacteriological warfare and claims falsity of Communist charges is
demonstrated by their refusal to allow impartial
investigation.

April 28______________ General Mark Clark is appointed Supreme Allied
Commander in Far East, succeeding General Ridg-
way who is appointed Supreme Allied Commander
in Europe.

     At a closed session of the full armistice delegations,
the U. N. delegation submits a new compromise
solution to settle all remaining differences.

     As later revealed, this solution provided, as a
"package" proposal to be accepted or rejected
in its entirety, the following: (1) That there
be no mention of prohibitions on rebuilding
airfields during armistice; (2) that Poland
and Czechoslovakia, but not the Soviet Union,
serve on the Commission of neutrals to oversee
the armistice; and (3) that prisoners of war
be exchanged under the principle of voluntary
repatriation.

May 2______________ The Communists at Panmunjom reject April 28 compromise proposal of the U. N.

May 7______________ Communist prisoners of war on Koje Island capture
the camp commandant Brig. Gen. Francis T. Dodd.

May 22______________ Maj. Gen. William K. Harrison, Jr., assumes his
duties as chief U. N. negotiator at Panmunjom, succeeding Vice Adm. Charles Turner Joy.

June 3______________ President Truman sends personal letter to President
Rhee in connection with impending election in
South Korea, urging him to observe democratic
procedure and to take "no irrevocable steps."

June 6______________ U. N. Secretary-General Trygve Lie expresses to
President Rhee his deep anxiety over conflict be-
tween Rhee and National Assembly in South Korea.

1951

June 9	U. N. Commission on Unification and Rehabilitation of Korea seeks to resolve political crisis brought on by differences between President Rhee and National Assembly.
	The U. N. Commission proposed that President Rhee lift martial law, release arrested assemblymen, and halt political squabblings for 10 days to ease tension.
June 12	South Korean Government suspends Voice of America broadcasts for carrying "bitterly anti-Government criticism, obviously insulting."
June 23	The tenure of President Rhee is extended indefinitely.
	This action was taken by resolution of the National Assembly on the day which was to have been set aside for the election of a President by the Assembly. The National Assembly was boycotted by the President's opponents. The resolution provided for the President to continue in office until a successor could be chosen and take office. Earlier the Assembly had passed a resolution extending Syngman Rhee's term to August 15.
June 24	Asia's largest hydroelectric projects, situated on North Korean side of Yalu River, are heavily bombed by U. N. airmen.
	Built by Japanese before World War II, Yalu River installations supplied 60 percent of their power output to Manchuria and the remainder to North Korean cities.
June 25	United States Army officers foil attempt on life of President Rhee.
July 3	United States request in Security Council for an International Red Cross investigation of the germ-warfare charges is vetoed by the Soviet delegate.
July 4	The National Assembly approves President Rhee's proposed amendments to constitution providing for popular election of the president and a bicameral Congress.
July 25	Truce delegations resume open meetings after eighteen meetings in secret session. U. N. delegation discloses Communists have refused to acept a revised list of 83,000 prisoners willing to be repatriated. Communists again reject principle of no forced repatriation.
August 10	Syngman Rhee is reelected President in the first popular presidential election.
August 29	Heaviest air raid of the war is made on Pyongyang.
September 28	General Harrison, senior U. N. truce delegate, in an attempt to break the deadlock, submits three alternative proposals for repatriation of prisoners, stating that the U. N. would sign an armistice on the acceptance of any one of them.
September 30	British Government confirms officially the presence of between 1,200 and 5,000 Russian technical troops in North Korea.
October 8	Communist delegation rejects U. N. proposals of September 28.
October 21	General Assembly rejects by vote of 46 to 5 a Soviet proposal that Communist representatives be invited to give support of charges that U. N. had adopted germ warfare in Korea.
November 10	General Van Fleet announces the mobilization of 2 new South Korean divisions and 6 regiments bringing total South Korean strength to between 14 and 15 divisions.

1951

December 3______________ General Assembly endorses by 54 votes to 5 Indian proposals on repatriation of prisoners of war.

December 5______________ General Eisenhower ends 3-day visit to Korea during which he saw frontline units and conferred with President Rhee.

Mr. Lester Pearson, President of the General Assembly, cables the text of the Indian proposals for a Korean armistice to the Peking Government and North Korean authorities and adds a personal appeal for their urgent consideration.

December 8______________ General Eisenhower is joined at Wake Island by three members-designate of his Cabinet for discussions on Korea.

December 13______________ United States Government expresses deep concern at the Chinese Communist rejection of Indian prisoner-of-war proposals and declares that responsibility for peace in Korea now lies clearly with the Peking and North Korean authorities.

1953

February 11______________ General Maxwell D. Taylor assumes formal command of the Eighth Army from General Van Fleet.

February 22______________ General Mark Clark sends letter to Chinese and North Korean commanders repeating his earlier proposal for immediate exchange of sick and wounded prisoners.

March 28______________ Communists accept General Clark's proposal of February 22 for an exchange of sick and wounded prisoners and propose reopening of armistice talks.

March 29______________ Chou En-lai, Premier of Communist China, proposes discussion of an armistice based on the transfer to a neutral state of all prisoners unwilling to repatriate.

April 11______________ U. N. and Communist truce delegates sign a formal agreement for exchange of sick and wounded prisoners.

April 20______________ Exchange of sick and wounded prisoners begins at Panmunjom.

April 26______________ Armistice talks are resumed.

April 29______________ President Rhee tells a press conference "The Republic of Korea cannot accept any armistice while the Chinese are still in Korea."

May 25______________ Negotiators meet in secret session at Panmunjom; the South Korean delegate boycotts the talks.

May 28______________ Yung Tai Pyun, Republic of Korea Foreign Minister, tells National Assembly that U. N. truce plan is unacceptable and if cease-fire were signed South Korea would go on fighting alone to unify the country.

May 30______________ President Eisenhower sends letter to President Rhee explaining the U. N. principles on repatriation of prisoners of war.

These principles were: (1) No prisoners would be sent back by force; (2) none would be intimidated or coerced in any way; (3) there must be a time limit to their captivity; (4) all procedures must reflect these principles.

June 7______________ In a letter to President Rhee, President Eisenhower urges moderation on the Government of the Republic of Korea. The president stated that the United States would not renounce its efforts to effect the unification of Korea "by all peaceful means" and that, subject to congressional approval, the United States would enter into a mutual defense treaty with the Republic of Korea and would continue economic assistance.

President Rhee proclaims state of emergency, and orders immediate return of Korean officers from the United States.

1953

June 9___________________ Antitruce demonstrations take place throughout South Korea.

June 18__________________ South Korean guards release 27,000 North Korean anti-Communist prisoners on orders of President Rhee.

June 19__________________ President Rhee, in letter to President Eisenhower, says acceptance of an armistice is a "death warrant" for the Korean nation.

President Eisenhower, in a note to President Rhee, demands the immediate recapture of the 27,000 North Koreans permitted to escape from U. N. prison camps.

June 22__________________ General Mark Clark confers with President Rhee and places the full responsibility for release of prisoners upon the Government of Korea.

June 24__________________ President Rhee formally notifies General Clark he would withdraw the South Korean Army from the U. N. command if a truce were signed on the present terms.

June 26__________________ Assistant Secretary of State Walter S. Robertson commences discussions with President Rhee in Seoul, concerning acceptance by latter of truce.

July 12__________________ Robertson-Rhee talks conclude with joint statement that conclusion of an armistice was now up to the Communists.

July 27__________________ United Nations and Communist representatives sign an armistice at Panmunjom, bringing hostilities in Korea to a halt.

The armistice agreement provided for: (1) Establishment of a neutral zone; (2) cease fire; (3) withdrawal of forces from designated coastal islands and waters; (4) no reinforcements; (5) a Military Armistice Commission, composed of 5 officers from each side, to supervise the armistice and settle any violations; (6) a Neutral Nations Supervisory Commission composed of officers of Sweden, Switzerland, Poland, and Czechoslovakia; (7) a Neutral Nations Repatriation Commission composed of officers of Sweden, Switzerland, Poland, Czechoslovakia, and India and a regular procedure for repatriation; (8) the convening within 3 months of a political conference of representatives of both sides to negotiate on the withdrawal of foreign forces from Korea and the peaceful settlement of the Korean question.

II. CONTRIBUTIONS TO KOREA ACTIVITIES

SUMMARIES OF MILITARY AND RELIEF ASSISTANCE FOR KOREA AS OF DECEMBER 31, 1952

Country	Date	Details of offer	Status
GROUND FORCES			
Australia	Aug. 3, 1950	Ground forces from Australian infantry force in Japan.	In action.
		Additional battalion of Australian troops.	Do.
Belgium	Sept. 13, 1950	Infantry battalion.	Do.
	May 3, 1951	Reinforcements	Do.
Bolivia	July 15, 1950	30 officers	Acceptance deferred.
Canada	Aug. 14, 1950.	Brigade group, including 3 infantry battalions, 1 field regiment of artillery, 1 squadron of self-propelled antitank guns, together with engineer, signal, medical, ordnance, and other services with appropriate reinforcements.	In action.

Summaries of Military and Relief Assistance for Korea as of December 31, 1952—Continued

Country	Date	Details of offer	Status
China	July 3, 1950	3 infantry divisions	Acceptance deferred.
Colombia	Nov. 14, 1950	1 infantry battalion	In action.
Costa Rica	July 27, 1950	Volunteers	Acceptance deferred.
Cuba	Nov. 30, 1950	1 infantry company	Accepted.
El Salvador	Aug. 15, 1950.	Volunteers	Acceptance deferred.
Ethiopia	Nov. 2, 1950	1,069 officers and men	In action.
France	Aug. 20, 1950	Infantry battalion	Do.
Greece	Sept. 1, 1950	Unit of land forces	Do.
	July 2, 1951	Additional unit of land forces	Transmitted to Unified Command.
Luxembourg	Mar. 15, 1951	Infantry company integrated into the Belgian forces	In action.
Netherlands	Sept. 8, 1950	1 infantry battalion	Do.
New Zealand	July 26, 1950	1 combat unit	Do.
Panama	Aug. 3, 1950	Contingent of volunteers and bases for training	Acceptance deferred.
Philippines	Aug. 10, 1950	Regimental combat team consisting of approximately 5,000 officers and men.	In action.
Thailand	July 23, 1950	Infantry combat team of about 4,000 officers and men.	Do.
Turkey	July 25, 1950	Infantry combat force of 4,500 men, later increased to 6,086 men.	Do.
United Kingdom	Aug. 21, 1950	Ground forces	Do.
	Official information communicated on June 12, 1951.	2 brigades composed of brigade headquarters, 5 infantry battalions, 1 field regiment, 1 armored regiment.	Do.
United States	Official information communicated on June 8, 1951.	3 army corps and 1 marine division with supporting elements.	Do.

NAVAL FORCES			
Australia	Sept. 4, 1952	1 destroyer and 1 frigate	Do.
Canada	July 12, 1950	3 destroyers	Do.
Colombia	Oct. 16, 1950	1 frigate, *Almirante Padilla* (replaced by *Capitan Tono*).	Do.
France	July 19, 1950	Patrol gunboat	Withdrawn.
Netherlands	July 5, 1950	1 destroyer, *Evertsen*	In action.
New Zealand	July 1, 1950	2 frigates, H.M.N.Z. *Tutira* and H.M.N.Z. *Pukaki*.	Do.
Thailand	Oct. 3, 1950	2 corvettes, *Prasae* and *Bangpakong* [1]	Do.
United Kingdom	June 28, 1950	Naval forces in Japanese waters diverted to Korea.	Do.
	Official information communicated on June 12, 1951, and Sept. 12, 1952.	1 aircraft carrier, 1 aircraft carrier maintenance ship, 1 hospital ship, 4 frigates, 1 headquarters ship, 2 cruisers, 4 destroyers.	Do.
United States	Official information communicated on June 8, 1951.	A fast carrier task group with a blockade and escort force, an amphibious force, reconnaissance and antisubmarine warfare units, supporting ships.	Do.
AIR FORCES			
Australia	June 30, 1950	1 R.A.A.F. fighter squadron, 1 air communication unit, base and maintenance personnel.	Do.
Canada	July 21, 1950	1 R.C.A.F. squadron	Do.
Union of South Africa	Aug. 4, 1950	1 fighter squadron, including ground personnel	Do.
United Kingdom	Official information communicated on June 12, 1951.	Elements of the air force	Do.
United States	Official information communicated on June 8, 1951.	1 tactical air force, 1 bombardment command, 1 combat cargo command, all with supporting elements.	Do.
MATERIAL			
Philippines	Aug. 3, 1950	17 Sherman tanks and 1 tank destroyer	Do.

[1] Destroyed on grounding.

Summaries of Military and Relief Assistance for Korea as of December 31, 1952—Continued

Country	Date	Details of offer	Status
TRANSPORT			
Belgium	Sept. 28, 1950	Air transport.	Available.
Canada	Aug. 11, 1950	Facilities of Canadian Pacific Airlines between Vancouver and Tokyo.	Do.
		Dry cargo vessels (10,000 tons)	Do.
China	July 3, 1950	20 C–47's	Acceptance deferred.
Denmark	July 22, 1950	Motor ship *Bella Dan*	Do.
Greece	July 20, 1950, and Oct. 13, 1950.	8 Dakota transport planes	In action.
Norway	July 18, 1950	Merchant ship tonnage	Do.
Panama	Aug. 3, 1950	Use of merchant marine for transportation of troops and supplies.	Do.
Thailand	Oct. 3, 1950	Transport *Sichang* to be attached to Thai troops	Do.
		Air transport.	Do.
United Kingdom	Official information communicated on June 12, 1951.	7 supply vessels	Do.
United States		(The Unified Command has arranged for transport of United States troops and material, as well as for the transport of some of the forces and material listed in the present summary.)	
MEDICAL			
Denmark	Aug. 18, 1950	Hospital ship *Jutlandia*	Do.
India	July 29, 1950	Field ambulance unit	Do.

Italy	Sept. 27, 1950	Field hospital unit	Do
Norway	Mar. 6, 1951	Surgical hospital unit	Do.
Sweden	July 20, 1950	Field hospital unit	Do.
United Kingdom	Official information communicated on June 12, 1951.	Hospital ship	Do.
United States		(The Unified Command has provided full medical facilities not only for United States troops but also for the troops of participating governments.)	
MISCELLANEOUS			
Costa Rica	July 27, 1950	Sea and air bases	Accepted.
Panama	Aug. 3, 1950	Bases for training	Acceptance deferred.
		Free use of highways	Accepted.
		Farmlands to supply troops	Pending.
Thailand	Feb. 2, 1951	Treatment for frostbite	Do.

UNIFIED COMMAND EMERGENCY RELIEF PROGRAM FOR KOREA
AS OF DECEMBER 31, 1952

Country	Date of offer	Details of offer	Value (U. S. dollar equiv.)	Status
MEMBER AND NONMEMBER STATES				
(1) *Offers made direct to Emergency Program*				
Australia	Nov. 28, 1950	Penicillin crystalline	67, 344	Arrived in Korean theater.
	Dec. 14, 1950	Distilled water	31, 836	Do.
		Laundry soap, 116,000 lb	8, 029	Do.
	Jan. 8, 1951	Procaine penicillin	108, 547	Do.
	Jan. 31, 1951	Barley, 2,000 long tons	196, 570	Do.
Belgium	Nov. 7, 1950	Sugar, 400 metric tons	60, 000	Do.
Brazil	Sept. 22, 1950	Cruzeiros, 50 million	2, 702, 703	Pending legislation.
Cambodia	May 11, 1951	Salted fish, 1,400 kg	389	Arrived in Korean theater.
	June 14, 1951	Rice, 5.2 metric tons	583	Do.
	Feb. 25, 1952	Rice, 100 sacks	1, 457	Do.
	Nov. 28, 1952	Rice, dried fish, timber	(¹)	Action pending.
China	Oct. 4, 1950	Coal, 9,900 metric tons; rice, 1,000 metric tons; salt, 3,000 metric tons; DDT, 20 metric tons.	613, 630	Arrived in Korean theater.
	July 17, 1951	Medical supplies	21, 152	Do.
Cuba	Oct. 2, 1950	Sugar, 2,000 metric tons; alcohol, 10,000 gal.	270, 962	Do.
Denmark	July 5, 1950	Medical supplies	142, 964	Do.
	Sept. 26, 1950	Sugar, 500 metric tons	95, 047	Do.
Ecuador	Oct. 13, 1950	Rice, 500 metric tons	99, 441	Do.

Country	Date	Commodity	Value	Remarks
France	Oct. 9, 1950	Medical supplies	74,286	Do.
	Dec. 29, 1950	. . . do		Do.
Germany, Federal Republic of.	Dec. 5, 1952	Medical supplies	47,619	Accepted by Unified Command.
Greece	Oct. 20, 1950	Soap, 113 metric tons	31,167	Arrived in Korean theater.
	Nov. 30, 1950	Notebooks and pencils, 25,000 each	1,333	Do.
	Dec. 27, 1950	Medical supplies	84,586	Do.
	Apr. 15, 1952	Salt, 10,000 tons	36,133	Under shipment.
Iceland	Sept. 14, 1950	Cod liver oil, 125 metric tons	45,400	Arrived in Korean theater.
India	Oct. 4, 1950	Jute bags, 400,000	167,696	Do.
	Oct. 11, 1950	Medical supplies	3,384	Do.
Israel	Aug. 22, 1950	Medical supplies	63,000	Do.
Liberia	July 17, 1950	Natural rubber	10,000	Do.
Mexico	Sept. 30, 1950	Pulses and rice; medical supplies	346,821	Do.
New Zealand	Oct. 6, 1950	Dried peas, 492 long tons	55,318	Do.
	Nov. 20, 1950	Milk powder, 150 metric tons	[2] 66,378	Do.
		Soap, 200 metric tons	[2] 49,644	Do.
	Mar. 14, 1951	Vitamin capsules	[2] 38,532	Do.
	May 26, 1952	Soap and vitamin capsules	69,725	Under shipment.
Nicaragua	Nov. 16, 1950	Rice, 1,000 quintals		Declined unless can be made available at U.S. port.
	Dec. 16, 1950	Rice, 2,000 quintals		
		Alcohol, 5,000 qt		
Norway	Feb. 13, 1951	Soap, 120,250 lb.	21,091	Arrived in Korean theater.
		Vitamins, 24,850 bottles	10,210	Do.
		Ether	[2] 39,699	Do.
Pakistan	Aug. 29, 1950	Wheat, 5,000 metric tons	378,285	Do.
Peru	Nov. 21, 1950	Clothing: cotton and wool; and cloth	58,723	Under shipment.
Philippines	July 7, 1950	Soap, 50,000 cakes	5,500	Do.
	Sept. 7, 1950	Vaccine	50,050	Arrived in Korean theater.

[1] No estimate available.
[2] Tentative value only.

Unified Command Emergency Relief Program for Korea as of December 31, 1952—Continued

Country	Date of offer	Details of offer	Value (U. S. dollar equiv.)	Status
MEMBER AND NONMEMBER STATES—continued				
(1) *Offers made direct to Emergency Program*—continued				
Philippines	Sept. 8, 1950	Rice, 10,000 metric tons	2, 255, 628	8,285 tons arrived in Korean theater, balance awaiting shipment. Tentative value only.
	Sept. 8, 1950	Fresh blood, 518 units.	19, 475	Arrived in Korean theater.
	Nov. 29, 1950	Fresh blood, 500 units.	. . . .	Declined owing to technical difficulties.
Sweden	May 14, 1952	Medical supplies	48, 326	Arrived in Korean theater.
Thailand	Sept. 20, 1950	Rice, 40,000 metric tons	4, 368, 000	Do.
Turkey	Aug. 29, 1950	Vaccines and serums	. . . . . .	Declined owing to difficulties of transportation.
United Kingdom of Great Britain and Northern Ireland.	Oct. 19, 1950	Salt, 6,000 long tons	139, 150	Arrived in Korean theater.
	Oct. 20, 1950	Sulfa drugs	48, 791	Do.
	Dec. 22, 1950	Food yeast, 50 long tons.	25, 167	Do.
	June 19, 1951	Supplies to the value of £400,000 including:	1, 120, 000	(Supplies to be made available at request of Unified Command.)
		Charcoal, 24,000 piculs.	. . . .	Under shipment.
		Salt, 8,200 long tons.	}	Arrived in Korean theater.
		Food yeast, 75 tons		Under shipments.
		Cotton sheeting.	. . . .	Accepted by Unified Command.
United States of America.	. . . .	Total contribution to emergency relief from June 25, 1950, to Dec. 31, 1952.	321, 688, 005	This total includes $313,964,320 for goods supplied or in process

				of supply from U.S. Army, including transportation costs; U.S. borne transportation for U.N. and other donations, $2,198,839; ECA relief assistance (exclusive of approximately $32,000,000 nonrelief ECA economic assistance), $5,524,846.
Uruguay	Sept. 14, 1950	$2,000,000 U.S.	2,000,000	Pending legislation.
	Oct. 28, 1950	Blankets, 70,000	250,780	Arrived in Korean theater.
Venezuela	Sept. 14, 1950	Medical supplies and foodstuffs	80,842	Do.
	Apr. 1, 1951	Clothing and food	70,000	Do.
Viet-Nam	Dec. 9, 1952	Rice, 10 tons	. . . .	Acceptance pending.

(2) *Offers made to the Negotiating Committee on Contributions to Programs of Relief and Rehabilitation but made available by UNKRA to the Emergency Program*

Argentina	Aug. 8, 1951	Corned meats, 13,950 cases	500,000	Arrived in Korean theater.
Burma	Feb. 1, 1951	Rice, 400 metric tons	49,934	Do.
Chile	Nov. 17, 1951	Nitrates, 5,000 tons	250,000	Pending legislation in Chile.
Israel	Feb. 19, 1951	Citrus products	33,600	Arrived in Korean theater.
Liberia	Feb. 23, 1951	Natural rubber	15,000	Do.

(3) *Cash contributions offered to the Emergency Program but credited to UNKRA*

Ethiopia	Aug. 5, 1950	£14,286 sterling	40,000	Do.
Lebanon	July 26, 1950	$50,000 U.S.	50,000	Do.
Paraguay	Nov. 3, 1950	$10,000 U.S.	10,000	Do.

Unified Command Emergency Relief Program for Korea as of December 31, 1952—Continued

Country	Date of offer	Details of offer	Value (U. S. dollar equiv.)	Status
NONGOVERNMENTAL ORGANIZATIONS (BY COUNTRY)				
Australia				
Save the Children Fund.	June 25, 1951	Services of 3 medical and welfare personnel.	. . . . .	1 doctor now working in Korea with UNCACK.
Canada				
Canadian Lutheran World Relief.	Nov. 28, 1952	Used clothing, 1 ton	2, 000	Accepted.
Unitarian Service Committee of Canada.	Dec. 31, 1952	Clothing, 2 tons	4, 000	Do.
United Church of Canada.	Apr. 19, 1951	Used clothing and shoes, 24,000 lb. . . .	24, 000	Arrived in Korean theater.
	Nov. 14, 1951	Used clothing, 30,000 lb.	30, 000	Do.
	Feb. 4, 1952	Used clothing, 30,000 lb.	30, 000	Do.
	May 7, 1952	Used clothing, 40,000 lb.	40, 000	Do.
	July 21, 1952	Used clothing, 40,000 lb.	40, 000	Under shipment.
	Oct. 30, 1952	Used clothing, 20 tons	40, 000	Do.
	Dec. 31, 1952	Used clothing, 20 tons	40, 000	Acceptance pending.
Colombia				
Commercial firms.	Mar. 3, 1951	Clothing—amount not specified . . .	. . . . . .	Declined unless made available in United States port.
	Mar. 19, 1951	Clothing—amount not specified . . .	500	
Japan				
Japan Canned and Bottled Foods Association.	Apr. 27, 1951	Preserved foods, 300 cases	3, 000	Arrived in Korean theater.

Japanese Catholic Organization AI RIN KAI.	June 17, 1952	Textiles and miscellaneous supplies . .	5, 400	Do.
New Zealand				
Council of Organizations for Relief Services Overseas.	Nov. 21, 1950	Used clothing, 71 cases.	11, 377	Do.
	Mar. 16, 1951	Used clothing, 48 cases.	19, 392	Do.
	Oct. 15, 1951	Used footwear and clothing, 104 cases .	44, 069	Do.
	Apr. 23, 1952	Used clothing, 15 cases.	12, 029	Do.
	Apr. 23, 1952	Clothing and footwear, 9 cases, 10 bales.	14, 052	Do.
	May 16, 1952	Medical books, 12 cases	1, 349	Accepted by UNKRA for medical library.
	Aug. 25, 1952	Medical books	(1)	Do.
	Oct. 17, 1952	Used clothing and footwear, 33 cubic tons.	(1)	Accepted.
	Dec. 5, 1952	Dental supplies.	(1)	Do.
Norway				
Europahjelpen . . .	Dec. 29, 1950	Clothing, 126 metric tons	277, 780	Arrived in Korean theater.
United Kingdom				
YWCA, Hong Kong.	Mar. 29, 1951	Clothing and cloth, 1,200 lb.	1, 200	Do.
United States of America.				
American Friends Service Committee.	Nov. 16, 1950	Used clothing, 103,000 lb. . . . . . . Soap, 5,000 lb.	104, 000	Do.
	Jan. 23, 1951	Used clothing, 10 metric tons	20, 000	Do.
	Feb. 14, 1951	Used clothing, 11,000 lb.	10, 000	Do.
	Mar. 12, 1951	Used clothing, 7,500 lb.	7, 500	Do.
	May 28, 1951	Used clothing, 24,233 lb.	24, 233	Do.
	July 12, 1951	Used clothing, 67,500 lb.	67, 500	Do.
	Aug. 28, 1951	Used clothing, 32,500 lb.	32, 500	Do.
	Sept. 11, 1951	Used clothing, 60,860 lb.	60, 860	Do.
		Soap, 3,700 lb.	370	Do.

[1] No estimate available.

Unified Command Emergency Relief Program for Korea as of December 31, 1952—Continued

Country	Date of offer	Details of offer	Value (U. S. dollar equiv.)	Status
NONGOVERNMENTAL ORGANIZATIONS (BY COUNTRY)—continued				
United States of America—continued				Arrived in Korean theater.
American Relief for Korea.	June 13, 1951	Used clothing and shoes, 500,000 lb. . .	480, 000	Do.
	Oct. 24, 1951	Used clothing and shoes, 3,868,403 lb. .		
		Hospital supplies, 1,135 lb.	3, 869, 650	Do.
		Powdered milk, 400 lb.		
	Mar. 3, 1952	Used clothing and shoes, 1,500,000 lb. .	1, 225, 000	Part arrived Korea, balance under shipment.
	Mar. 13, 1952	Rice, 20,000 lb	2, 000	Arrived in Korean theater.
	May 21, 1952	Canned goods, 150 lb	30	Do.
		Children's supplies, 315 lb	315	Do.
		Physician's samples, 177 lb. (no commercial value).	. . . . . .	Do.
	Aug. 18, 1952	Used clothing and shoes. 1,500,000 lb .	1, 225, 000	Under shipment.
		Laundry and toilet soap, 12,000 lb . .	2, 160	Do.
	Nov. 18, 1952	Toilet and laundry soap, 25.000 lb . .	4, 500	Do.
	Nov. 20, 1952	Used clothing and shoes, 1,500,000 lb .	1, 500, 000	Do.
Church World Service.	Sept. 25, 1950	Used clothing and miscellaneous supplies.	104, 958	Arrived in Korean theater.
	Nov. 6, 1950	Vitamin tablets, 1,000,000	5, 500	Do.
		Used clothing, 100.000 lb	100, 000	Do.
	Jan. 30, 1951	Used clothing, 60,000 lb	60, 000	Do.
	Feb. 19, 1951	Used clothing, 12,000 lb	12, 000	Do.
	Feb. 21, 1951	Used clothing, 40,000 lb	40, 000	Do.

	Apr. 2, 1951	Used clothing, 10,000 lb	10,000	Do.
	May 18, 1951	Used clothing, 50,000 lb	50,000	Do.
	Mar. 28, 1952	Hospital supplies (includes 1,000,000 vitamin tablets), 6,720 lb.	33,600	Do.
		Used clothing, 268,567 lb	268,567	Do.
		Food, 54,248 lb	14,595	Do.
		Soap, 2,433 lb	243	Do.
Committee for Free Asia.	Aug. 8, 1951	Newsprint, 1,000 tons	150,000	Do.
Cooperative Agencies for Remittances to Europe, Inc. (CARE).	Sept. 21, 1950	Food and clothing pkg	100,000	Do.
	Nov. 20, 1950	Blankets and textile pkg	154,294	Do.
	Apr. 10, 1951	Food pkg	100,000	Do.
	June 19, 1951	Food pkg	100,000	Do.
		Blanket pkg	28,000	Do.
	July 25, 1951	Food pkg	110,000	Do.
	Aug. 13, 1951	Dress material, soap, food	1,565	Do.
	Aug. 22, 1951	Food pkg	100,000	Do.
	Oct. 19, 1951	Knitting wool pkg	25,000	Do.
	Dec. 3, 1951	Clothing and blanket pkg	85,000	Do.
		Food pkg	100,000	Do.
	Jan. 9, 1952	Soap pkg	38,800	Do.
	Jan. 21, 1952	Blankets and underwear	80,000	Do.
	Feb. 21, 1952	Food pkg	100,000	Do.
	Mar. 10, 1952	Food pkg	230,000	Part delivered Korea, balance under shipment.
	Mar. 21, 1952	Cotton pkg	17,500	Arrived in Korean theater.
	Apr. 25, 1952	Food pkg	140,000	Under shipment.
	May 23, 1952	Knitting pkg	25,000	Part arrived in Korea.
	July 14, 1952	Food pkg	100,000	Under shipment.
	July 31, 1952	Cloth, 13,595 lb	10,000	Do.
	Aug. 19, 1952	Food pkgs., 14,870 lb	74,350	Do.

Unified Command Emergency Relief Program for Korea as of December 31, 1952—Continued

Country	Date of offer	Details of offer	Value (U. S. dollar equiv.)	Status
NONGOVERNMENTAL ORGANIZATIONS (BY COUNTRY)—continued				
United States of America—Con.				
Cooperative Agencies for Remittances to Europe, Inc. (CARE).	Oct. 24, 1952	Special cotton-wool blankets. 2, 500 . .	17, 500	Under shipment.
		Special underwear pkg., 2,500	25, 000	Do.
	Oct. 24, 1952	Cloth remnants	500	Do.
	Nov. 4, 1952	Cotton pkg., 200	20, 000	Do.
	Nov. 18, 1952	Special knitting wool, 2,030 pkg	20, 300	Do.
	Nov. 21, 1952	Underwear, 1,500 pkg..	15, 000	Do.
		Food, 5,000 pkg.	50, 000	Do.
	Oct. 10, 1952	Vitamin compound and vitamin B complex, 350 cartons.	9, 500	Do.
Friendship Among Children and Youth Around the World, Inc.	Feb. 26, 1952	Relief parcels, clothing, shoes	8, 700	Do.
	Dec. 9, 1952	Miscellaneous items of children's clothing, 78 crates.	12, 000	Do.
General Conference of Seventh-Day Adventists.	Apr. 11, 1951	Used clothing, 19,000 lb	10, 000	Arrived in Korean theater.
Heifer Project Committee.	Mar. 6, 1952	Hatching eggs 250,000	17, 500	Do.
	June 19, 1952	Goats, 100; pigs, 300.	25, 000	(Offers originally made to UNKRA which in turn offered this donation to Unified Command.

Organization	Date	Supplies	Quantity	Remarks
Lutheran World Relief.	Feb. 23, 1951	Used clothing, 44,500 lb	44,550	Arrived in Korean theater.
	Mar. 26, 1951	Used clothing and soap, 12,851 lb.	12,851	Do.
	Apr. 26, 1951	Used clothing, 200 bales	25,287	Do.
	July 18, 1951	Used clothing, 290 bales	29,000	Do.
	Apr. 15, 1952	Used clothing and bedding, 21,750 lb.	21,750	Do.
	May 1, 1952	Used clothing, 60,000 lb.	60,000	Do.
	June 19, 1952	Used clothing and bedding	14,031	Do.
Manget Foundation.	Sept. 26, 1951	Used clothing, 101 bales	9,000	Do.
Mennonite Central Committee.	Oct. 1951	Services of 1 supply officer	. . . . . .	Services made available for 1 year from October 1951.
Oriental Missionary Society.	Feb. 19, 1951	Used clothing, 102,883 lb.	102,883	Arrived in Korean theater.
Presbyterian Church in the United States.	Sept. 10, 1951	Medical supplies	950	Do.
Save the Children Federation.	Dec. 12, 1950	Used clothing, 4,913 lb.	5,033	Do.
	Feb. 16, 1951	Used clothing, 10,011 lb.	10,087	Do.
	Apr. 23, 1951	Used clothing, 13,512 lb.	13,610	Do.
	July 9, 1951	Used clothing, 15,700 lb.	15,395	Do.
	July 20, 1951	School equipment.	1,200	Do.
	Oct. 10, 1951	Used clothing, 15,136 lb.	15,115	Do.
	Oct. 10, 1951	School equipment and gift pkg.	7,500	Do.
	Oct. 22, 1951	Used clothing, 4,826 lb.	4,826	Do.
	Dec. 10, 1951	Used clothing, 9,867 lb.	9,867	Do.
	Jan. 21, 1952	Gift pkg. and tents	2,900	Do.
	Apr. 28, 1952	School equipment	5,000	Do.
	Apr. 28, 1952	Used clothing, 10,257 lb.	10,326	Do.
	July 9, 1952	Tents and poles	360	Under shipment.
	Aug. 4, 1952	Layettes.	900	Do.

Unified Command Emergency Relief Program for Korea as of December 31, 1952—Continued

Country	Date of offer	Details of offer	Value (U. S. dollar equiv.)	Status
NONGOVERNMENTAL ORGANIZATIONS (BY COUNTRY)—continued				
United States of America—Con.				
War Relief Services, National Catholic Welfare Conference.	Oct. 17, 1950	Used clothing, soap, medicinal supplies.	290, 749	Arrived in Korean theater.
	Oct. 27, 1950	Services of medical team		Declined.
	Nov. 17, 1950	Clothing, shoes, soap	99, 739	Arrived in Korean theater.
	Nov. 29, 1950	Used clothing, 1,000,000 lb.	1, 000, 000	Do.
	Dec. 7, 1950	Used clothing, 1,000,000 lb.	1, 000, 000	Do.
	Dec. 7, 1950	Used clothing, 70,000 lb.	70, 000	Do.
	Feb. 16, 1951	Medicinals.	2, 600	Do.
		Used clothing, 20,000 lb.	20, 000	Do.
	Mar. 26, 1951	Dried milk, 1,000,000 lb.	125, 000	Do.
		Dried eggs, 100,000 lb.	40, 000	Do.
	Aug. 30, 1951	Used clothing, 10,000 lb.	10, 000	Do.
	Oct. 22, 1951	Used clothing, 950,000 lb.	950, 000	Do.
	Dec. 6, 1951	Used clothing, 400,000 lb.	400, 000	Do.
	Dec. 27, 1951	Used clothing, 115,000 lb.	115, 000	Under shipment.
	Feb. 15, 1952	Used clothing, 12,000 lb.	12, 000	Part delivered Korean theater; balance under shipment.
	Mar. 12, 1952	Baby foods, 31,844 lb.	8, 250	Under shipment.
Miscellaneous United States Sources.				
Anonymous donors.		Used clothing, 130,802 lb.	130, 802	Arrived in Korean theater.
		Chaplain's supplies	3, 360	Do.
		Canned milk and food.	250	Do.
		Law books: 1 set	600	Do.

Mrs. J. M. Lee, Chicago.	. . . .	Used clothing, 1,120 lb.	1, 120	Do.
Korean Consul General, San Francisco.	. . . .	Used clothing, 756 lb.	750	Do.
School Children of San Francisco.	. . . .	Rice, 800 lb	80	Do.
U.S. Naval Hospital, Bethesda.	. . . .	Medical books, 2 cases	500	Do.
U.S. Third Army .	. . . .	Baby clothes and used clothing	10, 857	Do.
U.S.A.F. 19th Bombardment Wing.	. . . .	Used clothing, 200 lb	120	Do.
Special Service Officer, U.S. Army in Pacific.	. . . .	Used clothing, 16 boxes	1, 120	Do.
Sharp and Dohme, Philadelphia.	. . . .	"Captivite." 600 bottles	1, 000	Do.
Cash donations .	. . . .	. . . .	1, 903	
U.S. Army Chapels in Alaska.	Oct. 24, 1952	Cash for food	1, 271. 30	Accepted.
Dr. William B. Neal.	Dec. 18, 1952	Medical library, 500–700 books . . .	2, 500	Do.
Religious Denominations of Ft. Devens, Mass.	Oct. 17, 1952	Cash donation	1, 000	Do.

SPECIALIZED AGENCIES

ILO	Nov. 29, 1950	Services of 2 labor advisers	. . . .	Services made available by ILO until Jan. 1, 1952.

Unified Command Emergency Relief Program for Korea as of December 31, 1952—Continued

Country	Date of offer	Details of offer	Value (U. S. dollar equiv.)	Status
NONGOVERNMENTAL ORGANIZATIONS (BY COUNTRY)—continued				
SPECIALIZED AGENCIES—continued				
IRO	Aug. 3, 1950	Clothing, cloth, thread, kitchen equipment, sewing machines.	179,000	Arrived in Korean theater.
	Aug. 8, 1950	Medical supplies, 2 M tons	12,177	Do.
	Aug. 19, 1950	Services of 5 medical team personnel Services of 4 medical team personnel Services of 5 supply officers		Services made available by IRO until Jan. 1, 1952.
UNESCO	Jan. 31, 1951	$100,000 for purchase of educational supplies.	100,000	Made available to Unified Command.
UNICEF	Sept. 27, 1950	Blankets, 312,020	535,006	Arrived in Korean theater.
		Powdered milk, 330,000 lb	10,054	Do.
	Sept. 28, 1950	Soap, 100,000 lb	7,167	Do.
		Medical supplies	1,964	Do.
	Jan. 26, 1951	Clothing	200,000	Do.
	Feb. 1, 1951	Clothing	199,586	Do.
		Freight charges on cod liver oil donated by Iceland.	3,729	Do.
	July 24, 1951	Cotton cloth, 2,400,000 yd	540,000	Do.
WHO	Aug. 8, 1950	Services of 10 medical team personnel		Services made available by WHO until Jan. 1, 1952.
	Sept. 4, 1950	Services of 3 public health advisers		Services made available by WHO until Jan. 1, 1952.
	Nov. 22, 1950	Services of 10 medical team personnel		

LEAGUE OF RED CROSS SOCIETIES

League of Red Cross Societies, Geneva.	Nov. 11, 1950	Services of 9 medical teams each of 3 persons.	. . . .	5 teams made available by Red Cross until Jan. 1, 1952.
		Tents, blankets, medical supplies, clothing.	. . . .	Supplied direct to the Korean Red Cross.
	May 7, 1952	Reconditioned clothing, knitting wool .	2,016	Arrived in Korean theater.
American Junior Red Cross.	June 8, 1951	Educational gift boxes	100,000	Do.
	July 27, 1951	School chests	7,600	Do.
	Aug. 2, 1951	Children's clothing	150,000	Do.
	Sept. 5, 1951	Educational gift boxes	100,000	Do.
	May 7, 1952	Duplicating machines	2,700	Do.
	July 1, 1952	School chests and educational gift boxes .	210,000	Under shipment.
American Red Cross Society.	Aug. 2, 1951	Layettes and blankets	46,000	Arrived in Korean theater.
Australian Red Cross Society.	July 31, 1951	Medical supplies	970	Do.
	Aug. 2, 1951	Used clothing	6,100	Do.
	Mar. 11, 1952	. . do	2,000	Do.
	May 7, 1952	. . do	6,720	Do.
	May 7, 1952	. . do	2,000	Do.
	Oct. 17, 1952	Reconditioned clothing, 95 cases, 4 tons gross.	. . . .	Accepted.
British Red Cross Society.	July 31, 1951	Woolen clothing	8,400	Arrived in Korean theater.
Canadian Red Cross Society.	May 7, 1952	Knitting wool	2,240	Do.
Costa Rican Red Cross Society.	Mar. 3, 1951	Used clothing	1,761	Do.
Greek Red Cross Society.	June 13, 1951	Dried fruits	686	Do.

Unified Command Emergency Relief Program for Korea as of December 31, 1952—Continued

Country	Date of offer	Details of offer	Value (U. S. dollar equiv.)	Status
LEAGUE OF RED CROSS SOCIETIES—continued				
Indian Red Cross Society.	June 13, 1951	Mepacrine tablets	6, 090	Arrived in Korean theater.
	Aug. 15, 1951	Medical supplies	2, 100	Do.
Iranian Red Lion and Sun Society.	July 31, 1951	Blankets and clothing	3, 900	Do.
Japan Red Cross Society.	June 19, 1951	Medical supplies, clothing and food	36, 000	Do.
	Jan. 22, 1952	Medical supplies	25, 000	Do.
New Zealand Red Cross Society.	May 7, 1952	Knitting wool and needles	194	Do.
Norwegian Red Cross Society.	July 31, 1951	Hospital supplies	5, 640	Do.
Swedish Red Cross Society.	Aug. 2, 1951	Used clothing	90, 000	Do.
	Feb. 28, 1952	. . do	82, 512	Do.
Turkish Red Crescent.	Jan. 10, 1951	Knitting wool and needles	898	Do.